ARGUMENT
A Guide to Formal
and Informal Debate

SECOND EDITION

ABNÉ M. EISENBERG
JOSEPH A. ILARDO

Herbert H. Lehman College
The City University of New York

Prentice-Hall, Inc., Englewood Cliffs, New Jersey 07632

Library of Congress Cataloging in Publication Data

Eisenberg, Abne M.
    Argument: a guide to formal and informal debate.

    (Prentice-Hall speech communication series)
    Bibliography: p. 215
    1. Debates and debating.   I. Ilardo, Joseph A.,
joint author.   II. Title.
PN4181.E49 1980   808.53   79-4562
ISBN   0-13-045989-5

The Prentice-Hall Series in Speech Communication

Larry L. Barker
Robert J. Kibler
    consulting editors

Printed in the United States of America

10   9   8   7   6   5   4

Editorial/production supervision by Joyce Turner
Cover design by Saiki & Sprung Design
Manufacturing buyer: Harry P. Baisley

Prentice-Hall International, Inc., *London*
Prentice-Hall of Australia Pty. Limited, *Sydney*
Prentice-Hall of Canada, Ltd., *Toronto*
Prentice-Hall of India Private Limited, *New Delhi*
Prentice-Hall of Japan, Inc., *Tokyo*
Prentice-Hall of Southeast Asia Pte. Ltd., *Singapore*
Whitehall Books Limited, *Wellington, New Zealand*

Contents

part one RHETORICAL ASPECTS OF ARGUMENT

part two INTERPERSONAL ASPECTS OF ARGUMENT

PROLOGUE

When the first edition of this book was published in 1972, the war in Viet Nam was at its height and the Nixon White House had begun adding its own unique coloring to the American political scene. College campuses across the country were in turmoil: Violent demonstrations erupted with startling regularity as students and faculty alike sought to influence public policy in whatever way they could. "Surely if the war is immoral and the government unresponsive to the will of the people," reasoned the demonstrators, "all forms of protest—violent or not—are justifiable." The authors disagreed. We sought to introduce reason and insight into a chaotic scene.

Today things are different.

The war, fortunately, is over. The Nixon White House is a distant—but, we hope, not a forgotten—memory. College campuses have settled down: education has replaced demonstration, order has supplanted chaos.

Many authors have mistaken the calm facade on college campuses as an indication of a pervasive tendency toward noninvolvement. "A return to the '50s," they call it—to unquestioning acceptance of traditional values, to blind conformity, and to emotional detachment from issues of public concern.

We think their conclusions are wrong. Beneath the calm facade lies a seething community of young adults seeking something more than empty success. Not only are they struggling with their own identity crises, they are living in an age of a national identity crisis. Today more than ever, American society is a society aware of itself. The media force us to confront ourselves much as they forced us to confront ourselves during the Viet Nam war when they brought the battlefield into our living rooms. We see the injustice, the inhumanity that sometimes characterizes our economic and political systems. We view the plight of the elderly, the poor, the victims of racism. We, as a people, consider who we are and where we are going. We look beyond what *is* toward what *can be*. College campuses house the young, the idealistic, the harbingers of change. They are still in need of the tools with which to effect change.

The calm of the campus can be misleading for yet another reason. The '60s marked a turning point in American history. We think the students should be taken seriously. Once a dawning of ethical sensitivity occurs, there is no turning back. The dream of the past decade hasn't been forgotten. Propelled by the same idealism, the same democratic impulses, the college population isn't about to turn away from the need to humanize America. Never again will the '50s return.

We are living in an age of change. Angry voices may have fallen silent. Protest marches may be rare. But the drive to improve, to grow, to transform America has not disappeared.

This book, then, will be used whenever and wherever advocates of change confront defenders of the status quo. It presents a plan for disciplined disagreement, rational rebuttal, and calm confrontation. In short, it is a manual for social transformation.

This book rests on the following premises: (1) In logic lies man's only hope for the future. (2) Since argumentation is engaged in by human beings, nonlogical and nonverbal factors always operate. The requirements of the real world force us to consider the nonverbal and nonlogical aspects of interpersonal disagreement. Only then can the supremacy of logic be assured. (3) The same principles apply in both formal and informal argumental settings. Indeed, much of the more meaningful argumentation in which most people engage occurs in informal, interpersonal settings—around the dinner table, driving to work in the car pool, or chatting with a neighbor.

Readers of the first edition of this volume will recognize these premises. There are, however, several important changes in this edition.

First, our discussion of the rules and customs of school debate has been expanded. A new chapter entitled "Formal Debate: Procedures and Evaluation" has been added. In it, close attention is paid to debate formats and case construction, as well as to the criteria used to judge debates. This material has been included to insure that the book meets the needs of those readers who do most of their arguing on the school circuit.

Second, a chapter entitled "Applied Argumentation" shows how the principles discussed between these covers can be applied in a variety of everyday settings. We provide excerpts of speeches and arguments on diverse issues and invite readers to participate in the analysis of the arguments presented.

Throughout we have updated, enriched, and revised the materials in the first edition.

We think our readers will find that this volume captures the spirit of our earlier one, while providing an even deeper and richer exposition of the principles of argumentation.

One last point: Authors, like all other communicators, appreciate feedback. We received many thoughtful comments from our readers the last time around. We would like to encourage you, colleague or student, to share with us your reactions to this edition.

A.M.E.

J.A.I.

ACKNOWLEDGMENT

We would like to take this opportunity to thank our many students and colleagues who provided invaluable stimulation and feedback during the preparation of this revision. In particular, we thank Professors Patricia Goss and Francis Giordano who were kind enough to review and make sensitive comments about Chapter 3, Formal Debate: Procedures and Evaluation.

On a more personal note, we owe a debt of gratitude to Pearl Eisenberg and Roberta Ilardo for their patience and understanding; without it our text on argumentation could never have been born. Each has been an unfailing source of support.

A.M.E.
J.A.I.

1

ORIENTATION
TO ARGUMENTATION

BEHAVIORAL OBJECTS:

After reading this chapter, you should have a better understanding of

1. the two meanings of the word *argument*
2. the difference between argument and persuasion
3. the limitations of argumentation
4. the element of "risk" and how it operates in the field of argumentation
5. the various kinds of arguments and how they differ from one another
6. the purpose of argumentation
7. how written and unwritten rules dictate the structure of arguments
8. how the setting of an argument can influence its course, character, and outcome
9. the role that language plays in an argument
10. why an individual's education and knowledge can play a significant part in the argumentative process

11. how to distinguish between a dialogue, discussion, debate, altercation, and fight

This chapter has two purposes. The first is to introduce you to the world of argument. We will show you around the argumental arena, pointing out what you'll need to know as you begin your study of argumentation. We'll make clear the two senses in which the word *argument* is used. Then we'll discuss the limitations of argumentation so you can establish a realistic set of expectations. Finally we'll point out the risks of arguing, for in our view, a well-conducted argument is simultaneously a challenge and an opportunity for personal growth. By the time you finish this part of the chapter, you will know the major landmarks of the territory that is argumentation. Armed with this knowledge, you will be on familiar ground as you move on to more detailed study.

The second purpose of this chapter is to familiarize you with the kinds of arguments in which people engage. You will learn the distinctions that separate a *dialogue*, a *discussion*, a *debate*, an *altercation*, and a *fight*.

ESSENCE OF ARGUMENT

Two Meanings of Argument

The word *argument* is used in two distinct senses. As an interpersonal event, an argument is a disagreement between people. The exchange may be heated, the language vulgar; as a result feelings are hurt: "I'm not talking to Shirley anymore; we had an argument!" In this sense of the term, an argument almost always implies a scene. Hence, most people hate to argue.

More than a few evenings have been ruined when a friendly disagreement turned into a shouting match. But an interpersonal disagreement can do more than spoil an evening. It can fracture a relationship, drive a wedge between parent and child, signal the death of a long-standing friendship. It can. But it need not.

We hope to show that interpersonal conflict is not always unfortunate. Nor does it necessarily imply the death of a relationship. Sometimes an argument can be healthy. When both parties know *how* to argue, constructive conflict can enrich and deepen any relationship. In short, by becoming familiar with the psychodynamics of argument, you can learn how to argue constructively.

But this is not all you'll need to know. You must also appreciate the rhetorical sense in which the word *argument* is used: *a line of reasoning, with evidence, in support of a conclusion.* When a lawyer says, "I'd like to present the arguments in defense of my client," he is referring to *argument* in the rhetorical sense. Take another example. One may speak of the arguments for and against capital punishment. They are the proofs offered by proponents and opponents to support their positions.

We advance arguments when we want to convince another person. We gather evidence—facts and opinions—we prepare our lines of reasoning, and we do our best to convince our listener. Consider the following dialogue:

Husband:	I think we should sell the car.
Wife:	Why?
Husband:	It gets poor mileage, and repairs have been costing too much.

Here the conclusion being advanced is "we should sell the car." The arguments are: (1) it gets poor mileage, and (2) repairs have been costing too much.

The husband's convincing his wife would depend on how thoroughly he has prepared his case. He should be prepared to answer questions such as these: (1) What mileage does the car get? How does this compare with newer cars? (2) How much has been spent on repairs? How does this compare with the cash outlay required to buy a new car?

These questions are logical. Unless they were satisfactorily answered, the husband and wife could not make a rational decision about whether to sell the car.

As a student of argumentation you will learn how to analyze thoroughly and correctly any topic about which you expect to argue. In addition, you will learn to intelligently evaluate your own reasoned discourse and that of others. Finally, you will be able to prepare the most logically exhaustive and powerful arguments on any topic.

By implication, then, you would become an effective persuader. But what exactly is the relationship between persuasion and argumentation? It is possible to extend a discussion of the relationship between the two for many pages. That is not our wish.[1] Rather, we intend to state simply what we believe the difference to be. There are two main areas of distinction: (1) the function of each and the consequent emphasis placed on various persuasive means; and (2) the criteria of evaluation. Generally speaking, persuasion has as its function the changing of minds by virtually any means short of physical force. Argumentation, conversely, has as its function the establishment of conclusions through reasoned discourse. Thus, most propaganda would fall within the realm of persuasion, not argumentation.

Our second basis of distinction involves the criteria of evaluation. The principal criterion of persuasion is *effectiveness*. If a persuader succeeds in changing people's minds, then he is labeled an effective ("good") persuader. However, the principal criterion of argumentation is *logical cogency*. It would be possible for a speaker to present a "perfect" argumental case and still fail to persuade a popular audience (although he would almost certainly persuade a judge qualified to interpret the evidence and evaluate the case).

---

[1] For a discussion of this topic, see Glen E. Mills, *Reason in Controversy*, 2nd ed. (Boston: Allyn & Bacon, Inc., 1968), pp. 18-29.

In a sense, this book has a dual purpose. We hope to contribute to the development of persons who are both highly skilled in argumentation *and* capable of persuading average audiences. We want to create advocates who possess a mastery of the logical aspects of argument and who know how to employ the various modes of ethical persuasion. Further, we seek to train listeners to be aware of appeals addressed to them by arguers, to be able to evaluate such appeals, and to respond to them intelligently. Our wish is that persuaders will eventually be bound by the same logical and ethical standards that bind practitioners of argumentation. Such an eventuality will provide the best insurance against the insidious growth of demogoguery.

Now that we have seen the two ways in which the word *argument* is used, we can pause a moment. The careful reader has already drawn a number of conclusions. Let's state them explicitly:

1. Argumentation, as defined by the authors, is concerned with the logical proof of propositions and with the psychodynamics of controversy. Subsequent chapters will deal with both the rhetorical and interpersonal aspects of argument.
2. Knowledge of both aspects of argumentation makes one a well-rounded advocate. By understanding the psychology of argument, you learn how to disagree without becoming disagreeable. You learn to avoid "scenes" when you argue. You learn to speak your mind without becoming aggressive and without belittling your opponent. This knowledge will serve you well whether you're arguing with your mother about the use of the family car or with your employer about a raise.
3. Familiarity with the rhetorical aspects of argument prepares you to answer such questions as: what does it mean to prove a conclusion? How does one assess the strengths or weaknesses of arguments for or against a given issue? On what grounds should an argument be accepted or rejected? What is required of someone who is attempting to convince you of a particular idea? This knowledge will prepare you for the rigorous demands imposed on you in formal argument settings. Whether you're arguing on the intercollegiate debate circuit or in small claims court, you'll find a knowledge of the rhetorical aspects of argument invaluable.
4. Knowledge of argumentation can help you prepare for your career. Students in a wide range of fields often comment that they value familiarity with the principles of argumentation. Whether your interest is law, political science, or business, you will be better prepared for your vocation on completing your study of argument.

Limitations of Argumentation

Students often ask us, "What are the limitations of argumentation?" They observe, correctly, that we are enthusiastic about our subject, but they note that if argumentation were such a perfect tool for resolving conflict, then warfare, armed police, and even psychotherapists would not be needed. Their point is well taken. There are limits to what can be accomplished by argumentation. It is important that you recognize them so that you will know what to expect from this book and from yourself.

Argumentation is a tool used by people. Because people are imperfect, argumentation can be misused. For example, the skills and knowledge conveyed between these covers may be employed unethically, to manipulate or to exploit. We certainly don't want to nurture little demagogues. Rather, we hope to help in creating enlightened, reasonable persons who are sensitive to themselves and to others. Alert to the misuse of argumentation, they will be valuable contributors to society.

Intentional misuse aside, a danger still exists. Even sincere and well-meaning people can misuse argumentation. To understand how, we must consider the society in which we live.

It's been said that the products of a society reflect its values. The computer, perhaps our most significant product, has made its way into many areas of our lives. Your registration for this course may have been accomplished with the aid of a computer. Semester grade reports often appear as computer printouts. Computers are used in business, in the medical profession, even in interplanetary space travel. What can the development of the computer tell us about ourselves? Primarily, that we are a logic-dominated society. We tend to view most problems as having logical solutions. Faced with a problem, our first impulse is to say, "Now, let's be logical about it!" We like to think that all problems can be solved by the application of reason and the tools of reason.

We are mistaken. Many of our most significant personal and interpersonal problems do not lend themselves to logical solutions. They are essentially non-logical. They occur on an emotional level.

Applying the principles of argumentation to such problems constitutes misuse. We cannot solve emotional problems by applying logical criteria. A child who is afraid of the dark cannot be argued out of his fear; illogical though it may be, the fear persists. In the same way, many personal and interpersonal conflicts cannot be resolved through logic alone. Whether you're choosing a mate, deciding on a career, or selecting a family doctor, you rely on more than mere logic. To limit consideration to the logical aspects of the problem is to exclude from awareness a major element in decision-making. Which suitor does JoAnn feel more comfortable with? Does Benny like the kind of work he's thinking about? Does the doctor seem approachable and concerned? Such considerations are essential to sound decision-making. Yet they are not logical considerations; they involve feelings, preferences, and emotions.

Because we live in a logic-dominated society it is easy to become sold on the principles of logical argument as a cure-all, a universally applicable method of arriving at the "correct" decision. They are not intended to be such. They constitute a tool. Like any tool, they are designed to perform a specific function. Inappropriate use constitutes misuse.

Let's now turn to another important limitation of argumentation: An argument is only as good as the information on which it is based.

We live in a world that is groaning and creaking under the strains of the information explosion. Experts proliferate like crabgrass. You and I are often confused and overwhelmed by contradictory facts and opinions. Take the assassinations of John Kennedy and Martin Luther King. Were these murders committed by Lee Harvey Oswald and James Earl Ray, respectively? Did the murderers act alone or as part of a national or international conspiracy? Such questions are complicated by the fact that conflicting evidence abounds. Expert testimony becomes self-nullifying as authorities on both sides cancel one another out.

Take nuclear energy. Is it safe? Can we rely on the expert testimony of Atomic Energy Commission officials and top echelon executives in the public utilities? Or should we listen to the engineers who have resigned their posts in the AEC and the utilities to alert the public to the dangers of nuclear energy?

The list could go on. Our point is this: faced with conflicting evidence and disputed facts, many of us are confused. How can we come to a decision? To what can we commit ourselves? Many people are paralyzed by this dilemma. They are unable to decide. They don't know whom to believe. They live in a perpetual state of indecision.

From this dilemma, many turn to argumentation to justify their not taking a stand. "Certainly," they say, "conflicting evidence justifies my indecision!"

In our view, it is a serious error to use conflicting factual information, or testimony, as an excuse for not taking a stand. To say, "I really can't decide" is often a way of saying, "I'm unwilling to commit myself." Sometimes a leap of faith is necessary. Sometimes we must weigh the evidence available, evaluate the sources of the information based on our past experience and knowledge, then let our basic feelings determine our position.

We are not implying that evidence and reasoning should be tossed to the wind. Rather, we want to stress that the applicability of the principles of rhetorical argument is often limited in our complex and confusing world. We must do what we can—assess the arguments we have heard, gather and weigh the evidence, test the reasoning. But we cannot live in a perpetual state of indecision. We must take a stand. No one is perfect, and our decisions may be wrong. But to evade social, political, and moral choices because "we cannot decide" is often an evasion of responsibility, a refusal to live as a human being.

One additional point: Ours is a practical, method-oriented society. We want to learn techniques, prescriptions, methods. "How-to" books abound. For many students, the principal criterion for evaluating a college course is, "What will it teach me to do?" Under these circumstances it is important to clarify what you can expect from the study of argumentation.

We have divided the subject of argumentation into interpersonal and rhetorical aspects. It should be obvious that the principles of rhetorical argument *do* convey a knowledge of specific objective methods and techniques for analyzing, constructing, and evaluating arguments. If you master the skills presented in this volume, you will most assuredly be an expert in logical argument.

The study of the interpersonal dimension of argumentation is only partially centered on technique. We can offer few specific "how-to" instructions about interacting with others on an interpersonal level. Although there are no infallible techniques for winning arguments, a knowledge of the psychodynamics of interpersonal argument can give you a decided advantage. Thus we hope to deepen your knowledge of the interpersonal dimension of argumentation, to heighten your sensitivity to the nonverbal and nonlogical aspects of argument. This will allow you to enter the argumental arena with sophisticated understanding and awareness. We hope also to sharpen your focus on what *you* personally bring to your interpersonal exchanges. Part II of this book addresses itself to this topic; however, we wish to begin here by pointing out how you as a person affect the course and outcome of your disagreements. Simultaneously, we will show why no simple, sure-fire techniques for winning such arguments are possible.

Communication is a form of human behavior. Your communication—the way you talk to others and the way you manage interpersonal conflict—is inseparable from who you are, how you have grown up, the influences that have shaped you. We can never know these. And without such detailed and personal knowledge, we would be foolish to make specific recommendations. (Would a doctor prescribe medication without knowing your illness, your symptoms, your tolerance for different drugs?) This much we can say: To learn to manage interpersonal conflict more effectively, you *must* answer three questions.

First, *what are your patterns of communication when engaged in interpersonal disagreements?* Do you "choke up" when confronted with a hostile opponent? Are you unable to tolerate conflict with certain people? Do you try to get what you want by pussyfooting around and indirectly implying your feelings and wants?

Second, *where do these communication behaviors come from?* All communication behavior is learned. The way your communicate in an argument is, therefore, a learned behavior. Where did it originate? How, for example, did your family handle conflict? Were you taught as a child that anger is "bad," that conflicts should be smoothed over rather than resolved? Did your younger sister or brother learn to handle conflict differently from you? (Maybe women are conditioned to be indirectly manipulative rather than forthright in making demands.[2])

Finally, *what purposes are served by your current ways of handling interpersonal conflict?* What do you gain by managing conflict as you do? All behavior

---

[2]Lynn Z. Bloom, Karen Coburn, and Joan Pearlman, *The New Assertive Woman* (New York: Dell Publishing Co., Inc., 1975), pp. 63-64.

is functional: it serves a purpose. If you can see the reasons behind your current behavior, you can free yourself from the need to go on arguing as you do now.

The interpersonal dimension of argumentation is too complex to make simple prescriptions possible. Consequently, we will not suggest specific techniques in this area. Rather, we will attempt to heighten your awareness of the interpersonal aspects of argument and of the part you play in arguing as you do. From these deeper understandings, perhaps coupled with help from your instructor and classmates, you can begin formulating tailor-made prescriptions for yourself.

Aware of the limitations of logical argument and of your role in conflicts with others, you can develop your skills as an advocate. As you do so, you should recognize the risks involved in arguing.

Risks of Arguing

Conflict is a universal experience of man. Only by confronting and resolving differences do we grow. It is the clash between organism and environment that holds the potential for growth. Faced with unsettling facts and circumstances, we can either retreat to the security of the known and the familiar, or we can venture out. If we venture out we make ourselves vulnerable. We open to scrutiny our time-honored convictions. We strive to comprehend and assimilate the new truths that are available to us.

Sometimes our conflicts are internal ones. Take this example: all his life, seventeen-year-old Chico has been taught that adults are responsible and trustworthy. But today he saw the manager of the supermarket where he works deliberately overprice several fair-traded items. How does Chico react? He must revise the principle on which he's operated for so long. Not *all* adults are responsible and trusthworthy; some clearly are not! Whatever the means by which Chico resolves the dilemma, he has been thrown into internal conflict by what he has observed.

Sometimes our conflicts are interpersonal. Joan and Morty, for example, have been engaged for two years. During that time, Joan has become less and less happy about the prospect of their upcoming marriage. She has grown and changed. She has been involved in the women's movement and as a result has become concerned with fulfilling herself; she's thinking about a medical career. She is even questioning whether she wants to marry and have children. But Morty—well, Morty is still acting like a high-school senior. He seems to have stopped maturing, or at least he's not kept up with Joan. All he thinks about are cars and sex. He has little interest in Joan's fulfillment; he views her as little more than a baby machine and housekeeper. Were Joan to tell Morty of her well-grounded hesitancies, they would certainly experience interpersonal conflict. Their differing expectations and values would surely become the focus of disagreement, which, if well handled, could result in positive change. But for our purposes, the important concept is that by living and growing, by being exposed to ideas, we become parties to interpersonal conflict. Every meaningful interpersonal disagreement holds within it the potential for growth. When we argue with sincerity, when we genuinely bring ourselves to a conflict with openness, we can expand ourselves as a result.

Needless to say, profound and far-reaching changes in one's identity rarely occur as a result of a one-time interpersonal disagreement, for personality is an enduring pheonomenon and it resists change.[3] But interpersonal conflict, whether it emerges in a single exchange or whether it occurs in a series of ongoing disagreements, always holds within it the potential for growth.

We began our introduction to argument with three purposes in mind: (1) to point out the two meanings of the term *argument,* (2) to specify the limitations of argumentation, and (3) to make clear the risks of arguing. We promised to orient you to the field of argument and to lay the groundwork for further study.

Argumentation, as we define the term, is a dualistic discipline. It includes both interpersonal elements (the psychodynamics of argument) and rhetorical ones (analysis and proof).

Under the interpersonal umbrella, you can acquire knowledge of strategies and a heightened awareness of the psychological factors that influence disagreements. Under the rhetorical umbrella, you can learn about proof (reasoning and evidence), logical analysis, and case construction.

Although the principles of argumentation are not universally applicable, they are very useful when applied properly. They can help us think through and solve problems that lend themselves to rational solutions. They represent a tool with which to resolve conflicts systematically, logically, and responsibly. Knowing the principles of argumentation, however, does not make these tasks simple.

When we argue, we take risks. We put ourselves on the line and scrutinize our own beliefs and convictions. In this conflict between organism and environment are the seeds of growth. Nurtured, they spring into bloom. Ignored, they wither.

KINDS OF ARGUMENTS

Strategy plays a central role in all conflict. Great generals have always known that a good commander with few men and supplies can defeat an incompetent one who is well supplied and has many men. Astute politicians recognize that a well-run campaign need not be enormously expensive, that a few well-

[3] See Chapter 8, Know Your Opponent.

timed appearances are worth more than many scheduled at odd times when few people will attend to hear the candidate.

The same principle applies in the world of argument. A well-prepared advocate, keenly aware of the dynamics of the conflict in which he is engaging, can easily outstrip an opponent who, though well-informed, is insensitive to the psychological dynamics of interpersonal disagreement.

In planning strategy, the first thing the advocate must do is to develop a sensitivity to the kind of argument in which he is participating. The nature of the disagreement can help him determine the appropriateness of logical and emotional appeals; it can dictate how much he should rely on his opponent's receptivity to new ideas. In short, it can help him make a number of decisions crucial to his strategy.

Accordingly, we now turn to the kinds of arguments in which people engage. Our discussion will heighten your awareness of some subtle differences that distinguish one kind of argument from another. Armed with this knowledge, you can plan an effective strategy.

To repeat: viewed interpersonally, an argument is *any kind of disagreement between two or more persons.* The many kinds of interpersonal arguments can be distinguished by answering some very important questions. The most fundamental is, *what is the perceived purpose of the exchange?*

Purpose

Are the two parties arguing primarily to satisfy psychological needs? Or is their exchange intended to serve as a basis for a rational decision? How often have you had the experience of talking to someone and at the same time thinking, "I know this guy's not listening to me; he's just waiting for me to finish so he can say his piece!" Perhaps you got this message because of the way he was standing—arms folded and a deadpan face—or because of the vacant look in his eyes. No matter the reason, you knew very well that he wasn't hearing you out for any reason other than to disagree. Your words, your evidence, your logic mattered not at all. What your opponent sought was simply the opportunity to challenge and perhaps to humiliate you.

How the participants view an exchange affects it profoundly. Their attitudes determine the extent to which the disagreement is *people-centered* or *issue-centered.* Do they see the exchange as a personal competition? Do the advocates place primary emphasis on winning—achieving a one-up status over their opponent? In people-centered conflicts the emotional level is high and the rationality index is low. Carl Jung rightly observed that, "rational argument can be conducted with some prospect of success only so long as the emotionality of a given situation does not exceed a certain critical degree. If the affective temperature rises above this level, the possibility of reason's having any effect ceases and its place is taken by slogans and chimerical wish-fantasies." [4] In people-centered conflicts the affective temperature is high, and reason takes a back seat to emotion. Further, the level of open-mindedness is low. Advocates are not receptive to new ideas, but seek only to show up their opponents and "beat" them. Name-calling, laying blame, vulgar language, and other forms of interpersonal aggression occur with great frequency. Discussion is irrational and hostile.

On the other hand, an issue-centered conflict leans to the opposite pole. The parties tend to view the exchange not so much as a personal conflict, but as a common quest for a satisfactory resolution of a problem. Their emphasis is on seeking out areas of mutual interest and common concern. They perceive themselves as engaged in an inquiry—a search for an answer, a solution, or a decision. Consequently, issue-centered conflicts are characterized by relatively low levels of emotionality. The levels of rationality and open-mindedness are high. Name-calling, vulgarity, and other forms of interpersonal aggression are rare, if indeed they occur at all. Hence, the disagreement is civilized. Both parties show respect and regard for each other in the interests of arriving at a satisfactory resolution of their disagreement.

The reader should not get the impression that all arguments fall into two discrete categories, that they can be easily classified as either issue-centered or people-centered. They do not. In the real world, arguments tend toward people-centeredness or issue-centeredness. They are not entirely one or the other. Take a look at the continuum in Figure 1-1 to see what we mean.

FIGURE 1-1   People-Centered and Issue-Centered Conflicts

For convenience we have listed five kinds of interpersonal disagreements, ranging from the *fight* (the most extreme form of people-centered conflict) to the *dialogue* (The most extreme form of issue-centered conflict). The five can be distinguished by the relative degree to which emotionality prevails over rationality. Figure 1-2 shows the extent to which emphasis is placed on winning over the discovery of a satisfactory resolution of the problem.

Figure 1-3 illustrates the levels of emotionality and rationality that characterize each kind of argument.

Figure 1-4 depicts the degree of openmindedness typically evidenced by advocates participating in each type of argument.

[4]C. G. Jung, *The Undiscovered Self* (Boston: Little, Brown & Co., 1958), p. 5.

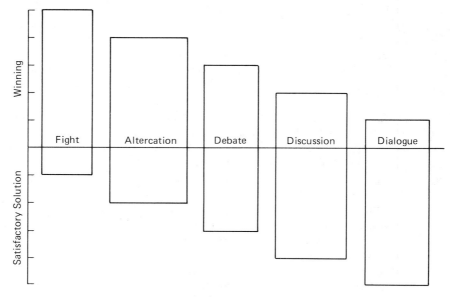

FIGURE 1-2   Emphasis on Winning Versus Finding a Satisfactory Solution:
A Basis for Distinguishing Between Kinds of Arguments

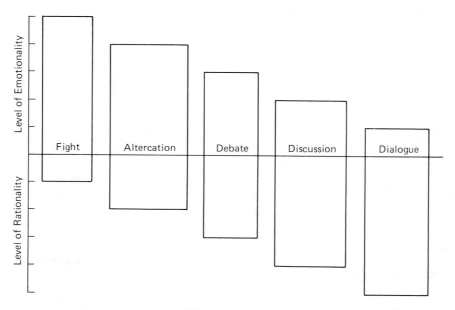

FIGURE 1-3   Levels of Emotionality and Rationality: A Basis for
Distinguishing Between Kinds of Arguments

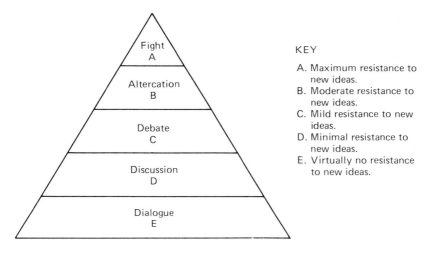

KEY

A. Maximum resistance to new ideas.
B. Moderate resistance to new ideas.
C. Mild resistance to new ideas.
D. Minimal resistance to new ideas.
E. Virtually no resistance to new ideas.

FIGURE 1-4   Degree of Openmindedness In Different Kinds of Arguments

Figure 1-5 shows the incidence of interpersonal aggression in each of the five kinds of arguments.

Thus far we have shown that the purpose of the exchange is one consideration in distinguishing between the various kinds of interpersonal disagreements. Next we turn to the degree of structure that characterizes an exchange.

Structure: Written and Unwritten Rules

Structure derives from rules and regulations. The more rules there are, the more structured the activity. Baseball is highly structured. Most sports are. With-

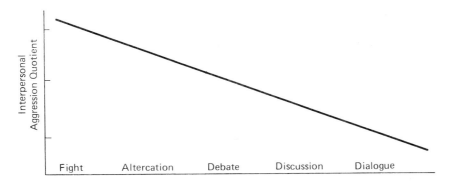

FIGURE 1-5   Interpersonal Aggression Quotient Characteristic of
Each Kind of Argument

out *some* structure, behavior becomes randomized and chaotic; cooperation becomes virtually impossible.

It is important to realize that not all rules and regulations are *written*. Some are unexpressed. They are "beneath the surface" and part of the lore of everyday argument. Nevertheless they are very real, and they exert a profound influence on the outcome of the arguments in which we engage. We must become aware of their presence if we are to learn to *use* structure to our advantage. To summarize, two kinds of rules and regulations give structure to a disagreement: *written rules* and *unwritten rules.*

Written Rules

Sometimes structure is *imposed* on the people who are arguing. In a courtroom or in an intercollegiate debate, for example, there are written rules and regulations (time limits, codes of proper behavior, rules dealing with evidence, witnesses, etc.).[5] Lawyers and intercollegiate debaters must become familiar with these rules if they intend to do an adequate job of defending their points of view. The rules serve to guarantee everyone a fair chance. If advocates start breaking the rules, confusion and inequalities often result. Consequently, there is usually a person present whose chief function is to see that the rules are observed. He may be a judge, a chairman, or the Speaker of the House.

Written rules are intended to serve the advocates—to help them do a thorough and fair job of arguing. Most people realize the value of rules and regulations. They are often set up during the course of an argument by people who know their advantages. Have you ever heard a comment like this: "Now wait a minute! We're never going to settle this if we just keep shouting at one another. You say your piece, then I'll say mine!" What has happened in this situation is that the advocates have agreed to establish definite rules to govern their disagreement. They have voluntarily imposed structure on their exchange. This happens when opinions are far apart and the advocates really *want* to settle their differences.

The presence or absence of written rules serves as a basis of distinction between the kinds of disagreements listed earlier. The situation can be viewed along a continuum. At both ends there are very few written rules. A dialogue has few written rules to go by; in a fight virtually anything goes. But as we move toward the center of the continuum, the influence of written rules tends to increase, peaking at the *debate* point in the scale. Parliamentary procedure is probably the most elaborate and refined system of rules for governing disputes. Knowledge of at least the essential rules is a *must* for anyone planning to argue in an organization regulated by parliamentary procedure.[6]

---

[5] See Chapter 3, Formal Debate: Procedures and Evaluation.

[6] See Bibliography under Parliamentary Procedure.

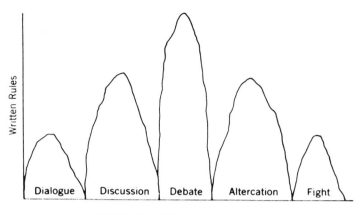

FIGURE 1-6   Written Rules Continuum

The continuum mentioned above can be visually depicted as shown in Figure 1-6.

Unwritten Rules

We are often unaware of the effect that certain unwritten rules and regulations can have on us. Sociologists call them *mores, norms of behavior,* or *customs.* In our society one of the unwritten rules we abide by is that of "no touching, except handshakes and such, unless in an intimate or sexual context." Picture this: You walk up to a stranger in the street and ask directions. As you're talking, he places his hand on your shoulder. What would your reaction be? Maybe you'd get suspicious or frightened; perhaps you would be pleased. But almost certainly you would sense that some unwritten rule of social intercourse had been broken. If he were to lean very close to you, you would really feel uncomfortable! We hesitate to predict what would happen if he said something like, "Excuse me for interrupting your question, but you look like a very nice person. I'd like to get to know you better. Would you come join me for a cup of coffee?" In each of his three actions, the man we innocently turned to for directions violated an unwritten norm or rule of social conduct.

The same kind of unwritten rules occur in our day-to-day exchanges. Generally, the fewer written rules governing our disputes, the more *unwritten rules* there are. Have you ever had this experience? You're talking with someone about a controversial subject. The exchange is pleasant and heated. You go on like this for a while, then suddenly—and perhaps unintentionally—you say or do something that causes a change in your listener's mood. Perhaps you raised your voice a bit too much or pounded the table a little too hard. Whatever happened, it cause a shift in the nature of the exchange. You moved from a

15

dialogue to a discussion or from a debate to an altercation. You feel as though you stepped over an invisible foul line or into an unmarked danger zone. But it's too late. Your friend is transformed into an opponent, and now you've got to save face! What happened is that you violated an unwritten, subsurface rule of argument.

The number of unwritten rules seems to increase as we move from debate toward either end of our continuum. It is almost as though in a debate, where there are so many written rules, unwritten ones are frequently unnecessary. But the fewer written rules we have to go by, the more we need unwritten rules. The situation can be depicted as shown in Figure 1-7.

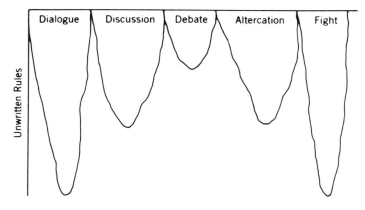

FIGURE 1-7   Unwritten Rules Continuum

It might be enlightening now to combine our two continua and look at the written-unwritten rules concepts together. See Figure 1-8.

In the chapters to follow you will learn more about written and unwritten rules that govern confrontations.[7]

Language

The language used in a disagreement can help us label it as a *dialogue,* a *discussion,* a *debate,* and so forth. Popular experience has demonstrated that the more crass and vulgar the language, the more apt we are to be witnessing a *fight.* However, as the language improves, we tend to ascend the scale, and we are perhaps witnessing a *debate,* a *discussion,* or a *dialogue.* Consider Figure 1-9.

---

[7] See Chapter 2, Rules of the Game, and Chapter 3, Formal Debate.

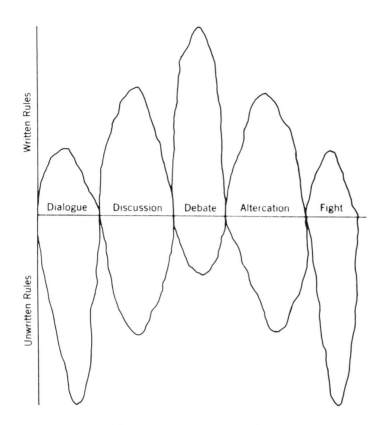

FIGURE 1-8   Written and Unwritten Rules Continua

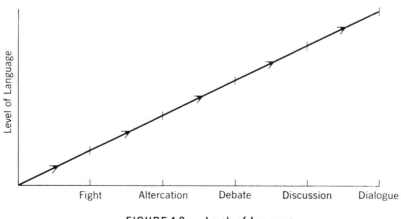

FIGURE 1-9   Levels of Language

17

Language reveals a wealth of information about the confrontation we may be observing or engaged in and about the people involved in it. We have already seen how the level of language can tell us the label we should apply to an argument. The words also reveal a great deal about the persons arguing. At a fairly obvious level, the words used by a person tell us something about how well educated he is and whether he's experienced or inexperienced in exchanging points of view. In addition, words tell us about the person's emotional state (is he calm or excited?), about his familiarity with the subject matter in question (does he know what he's talking about? does he use the proper words to express his ideas?), and often about his motive or goal in arguing (is he trying to impress us? confuse us?). Every word and utterance involves: (1) *representation*—words perform a symbolic function; they stand for the things we are talking about; (2) *expression*—words reveal emotion, the subjective feelings of the person using them; and (3) *appeal*—words often reveal the purpose or goal of the person using them.[8]

Education and Knowledge

Often the amount of formal education, as well as the knowledge each person has about the subject, makes a difference in the nature of their exchange. Usually, the better educated and more intelligent the participants, the more likely they are to avoid *altercations* and *fights* and to engage in *dialogues* and *discussions*. Along the same lines, the more the participants know about the subject of the disagreement, the more likely they are to handle themselves in a cool and rational manner. In other words, the *probability* that a disagreement will turn into a *fight decreases* as the participants' amount of formal education and knowledge of the subject matter *increases*. The scale can be drawn as in Figure 1-10.

Of course, this graph does not set down an absolute rule. We can't *guarantee* that well-educated or intelligent people never have arguments or fights. So many factors come into play—including the education, intelligence, and knowledge of the *other* party in the disagreement, the emotionality of the topic—that we dare not set down rigid rules. We have to deal with *probabilities,* which are always subject to exceptions.

One last note: We have made an important distinction here between *an educated person* and *an intelligent one.* An educated person is not necessarily intelligent nor is an intelligent one necessarily educated. Although the odds are heavily weighted on the side of the intelligent person's being educated, this is not an infallible rule.

Educated people are expected to carry around in their heads more information than uneducated people. But even if we admit that educated people are

---

[8] See Chapter 8, Know Your Opponent, for more about language.

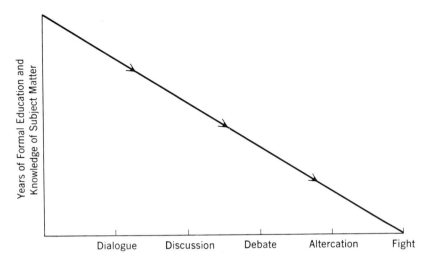

FIGURE 1-10   Probability of Occurrence of Different Types of Disagreements
Based on Participants' Formal Education and Knowledge of
Subject Matter

walking storehouses of data, which is usually not so, their data is useless unless
they also have:

1. the ability to recall information from their memory banks when
    needed
2. the intelligence to know what information to recall in response to a
    specific situation
3. the ability to manipulate the information recalled
4. the ability to see associations among bits of information

Having a superior education does not, in itself, give one an argumental edge. Few
arguments will be won by educated people if education succeeds only in turning
out warehouses groaning with bits and pieces of information rather than transforming the mind into a finely-honed instrument of communication.

Setting

Few people realize how much an interaction is affected by the setting or
context in which it occurs. By setting we mean *physical place*. An encounter
between two women in a law library would probably differ from an encounter in
a tavern. Setting also refers to the *physical makeup of the place* (furniture style,
wall colors, etc.); everyone knows that certain colors are exciting (red), others

soothing (green), and still others depressing (black). Yet it is the rare advocate who considers the impact of these factors on his disagreements.

Among the influential factors relating to the location of a disagreement are these: (1) *Who owns the place?* Is it likely that you would get into an argument with a host in his own home? (2) *What is the nature of the place?* The familiar admonitions, "That's no way to talk in church!" and, "That's not a topic we should talk about in a funeral parlor!" reveal that the nature of a place may influence the development and course of an argument. (3) *Why have people come together here?* Surely you've heard a wife say to her husband at a party, "Would you mind not discussing that now? Can't it wait till we get home?" Such factors as these reveal that *where* an exchange takes place can vitally affect its nature in two basic ways: First, the setting, context, or location can prevent *a discord* (even at the *dialogue* level) *from developing*—the wife's "Do you mind not discussing that now?" is really a request (or an order) to avoid the introduction of a potentially or actually controversial topic. If she were forced to go on with her admonition, she might well add something like: "We're all here to relax and have a good time. Why bring up my mother again?"

Second, the setting, context, or location of a disagreement can affect *the cutting off of a confrontation at a certain level.* The guest who politely sidesteps a heated encounter with his host is probably unconscious of his action. What he did was to avoid the risk of a heated *debate* or *altercation* by terminating the exchange at the *discussion* level.

The word *context* should be interpreted broadly so as to include psychological as well as physical elements. With this in mind, we consider two additional contextual factors capable of influencing an exchange: psychological climate and persons present.

PSYCHOLOGICAL CLIMATE

Are the participants happy? If so, they'll probably try to avoid spoiling their mood by arguing. Are they angry or resentful? If so, they'll probably encourage a scrap. It should not go unnoticed that the physical setting, temperature, humidity, room colors, and so on, do create and affect the psychological climate.

PERSONS PRESENT

The people with us strongly influence the prevailing psychological climate. If we like them and are comfortable with them, we tend to feel good. But if we don't like them (we may be suspicious of a fellow worker or bored by dull company), then we'll probably contribute to a bad psychological climate. The very real psychological phenomenon described by the slang term "bad vibes" can travel around a room with surprising speed. Have you ever purposely avoided inviting two particular guests to the same party because you knew what would happen when they came together? If you have, then you know what we mean when we say that the psychological climate can be affected by the people present.

WRAP-UP

The goal of this chapter was to introduce you to the world of argument and, by so doing, to improve your ability to disagree without being disagreeable. Another of its objectives was to make you aware of the fact that the word *argument* can be used in two senses: as an *interpersonal* event, or as a *rhetorical* event.

Also stressed in this opening section was the notion that argumentation is a field of inquiry made up of the basic principles of logic and rhetoric that underlie reasoned discourse. The chapter provides guidelines that help answer such questions as: what constitutes a sound argument and how we know when a conclusion is proved. Although principally concerned with the logical proof of propositions, argumentation has application when persuasion, and not just logical demonstration, is called for.

To argue is to take a risk. We encourage you to embark on a serious study of argumentation and, by so doing to take such risks. If approached sensibly, argument can contribute to personal growth and maturity.

We differentiated between five kinds of disagreements on the basis of the following criteria: (1) level of emotionality; (2) openmindedness; (3) structure of an exchange; (4) language used; (5) educational level; (6) advocates' knowledge of subject matter; and (7) setting of the disagreement.

Overall, the success of this chapter hinges on the ability of the reader to come away from it with a somewhat revised conception of argumentation and its role in today's world.

PROBES, PRODS, AND PROJECTS

Are the people who think logically inclined to be more OPEN- or CLOSED-minded? Why?

What do you think would happen in a society where courses in argumentation and persuasion were made compulsory in public schools and colleges?

Ordinarily, can you tell who won an argument solely by analyzing WHAT WAS SAID?

If the rules of logic were strictly applied in the business world, what do you think would happen?

Would you agree that you can have PERSUASION without ARGUMENT, but not ARGUMENT without PERSUASION? Why?

Is it realistic to ask an advocate to adjust to such things as wall colors and room temperatures?

Recall the distinctions among dialogues, discussions, debates, altercations, and fights. The next time you're in an argument, try "shifting gears." If your opponent speaks to you on a dialogue level, try responding as though you were in a debate; if you are having an altercation, try moving up to the dialogue level. This exercise can also be staged before a group of observers to see what their reaction is.

Americans are up tight about physical contact. Familiar expressions like "Hands off," "Keep your hands to yourself," "Do not handle" bespeak this preoccupation. To know the effects of touching in an argument, try holding hands with your opponent. Next, try placing your hand on his forearm, shoulder, or knee. Whereas some people are impervious to physical contact, others are disconcerted by it. Many, as soon as they are touched, can't think straight. Are you one of the "untouchables"?

It has been said that position is everything in life. If this were true, it would play an important role in an argument. People argue in varying positions. Married people often argue horizontally. Mothers insist that their sons or daughters sit when they argue with them. "Sit down, young man, I want to talk to you." It's difficult to argue if you must constantly look up at someone. Try arguing in different positions: one person seated and one standing; both lying down; one standing with the other lying down; back to back. Perhaps you have some ideas of your own. Try them.

Part One

Rhetorical Aspects
of Argument

2

RULES OF THE GAME: PROPOSITIONS, PROOF, and PREPARATION

BEHAVIORAL OBJECTIVES

After reading this chapter, you should have a better understanding of

1. why rules are so important in the world of argumentation
2. what propositions are and how best to analyze them
3. the difference between inquiry and advocacy
4. what the term *burden of proof* means and how it operates in a debate
5. how the terms *status quo* and *presumption* are applied to the debate situation
6. a *prima facie* case, and who has the responsibility of establishing it in a debate
7. the three kinds of propositions: fact, value, and policy
8. how a debater should go about gathering data in preparation for a debate
9. the nature of proof, its significance to the debater, and the role it plays in a debate

10. the Toulmin Model and how to use it
11. the different kinds of evidence and their tests
12. the various ways one may "reason" when engaged in a debate
13. a debate brief and how one goes about preparing it

In sports, politics, business, and love, there are rules. Adhering to them raises not only the level of efficiency but also the level of enjoyment. This applies equally to argumentation. People should learn to disagree without becoming disagreeable. Knowing the rules of argument and abiding by them helps one achieve this goal.

Before going further, a clarification is in order. There are two classes of rules that govern interpersonal argument. One is of interest primarily to the formal debater. It includes rules concerning the format employed in debate tournaments—for example, time limits and rules governing the order of speakers.

The other set of rules is of universal interest and utility. Rules and procedures concerning the analysis of propositions, for instance, are of critical importance to *anyone* engaging in interpersonal argument.

The school debater must, of course, master all the material presented on the following pages. However, casual renders may elect to skip material that pertains only to school debate.

What, then, do we set out to do on the pages to follow? Argumentation is principally concerned with the logical proof of propositions. In this chapter, we study the essence of argumentation: propositions and proof. The chapter is divided into four sections. In the first, we define word *proposition,* point out the kinds of propositions one may argue, and present guidelines for their analysis. The second section consists of an examination of the concept of proof. In it, we distinguish between reasoning and evidence and present seven kinds of evidence and their tests. In the third section of the chapter, we sent down the seven most commonly encountered patterns of reasoning and the tests of their validity. The fourth section describes the debate brief and offers suggestions for its preparation. In the next chapter, Formal Debate: Procedures and Evaluation, you will find other rules that apply specifically to the school debate.

NATURE OF PROPOSITIONS

Here is a formal definition of the word *proposition.*

> *A proposition is a statement growing out of and providing focus for a controversy; properly worded, a proposition calls for some change in belief, action, or both, thereby placing the burden of proof on its pro-*

> *ponents and giving the presumption to its*
> *opponents.*

Let us now look at each of the elements in our defintion.

> *A proposition is a statement growing out of*
> *and providing focus for a controversy. . .*

Controversy occurs when two or more people disagree about something. Current national controversies include nuclear disarmament, energy policy, the urban fiscal crisis, ecology, and a national health care plan. Doubtless, others will arise as time passes. The editorial page of your local newspaper will reveal any number of public controversies. Such controversies are the stuff of which debate propositions are made. Here are two examples of formal propositions springing from controversies.

> *RESOLVED, That the federal government*
> *should establish a program of national health*
> *care.*

> *RESOLVED, That the federal government*
> *should allocate funds for the relief of the*
> *urban fiscal crisis.*

When they are well worded, formal propositions like these provide rallying points for the advocate. Hence, propositions do not simply grow out of controversies. They provide a focus for disagreement by embodying the essence of a controversy and give all parties an opportunity to express their views.

Inquiry and Advocacy

It is important to recognize that controversies can give rise to questions as well as propositions. The nuclear disarmament controversy, for instance, can spawn the question, "What should be this nation's policy with respect to nuclear disarmament?" Or, it can spawn the proposition: "RESOLVED, That the United States undertake a policy of unilateral nuclear disarmament."

A question places emphasis on inquiry—the search for an answer. A proposition, on the other hand, places emphasis on advocacy—the urging of a particular conclusion about a controversy. For several reasons (among them, man's quest for power and influence over his fellows), advocacy seems to be practiced more often than inquiry. Neither is inherently superior; both can go wrong. With knowledge and proper guidance, however, both may serve as useful and effective tools.

One of the potential dangers in advocacy is that it may occur before the topic under discussion has been thoroughly explored. Surely you've met the person who knows pitifully little about a given topic but insists on arguing for or against it. In many people's minds, advocacy is separate from inquiry. However, it is important to recognize that argumentation involves inquiry as well as advocacy.

We intend to show that the inquiry phase of advocacy is more than mere mental gymnastics; it is a practical, common-sensical preparation for argument. Let us now turn to the second element in our definition of *proposition:*

> *. . . properly worded, a proposition calls for some change in belief, action, or both, thereby placing the burden of proof on its proponents and giving the presumption to its opponents.*

Consider the propositions in Figure 2-1.

We are bombarded by messages like these every day. All have one thing in common: *they call for some change in belief, action, or both.* Propositions properly worded for argument do this. The reason is simple: What is the point of arguing an already established policy? Why would you argue in favor of the proposition, "Students' work in college courses should be graded," unless someone had argued *against* the policy? There is simply no point in arguing for an existing policy unless someone contests it. And the person who argues *against* it thereby advocates some kind of change. He "initiates the action" (a phrase borrowed from the courts) because he is dissatisifed with the existing state of affairs. This advocate is said to have the *burden of proof*—a term referring to the responsibility of the supporter of a proposition to establish it beyond a reasonable doubt.

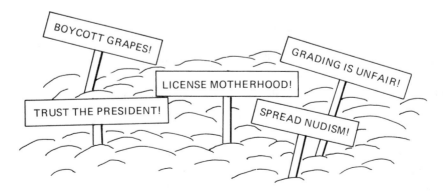

FIGURE 2-1   Propositions

To discharge the burden of proof in a formal debate, the affirmative (supporter of the proposition) must do two things. First, it must show that the present state of affairs is inherently inferior, possessing shortcomings that are derived from its very nature and that the proposal advanced will overcome.[1] Next, it must demonstrate that the proposal will improve the present situation without creating new and more serious evils.

Beware of the sophist who argues for change but refuses to assume the burden of proof. Point out that his accepting the burden of proof goes hand-in-hand with his advocating a change. This strategy serves to prevent undisciplined advocacy. Tell your opponent when he has the burden of proof. Consider the following:

Student:	I think final exams should be abolished.
Professor:	Why?
Student:	Because I don't think they serve any purpose.
Professor:	You can't just demand a change without giving convincing reasons for it. Back up your argument!

If this student cannot fulfill the burden of proof by offering reasonable and convincing arguments, he will fail to convince the professor.

Burden of proof is the counterpart of *presumption.* The latter refers to the "logical advantage" held by an opponent of a proposition. In our courts of law, a man is *presumed* innocent until proven guilty. The presumption is in his favor; the burden of proof rests on the prosecution. Actually, the presumption is often arbitrarily decided upon. It may be convenient, however, to think in terms of their being a presumption in favor of existing institutions.[2] In our society, we generally presume that monogamy is the "best" form of marriage. Anyone arguing for polygamy would assume the burden of proof. He would be proposing a departure from the *status quo,* the existing state of affairs. By the same yardstick, an American arguing for monogamy in a polygamous society would shoulder the burden of proof. The defenders of polygamy, in this case, would have the presumption in their favor.

In formal debate, the negative side has the *presumption* in its favor. It is the affirmative team that is advocating a change and must prove the need for its proposal as well as its workability. The negative side need only oppose the position advanced by the affirmative. They may wish to amass arguments showing there is little or nothing wrong with the present situation. Second, the negative may concede there is a minor problem, but that its solution does not require the elaborate plan proposed by the affirmative.

---

[1] See Chapter 3, Formal Debate: Procedures and Evaluation, for a more detailed treatment of each side's options and responsibilities.

[2] See Richard Whately, *Elements of Rhetoric* (London: John W. Parker, 1846), pp. 140-46.

> *Thus, a proposition is a statement growing out of and providing focus for a controversy; properly worded, a proposition calls for some change in belief, action, or both, thereby placing the burden of proof on its supporters and giving the presumption to its opponents.*

Another term that the advocate must be familiar with is *burden of rebuttal.* It refers to the responsibility each side has to respond to the arguments advanced by the opposition. Each side is required not only to refute opposing proofs but to defend its own case against attack.[3] Unlike the presumption and burden of proof (both of which remain constant during the debate), the burden of rebuttal continually shifts back and forth. It accounts for the give-and-take of a debate.

Neither the affirmative nor the negative is required to present absolute proofs. Debaters argue alternatives—the choices available by which to solve problems. To establish a conclusion, the advocate must show his position is reasonable and practical. To argue in favor of the government's support of solar energy research, you would want to establish the rationale for such a policy. You need not establish public support for such an endeavor. No one can know for certain what the public mood will be several months from now. It is important only to show that your position on solar energy is rational and practical.

The development of a *prima facie* case is the responsibility of the affirmative team. For a case to be *prima facie,* it must contain logical and convincing arguments, it must make sense, and it must stand on its own merits until arguments are leveled against it. In debate theory, a *prima facie* case implies the following: (1) a need exists and can be demonstrated, (2) the existing problem cannot be solved within the *status quo,* and (3) the affirmative plan is workable and will meet the need.

Kinds of Propositions

Three types of propositions can be argued. Can you distinguish among the following?

Mr. Thompson is a better teacher than Miss Burrage.

Peter Piper is a pimp.

A law should be passed declaring people over forty ineligible to vote.

---

[3]The word *case* in this context means the response to the proposition. A case is a detailed and complete stand or position taken with respect to a proposition. See Chapter 3 for additional information.

The first proposition is a *value* statement. The second is a proposition of *fact.* The third is a proposition of *policy* or *action.* These differences are significant because each statement requires a slightly different proof approach. You cannot argue a proposition of fact as though it were a proposition of action. Before getting into the details, however, a distinction should be made between propositions of fact, value, and policy.

Propositions of fact assert a relationship between two things. Factual propositions are objectively verifiable—that is, we can prove a proposition of fact without depending on subjective feelings or beliefs. A fact is a fact, and careful scrutiny of observables will verify it.

Propositions of value are based on subjective reactions. The proof of value propositions (which assert that something is good, bad, right, wrong, better than, worse than, etc.) often depends on subjective feelings and evaluations. Proof that Mr. Thompson is a better teacher than Miss Burrage would ultimately be contingent on one's subjective beliefs about what makes a good teacher.

Proof of factual propositions, however, is not dependent on subjective evaluations. Peter Piper either is or is not a pimp. Proof of the proposition must be established through an analysis of objective data. The law defines crimes associated with prostitution. Therefore, if Peter Piper is to be found guilty of pimping, it would have to be established that he did, in fact, sell flesh. If Peter Piper is to be convicted of pimping, this element in the legal definition of the crime must be established. It is objectively verifiable—that is, capable of being proven without a dependence on subjective feelings or evaluations. For instance, if it could be established that Peter Piper had no knowledge of, or dealing with, the prostitutes in question, he could not be convicted of pimping. A fact is a fact!

Although the distinction between facts and values is not as clear-cut as many people imagine,[4] the following principle is generally true: The more the proof of a proposition is dependent on the subjective feelings or emotional reactions of its supporters, the more likely it is to be a proposition of value; conversely, the less dependent it is on those subjective feelings and emotional reactions, the more likely it is to be a proposition of fact.

Propositions of policy or action are so named because they demand that something be *done.* "Yankee go home" calls for more than a belief; it calls for action. The proposition, *a law should be passed declaring people over forty ineligible to vote,* is a policy proposition. It is, like all propositions of policy, based upon subpropositions of both fact and value, as depicted below:

(Policy)   A law should be passed declaring people over forty ineligible to vote.

[4]Kenneth Boulding, *The Image* (Ann Arbor, Michigan: University of Michigan Press, 1956), pp. 173-74.

(Fact)   People over forty are incapable of making responsible political judgments.

(Value)   Failure to disenfranchise people over forty would create a real and present danger to the security and well-being of this nation.

Of the three kinds of propositions, the most sophisticated, and the one requiring the most elaborate proof, is the proposition of policy.

Proposition Analysis

Chemists analyze compounds in order to understand them. For the same reason, advocates analyze propositions. Presently we will suggest a number of considerations that should be made in analyzing a proposition prior to a confrontation. The order in which these considerations appear here follows the natural sequence occurring in a common-sensical approach. Although other sequential arrangements may work better for you, we recommend the use of this order as a starting point.

EVOLUTION OF A PROPOSITION

Understanding someone means understanding how they came to be what they are. Propositions, like people, have elaborate and complex histories. We can best understand them by considering the situations and context from which they emerged.

Earlier we said that propositions grow out of and provide focus for controversy. It is possible to identify a prepositional phase occurring in the genesis of a proposition. The state is characterized by vague feelings of dissatisfaction on the part of concerned people. For example, I may be vaguely dissatisfied with the current state of affairs in my neighborhood. There's been trouble between groups of young people. Homeowners complain that their property is being damaged. Loud music from a few houses keeps people awake nights. Teenagers complain about crabby adults and nagging parents. I have the suspicion that something constructive can come out of this ill will. All these feelings, experiences, and ideas remain in an amorphous mass, swirling around inside my head, possessing neither form nor force. If I were sufficiently concerned, I would refine my thinking, order my resentments, and formulate a proposition: *A neighborhood citizen group concerned of equal numbers of young people and adults should be organized.* Here, simply put, is how a proposition evolves. More complicated propositions have longer and more elaborate histories. But however simple or elaborate, the same phases can be identified. These phases are illustrated in the flow chart shown in Figure 2-2.

Tracing the evolution of a proposition often involves placing it in context.

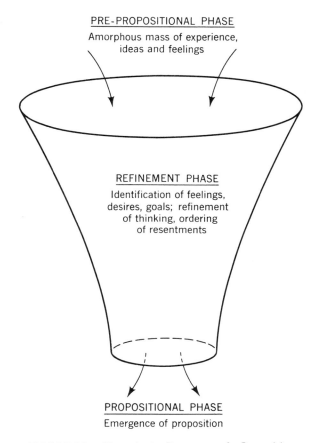

PRE-PROPOSITIONAL PHASE
Amorphous mass of experience,
ideas and feelings

REFINEMENT PHASE
Identification of feelings,
desires, goals; refinement
of thinking, ordering
of resentments

PROPOSITIONAL PHASE
Emergence of proposition

FIGURE 2-2 Phases in the Emergence of a Proposition

It is advisable to consider how the proposition is related to the things around it, including broad historical and intellectual contexts. Understanding a proposition referring to women's liberation may require a knowledge of feminism in American history. Likely, we could better understand this cause if it were placed in an historical context.

To wit, an advocate cannot properly understand a proposition unless he has some conception of its history and context. Without such insight, advocacy becomes little more than a dehumanized exercise in word-play.

SEMANTIC ANALYSIS OF A PROPOSITION

A proposition is a sequential arrangement of words having meaning. Preparation for an argument demands a knowledge of the meanings of all the key words in a proposition. For example, what do I mean when I say that certain

33

doctors perform *unnecessary* surgery? What makes surgery *necessary?* When is it *unnecessary?* Another manifestation of the results of semantic confusion was a recent debate over school *decentralization.* The controversy was compounded because different factions used the word in more than one sense, and nobody seemed to realize it! Opponents in an argument should agree on the meanings of the key words in their proposition. If they cannot agree, they ought to arbitrate a decision, for this may strike at the heart of their disagreement!

To spare the reader a lengthy discussion of semantics, we will present a selected number of facts that the advocate should be aware of when conducting the semantic analysis of a proposition.

1. Language—a retreat from reality. Words are not their referents (the things they represent), just as a map is not the territory it charts. Language is a shared, structured, social code having no direct connection with reality. Words are symbols and are arbitrary (a *chair* might just as well be called a *flegnis*). Language is a human contrivance. We should rule over language, but often it rules us (like many institutions created by man). Edward Sapir, Benjamin Whorf, and others have argued for the concept of linguistic relativity, which states that language determines our perception. We can only "see" what our language tells us is there. Eskimos have several words for snow, words that take into account its qualities—packed powder, glassy surface, whatever; hence, they can more readily see differences in snow. It has been said that the limits of our language are the limits of our world.

The more abstract the language we use, the further removed it is from tangible reality. Words like *peace* and *faith* are high-level abstractions because they have less specific referents than low-level abstractions like *electric typewriter* and *steak knife.*

The more abstract a word, the greater the likelihood of its being misunderstood, and the more emotionality it invites. Words can have both a denotative and a connotative meaning. Such words as *communist* and *right-wing* are endowed with the potential to evoke personal meanings and subjective associations well beyond their denotative (or dictionary) definitions. It is interesting to speculate whether the millions of men throughout history who have died for the causes of *justice, truth,* and *humanity* would have done so for such low-level abstractions as *chocolate cookies* or *ice cream.*[5]

2. Nonallness. You can never say all there is to say about anything. Everything is probable. Absolute statements (for example, John is a bad student) may conceal more than they reveal. They fail to consider that not all members of a group are the same. Second, they overlook the fact that people behave differently according to time, place, and circumstance. General semanticists encourage us to be oriented toward "someness" rather than "allness."

---

[5] On this subject, see "Conversation with Arthur Koestler" in *Psychology Today,* IV (June 1970), especially pp. 80-84.

3. Labels specify continua. When we read a word, we often assume that it means one thing and only one thing. But words may encompass a wide range of meanings. The political label *Republican,* for example, refers to a party in which a wide range of opinion exists. Thus, we can illustrate the meaning of the label *Republican* as shown in Figure 2-3.

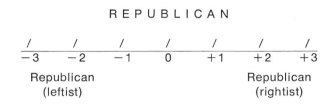

FIGURE 2-3   Range of Word Meanings

An awareness of the dangers inherent in the use of language can ensure against the occurrence of nonproductive advocacy. Whenever possible, come to some agreement with your opponent on the meanings of terms to be used in an argument. In some cases, such as propositions of fact, the entire controversy hinges on the meaning of a word. Consider this proposition: The traditional role of the housewife is anachronistic. Before the controversy can be resolved, we must establish the meaning of *anachronistic;* it is very likely that most, if not all, of the argument will be devoted to establishing that meaning.

Issues

Determining the issues underlying a proposition is one of the most important steps in proposition analysis. What are issues? They are questions that must be answered in the course of arguing a proposition. For example, you are sitting in class, and a student enters, interrupts the proceedings, and urges everyone to come to join a march on the administration building. He gives no reason for the march; he just says, "Come join us!" Would you leave the room and follow him? Would it be logical for you to do this? Most likely, if you had the chance, you would ask him a question or two: "Is there some problem or conflict with the administration that warrants our marching on the building?" What you have done is to formulate an *issue.* Unless the student were able to give you a satisfactory answer, you'd probably stay put, convinced that there's no need to do what he advocates.

Issues are questions. They are inherent and crucial questions within a proposition. By *inherent,* we mean that issues exist within a proposition. They are discovered or found, not arbitrarily chosen. You have heard of advocates who argue *irrelevant issues.* These are issues that have no central bearing on the proposition; they are fabricated, as when a political candidate, accused of corruption, argues that his voting record reflects support for the working class. This matter is irrelevant to the charge of corruption. He is arguing an *irrelevant issue*.

When we say that an issue is a *crucial* question, we mean that *each* issue *must* be dealt with by the supporters of a proposition (unless waived or admitted by the opposition) if the proposition is to be established. Take the following case: John lives in an apartment house. One day there is a knock on his door. His neighbor explains that she will be going away for a few days and asks John to take care of her Siamese cat. She gives John a key to her apartment and tells him to go in once a day to feed the cat, change the drinking water, and such. John agrees. The next night John decides to feed the cat at 7:30, but he cannot find the key to the adjacent apartment! Feeling responsible for the cat's well-being, John takes a hairpin and screwdriver and picks the lock. He spends fifteen minutes tinkering with it. Finally the door swings open. John enters, turns on the light, places the hairpin and screwdriver on the kitchen table, and proceeds to feed the cat. Ten minutes later the police appear, take John into custody, and book him on the charge of burglary. The hairpin and screwdriver are confiscated as evidence.

The law defines burglary as the crime of (1) breaking and (2) entering (3) a private dwelling (4) at night (5) with felonious intent. For John to be convicted of burglary, *all* these issues must be answered in the affirmative by the prosecution:

1.   Did John break into the room in question?
2.   Did he enter the room?
3.   Is the room a private dwelling or part of a private dwelling?
4.   Did John commit the act at night?
5.   Did John have felonious intent?

If the prosecution fails to establish *any one of these,* John will be found innocent.

How about John's defense attorney? Must he argue all these issues? Is each of these issues crucial so far as he is concerned? The answer is no. The defense (or the opposition to the proposition) has the option of dealing with as few as one or as many as all the issues inherent in the proposition. In other words, the defense attorney need answer only one issue in the negative. By so doing, he can disprove the proposition. In John's case, the defense attorney would *waive* or *admit* the first four issues. He would agree that John (1) broke into and (2) entered (3) a private dwelling (4) at night. But he would argue that *John did not have felonious intent.* The testimony of John's next-door neighbor would, in this case, be sufficient to establish John's innocence.

In a sense, then, the supporters of a proposition have a more difficult task than the opponents. The supporters must answer *all* the issues. They must present what is called in debate jargon a *prima facie* (complete or logically adequate) *case.* The opponents, by contrast, need only establish *one* issue in the negative. This seems proper because, as we explained earlier, the supporters of a proposition take upon themselves the *burden of proof;* whereas the opponents are said to have the *presumption* in their favor.

Although few of us will ever have the opportunity to argue a burglary case in court, we ought to be cognizant of the fact that the same principles regarding issues apply to *any* argument. Awareness of the issues in a controversy facilitates systematic advocacy. Below is a list of propositions and the issues inherent in them. Study them. Form the habit of analyzing propositions to determine the issues to be argued.

My wife is guilty of adultery. (Proposition of fact)
Issues:

1. Has my wife performed an act of sexual intercourse with another man?

Buying a farm is a good financial investment for me. (Proposition of value)
Issues:

1. Have farm values been increasing for a reasonably long time?
2. Is it highly probable that farm values will continue to increase?
3. Would buying a farm meet my personal financial objectives?

Marlowe is a better playwright than Shakespeare. (Proposition of value)
Issues:

1. Are Marlowe's plots more intricate and clearly developed than those of Shakespeare?
2. Are Marlowe's characters more clearly defined and alive than those of Shakespeare?
3. Is the language of Marlowe's plays more beautiful than that of Shakespeare's?

The Predmobile is more economical than the Kratmobile. (Proposition of fact)
Issues:

1. Does the Predmobile get better gas mileage?
2. Is the Predmobile less costly to maintain?
3. Does the Predmobile have a greater resale value?

Among the preceding examples, a proposition of policy was not included. The reason is that the issues in a proposition of policy can be derived by applying the following four *stock issues* to the proposition in question:

1. Is there a need for the proposed change?
2. Will the proposed change bring about a substantial improvement in the present situation?
3. Will the proposed change bring about those improvements without creating new and more serious problems?
4. Is the proposed plan workable and practical?

Stock issues are generalized formulations, abstractions that must be applied in every specific instance. They raise questions that arise in all propositions of policy, regardless of subject. Below are listed two policy propositions and the issues inherent in them. Our examples show: (1) the usefulness of stock issues, and (2) how stock issues are applied.

The People's Republic of Lilliput should be admitted to the U.N. (Proposition of policy)
Issues:

1. Does the world situation warrant the admission of the People's Republic of Lilliput to the U.N.?
2. Would the admission of the People's Republic of Lilliput result in a substantial improvement in the world situation?
3. Would the admission of the People's Republic of Lilliput come about without endangering the existence or meaningful functioning of the U.N.?
4. Is the proposed plan whereby the People's Republic of Lilliput would be admitted to the U.N. workable and practical?[6]

We should go on a vacation to Africa. (Proposition of policy)
Issues:

1. Would we enjoy a vacation in Africa?
2. Will a trip to Africa provide us with needed relaxation, diversion, and intellectual stimulation?
3. Will a trip to Africa provide those advantages without significantly depleting our bank balance or interfering with the fulfilling of our commitments?
4. Is the idea of a trip to Africa feasible now, since such a trip would require passports, shots, airline tickets, hotel reservations, wardrobe, etc.?

[6] We have not explored the topic of subissues, but the reader should recognize that beneath each issue there are subordinate issues that support the broader ones. For example, beneath the issue, "Is the proposed plan whereby the People's Republic of Lilliput would be admitted to the U.N. workable and practical?" lies the subissue, "Is the plan likely to win the approval of the major powers in the U.N.?" To determine subissues, convert the main issue into a proposition and then analyze it with a view toward uncovering its inherent issues.

Gathering Data

A cross-country drive requires a great deal of planning. The travelers must decide what route to take and, perhaps more important, what to take along with them. In deciding their needs, they follow a step closely parallel to the advocate who studies a proposition to determine what documentation and proof are needed to buttress his position. Entering a controversy without the necessary evidence is like starting on a cross-country trip without the necessary equipment.

Sources of evidence vary, ranging from personal experience to library research. To spare the reader a lengthy dissertation on the major sources of information in the library, we recommend the excellent sourcebooks and library guides available.[7] We will, however, make two general statements about library research.

Although research is usually undertaken at the end of the analysis process, the material you gather may make it necessary for you to rethink your proposition analysis. Don't feel that you need be inseparably bound to your first judgments about a proposition. Prepare to constantly revise your thinking as new information becomes available.

Research may reveal that the issues you have formulated need revision; if so, revise them. Research can enhance your understanding of the key terms in a proposition. Whatever its effects, remember that flexibility and awareness are the indispensable tools of the advocate.

Second, select your evidence carefully. Refer to the discussion of the tests of evidence in the next section of this chapter. Bear them in mind as you gather and analyze the materials for your confrontation.

Third, keep track of your sources. For a school debater, this is absolutely essential. We suggest the following procedure: On an index card, record the fact, statistic, quotation, or data you wish to preserve. Then, fully record the source of the data. For instance, if you were to draw a quotation from Abné M. Eisenberg's *Understanding Communication in Business and the Professions,* you should note the author, title, publisher, date of publication and the page on which the reference appeared. In the upper left-hand corner of the card, note the subject heading: "Dynamics of Interpersonal Communication." Include any supplemental information that might be useful, such as the qualifications of the source being quoted. In Figure 2-4, we have reproduced a typical data card. Note its structure and content.

PROOF

Among the demands most frequently heard during an argument is *prove it.* Exactly what is proof? What does *prove it* mean? Simply put, it means *establish your contentions through evidence and reasoning.* In another sense, *prove it*

---

[7]See Bibliography under Library Research and Report Writing Guides.

Territoriality in Interpersonal Communication

"Each of us is surrounded by an invisible bubble of space—a personal bubble. Not only does it vary in size from person to person, but also from situation to situation."

Eisenberg, Abne M. Understanding Communication in Business and the Professions (New York: Macmillan Publishing Co., Inc., 1978), p. 62.

Dr. Eisenberg is on the faculty of the City University of New York. He has authored several textbooks on Communication.

FIGURE 2-4 Debater's Index Card

means *convince me.* This distinction is important because it suggests that the word *proof* means at least two different things:

1. *Proof* refers to the establishment of contentions through evidence and reasoning—or again, proof refers to the logical demonstration of a contention's validity; and
2. *Proof* refers to whatever rhetorical methods are used to convince your audience.

These two definitions suggest that on the one hand *proof* means the valid, logical demonstration of a contention—*regardless of any audience.* Here the proof of a proposition can be tested impartially and objectively by a judge trained in evaluating evidence and testing patterns of reasoning.[8]

In our second definition, we recognize that proof, in most cases, must be directed toward a particular audience and that their reaction to it is all-important. When a person says "convince me," he means "use proof that I will accept; persuade me." He is not concerned with objective verifiability. He is concerned with being persuaded in terms of his beliefs, attitudes, and values.

If this were a book in logic, we would concern ourselves only with the first definition. However, since we are dealing with disagreements between people, we are obliged to address ourselves to the second one as well. Thus, the pages to follow reflect a dualistic approach to the subject of proof.[9]

[8]The letters Q.E.D. (used in geometry to indicate that "it has been established") come to mind here. Through purely objective evaluation of the evidence and reasoning, an observer concludes that the proposition in question has been proved.

[9]See Chapter 8, Know Your Opponent.

It is convenient to examine the topics of reasoning and evidence by noting that proof occurs in units. A proof unit can be defined as a *conclusion plus a reason.* This definition encompasses a great deal. All the following statements are proof units, according to our definition.

1. Dick is a nice person, *because* he observes the Sabbath.
2. Seatbelts save lives, *because* the National Safety Council reports that fatalities in eight out of ten traffic accidents could be prevented if passengers wore seatbelts.
3. Joan is fatter than Edith, *because* Joan drinks too much beer.

Although not all these proof units are of equal quality, they demonstrate that many kinds of statements function as proof units. Any such unit can be broken down into two parts: *claim* and *support.* The claim is the conclusion advanced in the proof unit. The support refers to the part of the unit that provides backing or substantiation for the claim (or conclusion). In our first example, the claim is, "Dick is a nice person"; the support is, "*because* he observes the Sabbath."

Support may be regarded as a synonym for evidence. When we ask for evidence, we are asking, "What have you got to go on? Upon what facts or authoritative opinions do you base your claim?" Evidence, then, refers to the raw material, stuff, or data of argument—the building blocks from which conclusions are constructed.

Although reasoning and evidence occur together, it is convenient for purposes of analysis to distinguish between them. Reasoning refers to the form or structure of an argument. One chooses his evidence, then marshals it, molds it, gives it form by means of reasoning. Thus, *support* (or *evidence*) plus *reasoning* yields *claim* (or *conclusion*). See Figure 2-5.

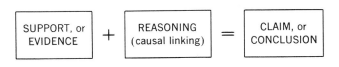

FIGURE 2-5   Proof Unit

Reasoning with the Toulmin Model

Another rather effective way of analyzing a proof unit has been suggested by Stephen Toulmin, an English logician. He expands on the preceding model, including the elements of *warrant backing,* and *rebuttal,* as shown in Figure 2-6.

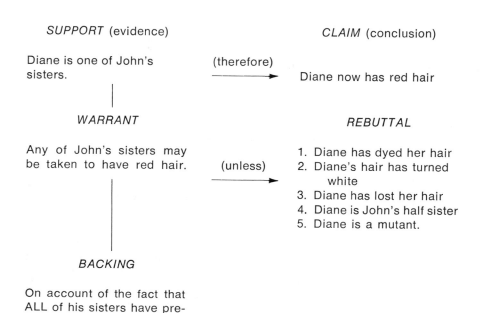

SUPPORT (evidence)

Diane is one of John's sisters.

CLAIM (conclusion)

(therefore) → Diane now has red hair

WARRANT

Any of John's sisters may be taken to have red hair.

(unless) →

REBUTTAL

1. Diane has dyed her hair
2. Diane's hair has turned white
3. Diane has lost her hair
4. Diane is John's half sister
5. Diane is a mutant.

BACKING

On account of the fact that ALL of his sisters have previously been observed to have red hair.

FIGURE 2-6   Sample Toulmin Model

HOW TO USE THE TOULMIN MODEL IN AN ACTUAL ARGUMENT

Step 1   The advocate should establish exactly what it is that his opponent is claiming ("Capitol punishment should be abolished." "Diane now has red hair.").

Step 2   After determining the claim that is being advanced, find out what evidence is being presented in support of such a claim. After all, a claim without evidence is worthless.

Step 3   At this stage, a warrant must be introduced. A warrant is information that justifies linking the claim with its supporting evidence. Referring back to our sample model, you will see that simply claiming that Diane now has red hair along with the fact that she is one of John's sisters is of no significance whatsoever. The warrant therefore introduces the basis for such a progression. It can be said this way: *Since* any of John's sisters may be taken to have red hair ⟶ Diane is one of John's sisters ⟶ *therefore* ⟶ Diane now has red hair.

Step 4   But this may still be insufficient evidence for some. You now must provide the backing for the argument. Backing is additional evidence that reinforces the warrant. The model can now be read like this: *since* any of John's sisters may be taken to have red hair ——*and* —— Diane is one of John's sisters —— *on account of* the fact that all of John's sisters have previously been observed to have red hair —— *therefore* —— Diane now has red hair.

Step 5 This, the rebuttal, is a critical element of the model. It attempts to either deny or cast doubt upon the conclusion or claim made by your opponent. Let us now read the entire argument—Toulmin style.

SINCE	Any of John's sisters may be taken to have red hair.
ON ACCOUNT OF	the fact that all of his sisters have previously been observed to have red hair.
AND	Diane is one of John's sisters.
THEREFORE	Diane now has red hair.
UNLESS	Diane has dyed her hair . . . or . . . her hair has turned white . . . or . . . she has gone bald . . . or . . . she is only John's half sister . . . or she is a mutant.[10]

Evidence

Evidence falls into two broad categories: *factual* and *authoritative.* Factual evidence refers to objective data—facts observed and reported objectively. Authoritative evidence refers to expert judgments about or interpretations of facts. The weekly news magazine that advertises it "separates fact from opinion" is cognizant of the distinction between these. So is the detective who wants "just the facts, ma'am." It is one thing to witness an automobile accident and report the facts as you saw them; it is another to make a judgment about who is to blame.

It is, of course, misleading to imply that every fact can be observed and reported objectively. Erroneous reports result from distorted perceptions, mistaken inferences, bias, and so on. What is reported as fact may not be such at all. That journalists, who are trained to observe and report impartially, are sometimes guilty of this failing has been shown many times.[11] It is probable, then, that untrained observers are more often guilty of this failing. The advocate should be watchful of his opponent's alleged facts, since they may be found wanting.

[10] Stephen Toulmin, *The Uses of Argument* (New York: Cambridge University Press, 1958).

[11] Russel Windes and Arthur Hastings, *Argumentation and Advocacy* (New York: Random House, Inc., 1965). pp. 100-102.

Next, we deal with four broad categories of evidence: *statistical* (a form of factual evidence), *authoritative, journalistic* (which falls between factual and authoritative), and *other forms* (including witnesses, documents, recordings, and objects). Under each heading, we present a number of pertinent questions to be asked when evaluating evidence falling into that category.

STATISTICAL EVIDENCE

Since statistical proof is so often relied on as "factual evidence," we present a series of questions designed to test its validity.

1. Who did the study? A knowledge of the source of a statistical survey can, and often should, affect our reactions to it. If an opponent confronted you with statistical evidence indicating excessive cruelty to experimental animals in research laboratories, what would your reaction be? Suppose you then found that the source of this study was a militant antivivisection league. Would that knowledge color your attitude toward the evidence? Why? The answer obviously rests on the fact that the source of the study invests its conclusions with doubt. More extreme examples of the same phenomenon include: (1) statistics about black Americans compiled by a white racist organization; (2) a particular religious organization's survey on the contributions of its members to the American way of life. While there is certainly not a one-to-one connection between the source of a study and the probable validity of its conclusions, the source certainly ought to be one criterion for formulating our judgment.

2. When was the study done? A study done on unemployment trends thirty years ago would have little contemporary relevance, unless it were being used for purposes of comparison. Knowledge expands so rapidly and changes occur so quickly that many studies are outdated almost as soon as they are finished. It is important, then, to determine when a study was done in order to intelligently evaluate the validity of its conclusions.

3. Where was the study done? The location in which a study is done can significantly influence its findings. Take a study that probes the attitudes of Americans toward social security benefits. Certainly its results would be influenced by the number of senior citizens living in the area surveyed. Suppose the questionnaire were distributed on a college campus? In a retirement community? It should be clear that *where* you ask the questions *does* make a difference.

4. Why was the study done? All statistical studies are done for particular reasons, and the motives behind them can influence the outcomes. When a company undertakes a study of the relationship between the consumption of its product and a danger to the public health, we can guess the motive behind the study. Hence we should not spend too much time awaiting the announcement of a positive correlation. But we might rightly anticipate a prompt, enthusiastic announcement of a negative correlation and view the announcement with a healthy skepticism. Often the intent of a study colors its outcome.

5. What statistical methods were used? There are various ways of collecting data. These differ according to the needs of a specific researcher. While some range of choice exists among these methods, the one selected can affect the outcome of a study. It is therefore advisable to determine the method used. Without going into detail, we present some of the more important aspects of inquiry and indicate their potential effects on the conclusions of a survey.[12]

Sampling techniques should yield a group of subjects that is representative of some larger body. In this context, a random sample could produce results different from those derived from a sampling technique whereby subjects were carefully chosen according to specific criteria. The *size of the sample* can also have an effect. Television commercials frequently speak of studies in which two out of three doctors are said to prefer Brand X without ever telling us how many or what type of doctors were asked.

If a study showed that fifty percent of the people surveyed studied yoga, you might get the impression that yoga is sweeping the country. Wouldn't you be shocked to learn that this study consisted of questioning two people on a bus!

The *kind of questions* asked in a survey can also distort its results. A question such as, "Are you or have you ever been a member of the Communist party?" is really asking two things at once. An affirmative answer can mean "I have been and still am" or "I was but I am no longer." A negative answer can mean "I never was and am not now" or "I have been but am not now." Often the answer to a question lends itself to misinterpretation. A question such as, "Are you a Christian?" might be answered, "No, I'm sorry; I'm not." In compiling the statistical results of the survey, an opportunist might be tempted to report that sixty four percent of the people polled said that they were *sorry they were not Christians.*

6. Who interpreted the findings of the study? The raw data accumulated in a particular study can often be interpreted in more than one way. Therefore it is advisable to consider the attitudes, values, and other possible sources of bias in the interpreters. Here we are not concerned so much with who *did* the study but with who *interprets* its results. Are the interpreters ethical? Biased? How much does their job security depend upon their interpretation? Unless you can ascertain the integrity of the interpreter, his interpretation stands open to challenge.[13]

[12] See Bibliography under Statistics.

[13] IQ scores for blacks might be interpreted one way by the NAACP, another way by the KKK.

AUTHORITATIVE EVIDENCE

"According to . . . " is a phrase frequently heard in argument. Yet it is amazing how few people know what questions to ask in evaluating arguments based on authoritative evidence. Below are seven key questions.

1. Exactly what are the authority's credentials? Although common sense tells us that credentials do not necessarily make the man, they do provide a yardstick with which to make a judgment about him as an authority. From the standpoint of probability, we should be more inclined to honor a certified theologian's statement about the Dead Sea Scrolls rather than an unqualified layman's.

Credentials in one field do not automatically imply competence in another. Yet a "halo effect" often occurs when a recognized authority in one field makes a statement about a subject outside his range of competence and is believed simply because of his primary credentials. Such is the case when a mathematician expounds on anthropology or a pediatrician on international politics.

2. Where and how were the authority's credentials earned? In certain cases, knowing the institution that granted a degree could be of great importance. Some universities have better reputations than others. Rightly or wrongly, a degree from an Ivy League school carries more prestige than one from a remote and little-known institution.

Academic degrees are not the only kind of credentials a person can possess. Many authorities have acquired their credentials through hard work and practical experience. These assuredly carry no less weight than formally earned degrees, although their worth is more difficult to evaluate.

3. When were the authority's credentials earned? Dating an authority's credentials provides insight into his reliability. In certain fields, the progress is so rapid that only exceptional persons are able to keep up. An M.D. degree earned fifty years ago may preclude certain skills and information recently introduced into the medical curriculum. Although the recency of a degree is not an infallible indicator of an authority's credibility (some would argue that credentials earned recently are worth less than those earned some time ago), it *does* provide important information for the advocate.

4. What is the authority's reputation among his peer group? On occasion, there is a disparity between a man's reputation among his peer group and with the general public. The standards by which each judges him may differ. We would argue that the more reliable index to a man's caliber and integrity can be gleaned from the opinions held of him by his peers, who are usually in a better position to judge his expertise.

5. What is the nature and extent of the authority's published works? An authority's published works, as well as the agency that published them, can be used as a basis for judging his scholarship. Like the institutions of higher learning mentioned earlier, magazines and publishing houses have well-defined reputations based not only on the kinds of works they will publish but also on their excellence. First impressions by professionals are at times based on who published a given work. In this connection, remember that one person's reaction to a magazine like *Playboy* or *Reader's Digest* might be different from another's. In the case of books, it's a good idea to inquire into the reviews and sales of a work; consistently unfavorable reviews and a very scanty sales record might reveal something significant about the work.[14]

6. *Does the authority have any practical experience in his field?* The stereotype of the ivory-tower scholar has some basis. At times we encounter "experts" who shock us with an almost entirely theoretical knowledge of their field. A white middle-class sociologist writing about the problems of ghetto living without ever having lived in or visited one would be less credible than an expert who had first-hand experience.

7. *Is the authority relatively objective and impartial?* Although few can be totally objective and impartial all the time, it is important to know whether the authority cited has a *reputation* for either intellectual honesty or subjectivity and bias. A person who consistently distorts facts and bastardizes evidence in order to have them do his bidding would be less credible than an objective reporter.

Again, we remind the reader to maintain a constant vigil for presence of bias in authoritative evidence.

JOURNALISTIC EVIDENCE

Many of the same questions presented earlier can be asked of evidence gleaned from newspapers and periodicals. Before we accept a newspaper story on a controversial topic as "factual," we must ask ourselves the following questions:

1. *In what newspaper or periodical did the story appear?*

2. *Has the journal a reputation of accurate reporting?*

3. *Does the journal have any record of bias in a particular political direction?*

4. *Who wrote the article?*

5. *What are the reporter's credentials?*

6. *Has the reporter a record of accurate and objective reporting?*

7. *Did he or she have access to all pertinent facts in preparing the story?*

---

[14] This should not be taken to mean that a book that received unfavorable reviews is necessarily lacking in authority or scholarship.

While most newspapers and periodicals make a sincere attempt to report news accurately and objectively, some are more successful than others. Some cater to sensational news stories. Others, such as underground newspapers, are staffed by relatively inexperienced journalists. The reputation a medium enjoys is to some extent a barometer of the confidence we should place in it. Whenever possible, we should depend less on its reputation than on our specific information about the story and reporter in question.

OTHER FORMS OF EVIDENCE

In addition to statistical, authoritative, and journalistic evidence, we now present four other forms of evidence and suggest pertinent analytical questions to be asked about them.

Witnesses

Are they willing witnesses? (Have they something to gain?)

Are they reluctant witnesses?

Have they been coached on what to say?

Are they competent on the subject in question?

Are they presenting facts or opinions?

Did they have first-hand experience with the events (did they actually see, hear, or feel the evidence at its source), or is their testimony based on hearsay (second-hand evidence)?

If they are first-hand witnesses, are their observations accurate?

If they are relating hearsay evidence, what assurance do you have of the accuracy of (a) the source of their testimony, (b) the transmission of the information from the source, (c) the testimony itself?

Documents

Are they primary or secondary source materials?

If secondary, the same questions listed above under journalistic evidence apply.

Are they the actual documents in question (not forgeries)? Have they been tampered with in any way?

Recordings

Are the voices recorded actually those of the persons in question?

How were the recordings obtained, by whom, and so forth?

Objects

Are these the objects actually involved?

Have they been tampered with in any way?

By whom were they collected? Under what circumstances?

Two Questions Applicable
to All Kinds of Evidence

Two final questions should be asked of all kinds of evidence:

1. Is the evidence internally consistent? Does the evidence contradict itself at any point? Such would be the case if a mayor reported: "All four hundred of the city's snow plows were in operation on the streets during the snow emergency, and a total labor force of three hundred and fifty men was on duty." Obviously, four hundred men would be needed to drive four hundred snow plows, yet the Mayor said there were only three hundred and fifty men on duty. Such inconsistencies appear from time to time, although often less obviously. Careful listening and close attention can help the advocate detect them.

2. Is the evidence consistent with external reality? Sometimes evidence contradicts known realities. If a survey showed that four out of five teen-agers are female, we could testify that the survey is in error.

Our own observations and experience should be used to cross-check evidence that seems questionable.

REASONING

Reasoning, as we have said, refers to the form or structure of a proof unit. When we reason, we make inferences. Imagine the following roadside scene: a young lady is standing beside a car, watching a young man change a tire. Behind the jacked-up auto is a flashy red sports car with its safety lights blinking on and off. Both cars look as though they had been pulled over to the side rather hurriedly and not too long ago. What inference can we make? We would probably infer that the young lady had had a flat tire and pulled over to the side of the road. While staring helplessly at her flat tire, the young gallant in the sports car (who happened to be passing by) saw her plight and stopped to lend a hand. A perfectly logical inference. We have reasoned. We have established relationships between the observed facts. In the majority of cases our reasoning would be correct. But are we *certain* that it is? Might it not be that the two people at the side of the road are members of a spy ring, exchanging classified information as part of an elaborately planned espionage operation? Perhaps the whole gambit was carefully planned and prearranged. To this interpretation of the facts observed, you might say that the second inference is less probable than the first. Your reply strikes at the very heart of reasoning—*probability*. Except in the cases of the physical sciences, mathematics, and related fields (in which some of the inferences drawn are virtually certain), much of our reasoning is probable to varying degrees. The espionage inference is less probable than the Good Samaritan one. But almost all reasoning is based on probability. We will return to this concept frequently in the discussion to follow.

It would be possible to write an entire book on reasoning. We prefer not to belabor the subject, and so we present seven of the more commonly used types of reasoning, along with tests for each.

Reasoning from Example

> *I have known five recent graduates of Quagmire College. Each of them was a dull, unintelligent bore. Quagmire College graduates are dull, unintelligent bores.*

Reasoning from example involves moving from one or more specific instances to a generalization. On the basis of a small number of cases, we *generalize* about a larger group. The more representative the sample on which we base our conclusion, the greater the probability that the generalization is correct. Five of Quagmire College's recent graduates were dull, unintelligent bores. But this does not necessarily mean that *all* their graduates are bores. Perhaps these five were exceptions; two hundred other graduates may have been interesting, brilliant, and charming.

There are two tests of reasoning from example:

1. Are the examples typical and representative? To yield valid generalization, examples must be representative of something outside themselves. Typicality implies ordinariness. To argue that all Germans are anti-Semitic because Hitler was anti-Semitic is to reason from an atypical and unrepresentative example. As implied here, stereotyping is often the result of reasoning from atypical and unrepresentative examples. The same kind of illogicality yields the following argument, which was advanced to one of the authors recently: "Seatbelts are unsafe; one friend of mine, whose car went off a bridge, died because he could not unfasten his seatbelt."

2. How large is the body of examples that form the basis for making the generalization? Although the size of a sample is no guarantee of a generalization's validity, the larger the sample the greater is the probability that the generalization is valid. If a group of thirty Quagmire College graduates included five dull, unintelligent bores, the other twenty-five would have acted as a leveling force, allowing for the formation of a more accurate generalization.

A relationship should now be seen between our present discussion and earlier comments about statistical surveys. The same basic principles apply in both cases: Generalization from statistics requires the same care as generalization from a few specific instances. The statistical population must be sufficiently large, representative, and typical if the conclusions of the survey are to have validity for any group larger than the number of persons consulted in the survey.

Reasoning from Comparison

> *A state lottery would provide needed revenue for Alaska, because such a lottery has done so for New York.*

The steps involved in reasoning by comparison are these:

1. observation of facts (The New York state lottery has provided revenue; Alaska needs revenue.)
2. comparison of two things (Alaska and New York are alike in many ways.)
3. inference (An Alaskan state lottery would provide needed revenue.)

This kind of reasoning involves comparing two different things. When the two have a sufficient number of significant attributes in common, it is possible to conclude that they are similar in other ways as well; therefore, what has worked for one will work for the other. Hence, we argue: Colleges X and Y are alike in many ways; since a pass-fail grading system has worked well at College X, the same program will work well at Y. Or again, socialized medicine has worked successfully in Scandinavia; since the United States and Scandinavia are alike in many respects, socialized medicine would work successfully here.

There are two tests of reasoning by comparison:

1. Are the facts established? Our first sample argument is based on the assertion that "the New York state lottery has provided needed revenue." But the argument must stand close scrutiny on this point before it can go forward. Argument by comparison frequently breaks down at this basic level. Too often such assertions, which provide a basis for the argument, go unsupported and unchallenged. We might want to ask: "How much money did the New York state lottery provide?" "Was the amount of revenue sufficient to warrant the effort and expense involved in running the lottery?" Only when these questions are answered ought we to allow the argument to proceed.

2. Do significant similarities outweigh significant dissimilarities in the things compared? Since this type of argument rests on similarities between different things, we must establish that these *similarities are significant in kind and number* before we can draw our conclusion. In other words, we must ask ourselves if the compared things are sufficiently similar on critical matters to warrant the conclusion we draw. Cars are like boats in that both run on liquid fuels, but do cars float? Obviously, the point of similarity between them does not warrant the conclusion of their being alike.

It must be emphasized that both quantity and quality of similarities are important here. Two things may be alike in ten ways, but these ways may be irrelevant to the point being argued. On the other hand, two objects may have only a few similarities, but if these are critical and relevant to the essence of the argument, then the conclusion of likeness may be justified.

Reasoning by Figurative Analogy

> *With respect to Communism, the nations in a particular area are like a row of dominoes standing side by side: If one falls the rest are sure to follow. Therefore, we must prevent the fall of each and every nation.*

This is an inherently weak form of argument, since it is always based on the comparison of two vastly different things. Yet arguments based on figurative analogies are used quite frequently. A war may be said to be like a fire—best extinguished quickly and at its source; or a child may be compared to a budding flower. Although these analogies are poetically pleasing, it is very dangerous to try to draw conclusions from them.

The tests for this kind of reasoning are the same as those for literal comparison: (1) Are the facts established? (2) Do significant similarities outweigh significant dissimilarities in the things compared? It is in answering the second question that the inherent weakness in this form of reasoning becomes apparent. Our advice is this: Be wary of arguments based on figurative analogy.

Reasoning from Effect to Cause

> *John is usually a friendly, enthusiastic person, but whenever he's in the presence of Cynthia, he becomes sulky; therefore, Cynthia is the cause of John's change in behavior.*

When two things occur together, we are sometimes justified in asserting that one is the cause of the other. Argument from effect to cause begins with observed data and proceeds to the judgment that a causal relationship exists between them. Not all these judgments are correct, because causality is at times quite a complicated phenomenon. Most of us would seriously doubt the conclusion of the following argument:

> *I walked under a ladder. I tripped and fell on the next block. Therefore my walking under the ladder was the cause of my accident.*

Why should we doubt this conclusion? Isn't the preceding case of Cynthia and John similar? The answer is no for a couple of reasons. First, the John-Cynthia case implied *regularity of occurrence*. The more often two events occur together, the greater is the probability that they are causally related. In addition, the nature of each situation is different. In the first, we are dealing with two people who interact. Experience teaches that being in the presence of a certain type of person can alter one's mood. People affect people. But how likely is it that inanimate objects can interact with or cast a spell on people?

John Stuart Mill established a number of tests of causal reasoning that are very useful, although somewhat technical. We offer them here with this comment: in dealing with causality we must be aware that it is frequently difficult to isolate *one* cause that alone produces an effect. Often causal factors work in concert, interacting with one another to produce a particular effect.

1. If an effect occurs when a certain factor is present but fails to occur when the same factor is absent, then that factor is either the cause or a contributing cause of the effect.

In symbolic form:

$$A \ C \ D \ E = 0 \text{ (no effect)}$$
$$A \ B \ C \ D \ E = X \text{ (the effect)}$$
$$\therefore B = \text{cause or part thereof.[15]}$$

In other words, if John is cheerful in the presence of Sam, Martha, George, and Frank, but he is sulky in the presence of the same people plus Cynthia, then Cynthia is the probable cause of John's sulkiness.

2. No factor can be a cause in whose presence the effect fails to emerge.

In symbolic form:

$$A \ B \ C \ D = 0$$
$$A \ B \ C \ D \ E \ F = 0$$
$$\therefore \text{ neither } A \ B \ C \ D \ E \text{ nor } F \text{ is a cause.}$$

If five other individuals are introduced to John, and neither they nor Sam, Martha, George, and Frank occasion sulkiness in John, then none of them can be the cause of his sulkiness.

3. No factor can be a cause in whose absence the effect emerges.

In symbolic form:

$$A \ B \ C \ D = X$$
$$D = X$$
$$\therefore \text{ neither } A \ B \text{ nor } C \text{ are causes or causal agents.}$$

---

[15] The symbol $\therefore$ means *therefore*.

If John is sulky in the presence of Sam, George, Martha, and Cynthia, but he remains sulky after Sam, George, and Martha leave, then we can be sure that none of them is a cause of his mood. By the process of elimination, we conclude that Cynthia is the cause of John's sulkiness.

4. If an effect varies in concomitance with the variations in a certain factor, then that factor is probably the cause (or a contributing cause) of the variation in the effect.

In symbolic form:

$$A\ B\ C\ D = X$$
$$A^2\ B\ C\ D = X^2$$
$$A^3\ B\ C\ D = X^3$$

$\therefore A$ is a factor or the cause of the variations of X.

If in the presence of Sam, Martha, George, Frank, and Cynthia, John becomes sulky in proportion to Cynthia's cheerfulness, then we can conclude that (1) Cynthia is the cause—or part of the cause of John's sulkiness and (2) the extent of her cheerfulness affects the degree of John's sulkiness.

Reasoning from Cause to Effect

> *Federal control of the contraceptive industry will result in lowered manufacturing efficiency, because whenever a government controls an industry, lower efficiency levels result.*

In this kind of reasoning a prediction is made on the basis of past instances. We may have observed ten cases in which event A caused event B to occur (for example, every time I go boating I become seasick). On the basis of this, we predict that when the eleventh case comes around, event A will again cause the occurrence of event B. Thus, we can predict that increasing import duties will result in a smaller volume of incoming goods (since past experience shows that increasing import duties *causes* a decline in the volume of a nation's incoming goods).

Since reasoning from cause to effect is based on a causal generalization (when A occurs, B follows), we must scrutinize that generalization to determine its validity.[16] Further, in testing this kind of argument we must analyze the situation to determine whether contravening causes would interfere with the regular occurrence of the effect. Put another way, although A usually causes B to occur, is there anything in this particular case that might alter that progres-

---

[16] Here the same tests apply as were listed for the types of reasoning preceding.

sion? For example: it may be that every time I go boating I become seasick; however, *this* time I'll be riding on a twenty-five thousand ton ocean liner rather than a fifteen-foot sailboat.

Hence, the questions to ask in reasoning from cause to effect are these:

1. Is the causal generalization valid? Suppose I argued:

> The opening of a new grocery store in our neighborhood will result in higher prices on grocery items, because competition results in increased prices.

You would be wise to challenge this argument by declaring that the causal generalization is invalid: competition does not cause increased prices but rather lower ones! Since the causal generalizations in this type of reasoning are often *implied* rather than made explicit, the advocate should train himself to listen carefully so that he can detect them even when they are not explicitly stated in his opponent's argument.

2. Do the facts of the case fit into the broad category of events and occurrences dealt with by the causal generalization? Suppose I argued as follows:

> The opening of a wholesale pharmacy in our neighborhood will result in lower prices of pharmaceuticals, because increased competition yields lower prices.

This argument is faulty, not because the causal generalization is invalid, but because the facts of the case don't fit into its scope. Prices of pharmaceuticals might decline, but not because the wholesale merchant would compete with the retail ones. Rather, he would compete with other wholesale merchants, which may or may not be in our neighborhood.

3. Are there factors present that would contravene the operation of the causal generalization? Although it is true that crying babies cause parents concern, the concern doesn't occur if the baby is out of hearing range. While it is true that most times event A causes event B to occur, it is possible for certain conditions to exist that would prevent the occurrence of event B in conjunction with its usual cause. Our earlier reference to seasickness illustrates this point.

Reasoning from Criteria to Labeling

> The electoral college system fails to give equal weight to the ballots of all voters; therefore, the electoral college system is undemocratic.

The assignment of labels is commonplace: Company A is a *monopoly;* the local power company is a *major polluter* in our area; Professor Peters is a *good* teacher. Reasoning that results in the assignment of a label follows three basic phases: (1) the observation of data; (2) the introduction of the label to be applied; and (3) the application of the label to the phenomenon in question.

For example, we may contend that the treatment of migrant workers is *inhumane.* In this case, the data observed may consist of substandard housing, inadequate sanitation facilities, improper diet, and so on. The label to be applied is *inhumane.* (Often in this sort of argument, the key word requires definition; more frequently advocates fail to define it. Hence, without having the key words defined, political activities are labeled *un-American;* wars are labeled *immoral;* and so on.) In the third phase of our sample argument, the label *inhumane* is applied to the treatment of migrant workers.

Whether the label to be applied is factual or evaluative, the tests of this kind of argument are the same:

1. Are the elements in the definition of the label valid, clear, explicit, complete, and acceptable to the audience? Rational disagreement is impossible when advocates use terms without defining them. Such labels as *honky* and *cracker* are loaded with subjective meaning. Therefore, it is risky to use them without proper definition and without being aware of the subjective meanings assigned to them. A definition that is clear (unambiguous, concrete), valid (based on authority or first-hand knowledge), explicit, and complete can do much to avert a great deal of fruitless and meaningless advocacy.

Because one person's definition may not be the same as another's, an arguer should try to define crucial terms in a way acceptable to his opponent. As noted earlier, to be effective, proof must be acceptable to your audience.

2. Do the data actually fit the definition of the label? Suppose I define a *good* teacher as one who is (1) effective in imparting knowledge, (2) fair and objective in grading, and (3) considerate of students. I further contend that Professor Bowdoin is a *good* teacher of history, basing my assertion on two facts: (1) his students consistently score well on standardized history tests (thus implying that he is effective in imparting knowledge),[17] and (2) he is always fair and objective in grading. Unless I could also establish that he is considerate of students, I would, strictly speaking, fail to satisfy the criteria of my definition of *good.* But in any list of elements in a definition, some items are more important than others. In this case, effectiveness in teaching and fairness and objectivity in grading may be *more* important than the third criterion of the definition—consideration for students. Hence, I *might* be justified in applying

---

[17]Other factors can account for the high scores made by Professor Bowdoin's students. They may all be naturally bright, they may have studied the subject before, and so on.

the label *good* to Professor Bowdoin. Or I might label him *good* in two respects and *not good* in a third.

3. Are the facts established? Reasoning from criteria to labeling rests on the existence of facts that fit the criteria in question. Therefore, it is important to determine whether or not the alleged facts have indeed been established. In our preceding example, it was reported that Professor Bowdoin was "always fair and objective in his grading." But what proof was advanced for that contention? None at all! Would you accept the assertion under those circumstances? You would be wise not to!

Reasoning from Circumstantial Evidence to a Hypothesis

> *The airplane has disappeared from the radar scope, and radio contact with it has been broken. Therefore, it has probably crashed.*

Many times we are confronted by facts that seem to indicate that a certain thing has taken place: I enter my apartment and find lights on, drawers open, and the contents scattered on the floor. I infer that I have been burglarized, and I am probably correct. But it is possible that another explanation can account for the same facts. Perhaps a friend has played a practical joke. Unlikely, but possible.

This kind of argument moves from observed data to some explanation of them. Darwin observed various forms of life and their relationships to one another and hypothesized (or theorized) that species of life evolve. Others see the same data and theorize that God created them in their present form. Because two or more explanations can often account for the same set of data, we must ask, how can this sort of argument be evaluated? In other words, what would make one explanation more probable than another?

1. Does the hypothesis account for all the data? An explanation failing to account for the observed facts should be rejected. I might venture a guess that a practical joker has made my apartment appear as though it has been burglarized, but would that hypothesis explain the broken window and missing valuables? Probably not, unless my prankster friend tended to go to extremes.

Awareness of all the facts of a case can help us judge the probable validity of a hypothesis. As more and more facts come to light, we are better able to test the alleged explanation. Arguments based on an incomplete set of facts run the risk of invalidity. This brings us to a second test of this sort of argument.

2. Is there any available information that would contradict the hypothesis? A defendant might be charged with a crime because (1) a person matching his description was observed at the scene of the crime, (2) his jacket was found there, and (3) a witness reports that the defendant told him that he was guilty. Although the case seems airtight, if his defense attorney could prove that his client was five hundred miles away at the time the crime was committed, the defendant would be found innocent. The fact that he was in another place negates the hypothesis.

It is important for an advocate to be objective in his analysis of facts and evidence. He should beware of the human tendency to reject information that appears to contradict a theory he holds. More than one wife has refused to believe obvious evidence that her husband has been unfaithful. They allow their belief in their partner's faithfulness to color their reactions to observed facts and/or authoritative testimony.[18]

3. Would another hypothesis be equally or more probable than the one advanced? Someone may argue:

> *Victor Pringle has cast his ballot for a Re-publican presidential candidate three times, for a Democrat four times, and for an Inde-pendent once. On the basis of this, I con-clude that Victor Pringle is a man of few (if any) political principles.*

The conclusion drawn from this data is questionable, for this reason: Mr. Pringle's voting pattern may indicate that he is a man of strong principle, not bound by party affiliations, and that he votes for whoever seems to espouse his political principles most faithfully. In other words, *a different explanation could account for the same set of data.* Before a final judgment can be made, the advocates must ascertain additional facts. After this has been done, it might be possible to decide which hypothesis is more probable. (Suppose additional investigation disclosed that Mr. Pringle was himself a politician and that in order to be returned to Congress he switched allegiance to the party of the stronger candidate. This might lend credence to the hypothesis of "no political" principles.)

PREPARATION

The Debate Brief

By the term *brief* we mean a sentence outline of all the evidence and argu-ment marshalled by the advocate in support of his response to the proposition. It is a systematic record of the ideas and proofs uncovered during the analysis phase of preparation.

---

[18]This is the basis of "the genetic fallacy" (i.e., good people do good things) to be discussed in Chapter 4, Exposing a Fallacy. Special attention is called to this fallacy because it is one of the most commonly encountered errors in thinking.

Briefs, customarily used by attorneys in the preparation of their court cases, are also useful to school debaters. A brief permits them to analyze their own thought processes, to test their reasoning, and to assess the weight of the evidence they have gathered. A brief provides an overview of the main contentions advanced and of all the support offered for those contentions.

Informal debaters usually organize their proofs and arguments mentally, rarely using a formal brief. Although this method is usually adequate, we recommend a modified form of the brief when the case being argued has special importance.

Here are some general suggestions for constructing a brief:

1. Begin with a statement of the proposition. On a separate line in the middle of the page, write the words *affirmative brief* or *negative brief.*

2. Organize the brief into three parts. Label the first *introduction,* the second *body,* and the third *conclusion.*

3. Use the conventional outlining system to organize your brief. Main contentions should be preceded by Roman numerals, flush to the left margin. Indented capital letters should precede statements that directly support the main idea. Additional supporting material should, in turn, be indented and preceded by Arabic numerals, then lower-case letters. Thus a typical outline employing this symbol and indentation system should look like this:

I. _____

   A. _____

      1. _____

         a) _____

            (1) _____

               (a) _____

                  (i) _____

                  (ii) _____

4. Include only one concept in each numbered or lettered statement. Several ideas should not be run together. Be certain you are saying only one thing at a time.

5. Express each idea in a simple, declarative sentence. Avoid phrases, single words, and sentence fragments. Avoid questions, except when listing issues. Use only one sentence per symbol, except when a quotation, standing as a whole, is used for support. If your item is longer than one line, the second and subsequent lines should be indented to conform with the first.

6. Do not include transitions. Remember, a brief is not a speech outline, nor is it a "chopped-up" speech. Any transitions, figures of speech, or rhetorical flourishes are inappropriate and confusing. (Some beginning debaters, the victims of bad habits, write the speech first, then construct the brief. This is working backwards. We cannot assert too strenuously that such a faulty procedure should be avoided.)

7. Test whether your supporting material is meaningful. This can be done by inserting the word *for* or *because* after each statement requiring support. Another good way to check your logic is to read from bottom to top, mentally inserting the word *therefore* between each piece of supporting material and the assertion it is designed to support.

8. Maintain an emotion-free style. Bear in mind that when outlining arguments and recording evidence for a brief, only an objective approach is considered appropriate.

Each component of a brief has its function and specific elements. To guide you, we briefly present the essential features of each component.

The *introduction* contains no arguments, only exposition. It should include:

1. a statement that indicates the timeliness of the proposition, the circumstances that suggest its importance, and the reason why it warrants immediate attention.
2. background information. The advocate should trace why and how the proposition evolved and the circumstances leading up to its emergence.
3. definition of terms. What are the critical terms in the proposition? Unclear words or phrases that are critical to the stand you have taken should be defined.[19]
4. proof requirements, waived and admitted matter, limitations, and exclusions. For example, if this is an affirmative brief, the introduction must contain answers to these questions: What must the affirmative team do to discharge the burden of proof? What admissions does the affirmative team make? What issues are waived? What matters are outside the scope of the debate?
5. issues. What issues are inherent in the proposition? The issues appear last in the introduction.

The *body* of the brief is the essence of your argument. It contains all the major contentions and proofs you plan to advance in support of the position you are taking. It is the longest part of the brief. All evidence must be documented. (Many experienced advocates use a numbering system whereby citations in the brief are correlated with evidence cards. This enables them to

---

[19]See Chapter 3, Formal Debate, for more information on defining terms.

immediately locate the card upon which the fact, statistic, quotation, or other piece of evidence appears. Ask your teacher or coach for specific advice.)

In the *conclusion,* the advocate restates the issues inherent in the proposition and demonstrates that as a result of his documented proof in support of each contention, his conclusions should be accepted.

Remember that a brief is not intended to serve as an outline for the debater's presentation. It is merely a convenient guide to the contentions and proofs the advocate is advancing. Typically, out of the mass of argument contained in the full brief, an advocate will select those arguments that are strongest and most clearly suited to the audience in question. He will organize them into a talk, constructing an introduction and a conclusion, writing transitions, making use of rhetorical devices, and so on. Properly prepared, a brief is an invaluable help to the advocate in the preparation and defense of his case.

WRAP-UP

In this chapter, the student has been exposed to the essential components of argumentation: propositions and proof. We defined a proposition as a statement growing out of and providing focus for a controversy. Properly worded, a proposition calls for some change in belief, action, or both, thereby placing the burden of proof on its proponents and giving the presumption to its opponents. In open debate, a proposition provides a rallying point for advocacy. By embodying the essence of a controversy, it gives all parties an opportunity to express their views.

We have defined proof as the establishment of contentions through evidence and reasoning. But we said that proof in argumentation means more than mere logical demonstration of a contention's validity. Because proof is offered to a specific audience, the concept must be broadened to include whatever rhetorical methods are used to convince an audience.

We discussed several types of evidence (among them, statistical, authoritative, and journalistic) and offered tests of each. Evidence, we said, refers to the substance or matter of argument. Reasoning, on the other hand, has to do with the form or structure of argument. When we reason, we make inferences—that is, we make a statement about the unknown based on the known. You have reasoned when you establish relationships among facts. In the chapter, we considered several of the most common forms of reasoning and offered illustrations and tests of each. They are, reasoning from example, from comparison, by figurative analogy, from effect to cause, from cause to effect, from criteria to labeling, and from circumstantial evidence to a hypothesis.

In the last section of the chapter, we gave advice on how to prepare a brief. A brief was described as a sentence outline of all the evidence and argument marshaled by the advocate in support of his response to the proposition.

A brief provides at a glance an overview of what an advocate is attempting to prove and shows exactly how that individual sets out to do it.

PROBES, PRODS, AND PROJECTS

What's the use of learning all these rules of argument if the next fellow, ignoring them, simply punches you in the mouth?

In what ways are the principles presented in this chapter impractical and unrealistic in real life?

What do you think it would be like to be married to an expert in argumentation? Would it be an asset or a liability to the marriage? Explain what you mean.

How does the average person usually support his point of view in an argument?

Since most people don't carry statistics around in their heads, what's the point in asking for statistical proof?

From a newspaper or magazine, gather samples of the following kinds of arguments:
a.   reasoning from effect to cause
b.   reasoning from analogy
c.   reasoning from circumstantial evidence to a hypothesis
d.   reasoning from criteria to labeling

Construct an affirmative brief on a proposition of fact, value, or policy.

Research a controversial topic at the library. Prepare a three-hundred word statement of the main arguments for and against the controversial idea. Be certain to buttress all claims and document all evidence.

3

FORMAL DEBATE: PROCEDURES and EVALUATION

BEHAVIORAL OBJECTIVES:

After reading this chapter, you should have a better understanding of

1. how a school debate is organized
2. case options available to the affirmative and negative teams
3. responsibilities to be assumed by the affirmative and negative speakers in a debate
4. such terminology as *status quo, prima facie, rebuttal, presumption, options, cases,* and *plans*
5. cross-examination debate
6. the basis of debate judging

This chapter is designed with school debaters in mind. It advances practical advice on debate formats and case construction, including information on (1) order of speakers in a school debate and responsibilities of each speaker, (2) time limits imposed on speakers, and (3) rules and procedures governing the exchanges. In addition, it contains information on judging debates. On what basis is a debate judged? What standards are applied? How is a winner determined?

Sample ballots are presented to give school debaters an awareness of precisely how their performance and the performance of their team will be judged.

DEBATE FORMATS
AND CASE CONSTRUCTION

A school debate is an exercise in argumentation. The participants are asked to apply their knowledge of proposition analysis, organization, evidence, and reasoning in a setting characterized by order. They present their cases orally rather than in writing, so that some attention (too little, we think) is paid to presentation. It is an opportunity for reasoned disagreement and calm confrontation.

The most common format for school debate looks like this:

Constructive Speeches

> First affirmative (10 minutes)
> First negative (10 minutes)
> Second affirmative (10 minutes)
> Second negative (10 minutes)

Rebuttal Speeches

> First negative (5 minutes)
> First affirmative (5 minutes)
> Second negative (5 minutes)
> Second affirmative (5 minutes)

Two important aspects of this format should be observed. First, the debate is divided into two parts. The first part, the *constructive phase,* consists of speeches designed to present the respective positions taken by each team. It is important to recognize that with the exception of the first affirmative speaker (who presents a preplanned response to the proposition), the constructive speeches involve much give-and-take. The negative team cannot present precise, preplanned talks, for the speeches they present must respond to the case offered by their opponents. In other words, the negative team must be prepared for whatever strategy the affirmative team employs. To use an analogy, the affirmative team is like the queen in a chess game, which can move in many different directions. The negative team must be prepared to attack, no matter what options are chosen by their opponents.

During the *rebuttal phase,* each side focuses on those central points of clash on which the debate hinges. Attention is focused on (1) attacking the opposition's case at its most vulnerable points, and (2) defending one's own case against attack by the opposition. Neither side may change its case during the rebuttal speeches. Once your team has decided on a particular response to the proposition, you are committed to it. Rebuttal speeches provide you with an opportunity to shoot down the opposition's case and to buttress your case against attack.[1]

Observe, too, that in this format the affirmative side begins and ends the debate. Although it might seem unfair to allow the affirmative side both the first and the last word, the reason for this apparent edge is that the affirmative team starts out at a disadvantage. It must advance and prove a proposition that runs counter to the *status quo*. As noted in Chapter 2, the affirmative side has the burden of proof; the presumption is in favor of the negative side. To equalize this imbalance, the affirmative team is allowed to begin and end the debate.

Within this format, each speaker has clear and distinct responsibilities. It is essential to bear in mind that debaters must function as a team, with each member assigned a job. In the format just outlined, the responsibilities usually assumed by each speaker are:

1. First Affirmative Speaker

The first affirmative speaker introduces the resolution to be debated. She sketches the background of the problem, showing how and why it has come about. She defines the critical terms in the resolution. (Words that are commonly understood need not be defined.) She demonstrates a need for the change proposed by her team and presents the affirmative's plan. When she has finished speaking, the audience should know and understand the nature of the problem to which the affirmative team is responding. Furthermore, the audience should also understand what the affirmative team is proposing. They should be persuaded to believe that there is a problem requiring attention, that the problem can be traced back to flaws inherent in the *status quo*, and finally, that the affirmative's plan makes sense.[2]

A typical ten-minute speech given by a first affirmative speaker conforms to the following outline:

    I.   Problem and definition of terms   (3 minutes)

---

[1] Some beginning debaters think that the give-and-take of debate (and rebuttal speeches in particular) involves only the restatement of arguments and evidence offered earlier in the debate. This is not so. Ideally, debaters on both sides further develop the arguments offered earlier by strengthening the evidence as the debate progresses. Technically this is called *extension of argument*.

[2] We assume here a traditional affirmative case. It is possible for the affirmative side to argue that present problems do not arise out of conditions inherent in the *status quo*. See note on p. 68 for discussion of the term *inherent*. See also p. 69-70 for our discussion of the "comparative advantages" case.

II.	Need (inadequacies of present system)	(3 minutes)
III.	Presentation of plan	(3 minutes)
IV.	Summary, conclusions	(1 minute)

2. First Negative Speaker

The first negative speaker immediately begins to attack the case presented by his opponents. Assuming that no major disagreements arise over the meanings of critical terms used in the proposition, he characteristically argues that no need exists for the proposal advanced by the affirmative team. His job is to prove that the present system is satisfactory. He may, for example, concede that there are flaws in existing right-to-privacy safeguards. He might also strenuously argue that such a drastic proposal as the one advanced by his opponents is not necessary to remedy existing flaws.[3] Finally, he should ask for clarification and specification of parts of the affirmative plan that are confusing.

An outline of his speech might look like this:

I.	Negative's view of the problem, possible disagreement on definitions	(2 minutes)
II.	Denial of need (including the charge that the affirmative has incompletely and/or incorrectly analyzed the present system)	(2 minutes)
III.	Defense of *status quo*	(3 minutes)
IV.	Request for clarification of affirmative plan	(2 minutes)
V.	Summary, conclusions	(1 minute)

3. Second Affirmative Speaker

By the time the second affirmative speaker takes the floor, the give-and-take of the debate has gotten into full swing. Arguments on both sides of the proposition are before the audience. Each side has begun to present its case. Questions have been raised by the affirmative as well as the negative. The audience waits.

In the event that no major disagreement on the definitions of terms has arisen, the second affirmative speaker is left with two major tasks. First, he must briefly review the cases advanced by each side thus far, pointing out the major areas of clash. For instance, he might mention that the first negative speaker has conceded the existence of flaws in the present right-to-privacy legislation, but has minimized those flaws and argued that minor modifications of present laws would remedy the situation. In reviewing this point of clash, the intent of the second affirmative speaker would be to pinpoint the audience's attention on it

---

[3]It is possible for the negative team to make no concessions of need. In the example given, we assume an "adjustment and repairs" case. See p. 70-72 for case options available to the negative team.

and to show that the central issue is whether or not the flaws grow out of something inherent in the *status quo*. If they do, the affirmative's plan is essential, for mere adjustments and repairs of the present situation would fail to solve the problem.

Second, he must respond to the negative's questions about the affirmative plan. In other words, he must clarify aspects of the affirmative plan. He must also demonstrate that the affirmative plan will meet the need he and his partner have demonstrated exists. Finally, he must show that the plan would do so without creating any new or more serious problems than those that already exist.

An outline of a typical second affirmative speech might look like this:

I.	Review of both cases and delineation of points of clash	(2 minutes)
II.	Answer negative questions regarding plan	(2 minutes)
III.	Rebuilding of need issue	(5 minutes)
IV.	Summary, conclusions	(1 minute)

4.   Second Negative Speaker

This speaker reviews the areas of clash that have emerged in the debate. She may (and usually does) restate the negative's stand on the need issue. Her primary job, however, is to attack the plan. She may elect to do this in one of several ways, or may employ a combination of means. She may deny that the affirmative's proposal would solve the problem they contend exists. Suppose the affirmative side has proposed legislation forbidding the establishment of data banks that would store information on every citizen in the United States. The second negative speaker might argue that such a prohibition would not solve the right-to-privacy problem, for other infringements on the privacy of citizens would be likely to occur.

She might choose to argue that the affirmative's plan is unworkable—that is, although the idea appears adequate on the surface, close scrutiny reveals that it is impractical and unworkable.

Another alternative open to the second negative speaker is to argue that the affirmative's plan would create new and more serious problems than those it would solve. This is called a disadvantage. The prohibition of data banks, a second negative speaker might point out, would make the keeping of proper employment or financial records impossible. A breakdown in the credit system might be the result. By arguing along these lines, the second negative speaker attempts to convince the audience (1) that her opponents' proposal is uncalled for, (2) that because it is inadequate or unworkable, her opponents' proposal would not solve the problem, and (3) that the affirmative plan would create new problems more serious than those it is designed to solve.

Here is a possible outline of a second negative speech:

I.	Review of negative's stand on need issue	(1 minute)
II.	Inadequacies of the plan proposed by the affirmative side	(7 minutes)
III.	Summary and conclusion	(2 minutes)

Rebuttal Speeches

The purpose of the rebuttal speech is to defend the case your side has advanced against the attacks of the opposition and to show weaknesses in the opposition's arguments. No new arguments may be presented in rebuttal. Rebuttal speeches require the debater to determine which arguments must be defended to support his own case. The rebuttal speech is very important (most debates are won or lost in rebuttal) and the debater must decide which arguments, of those originally advanced, should be extended (or further developed). It is fairly obvious that, because of time restrictions, not all arguments can effectively be extended into rebuttal.

The first negative rebuttal speaker usually attacks the need for change. The first affirmative rebuttal speaker answers the attacks and returns to crucial issues on the need. It is understood that the last speaker on each team will summarize the main thrust of his side's arguments and will attack the opposition's most vulnerable points.

Before returning to other formats that may be employed in school debates, we wish to make a point about case options available to the affirmative and negative sides.

Affirmative Case Options

In the preceding example, we have sketched a traditional affirmative case. It is characterized by the claim that the present situation is seriously in need of repair and that the existing problems are attributable to conditions inherent in the *status quo*. This means that no mere alteration of the present situation would solve the problems that exist. Instead, a major and fundamental change is required.[4]

---

[4] To argue *inherency* is to demonstrate that problems arise necessarily out of the present situation, that they are inseparable from it. Thus one might legitimately argue that existing programs designed to provide public assistance (welfare) are inherently flawed. A complete revision of current laws and policies is required to more fairly distribute the burden of welfare costs. Consider, too, these examples: an ingrown toenail does not justify amputating a foot (the problem is not inherent); a leaky faucet does not justify selling a house. But an automobile without an engine or a transmission would be considered by most people to be inherently flawed. See Wayne Thompson, *Modern Argumentation and Debate: Principles and Practices* (New York: Harper and Row, Publishers, Inc., 1971), especially pp. 82-83.

COMPARATIVE ADVANTAGES CASE

Another option open to the affirmative side is to argue the *comparative advantages* case. The affirmative concedes that while there are serious problems with the present situation, those problems may not arise out of conditions inherent in the *status quo*.[5] There are flaws, and they are serious. The affirmative argues advantages of the adoption of the resolution over the present system.

We wish to emphasize that the comparative advantages case does not eliminate the affirmative's obligation to present a rationale for change. If no significant advantages would follow from the affirmative's proposal, why offer it? In the comparative advantages case, the affirmative team must show that the present system is flawed in some way—that it is not equipped to solve the problems that exist or those that are likely to arise in the future—and it must present advantages that are unique to the adoption of the resolution—that is, the advantages cannot be accrued by the present system. In addition, the affirmative team must demonstrate that its plan will solve both sets of problems without creating new and more serious ones. Thus, prediction is at the heart of the comparative advantages case. Often, the affirmative team will predict the emergence of problems that will be insoluble within the existing framework. For example, they might wish to argue that although current environmental safeguards used for the storage of nuclear waste are now adequate, they will be unable to protect the population against the dangers of nuclear contamination in the future. Further, they might argue that in view of this approaching problem, solar power should replace nuclear power as the major source of energy, and they might give advantages to doing so.

Here is a delineation of the responsibilities typically assumed by affirmative speakers who choose to argue the comparative advantages case:

First Affirmative Speaker

He must introduce the resolution, define critical terms, and sketch the background of the problem. (So far, his responsibilities are the same as in the traditional case.) Next, he must demonstrate the rationale for change: he must delineate present problems and those that are likely to arise, and he must show that there are signficant advantages to adopting the resolution and that these advantages do not exist in the *status quo*. The advantages must be well developed and substantiated. Finally, he must present the affirmative plan, a new and desirable alternative capable of solving existing or anticipated problems.

---

[5] Philosophically, debate theorists differ on the question of whether or not the affirmative team, having elected to argue the comparative advantages case, must prove inherency. See David Zarefsky, "The 'Traditional Case'-'Comparative Advantages Case' Dichotomy: Another Look," *Journal of the American Forensic Association,* VI (Winter 1969), 12-20.

Second Affirmative Speaker

She must reestablish the rationale for change (that is, defend the affirmative's case against the attacks of the first negative speaker). Then, she must answer negative questions about the affirmative plan. Finally, she must demonstrate how her team's plan would solve the present problems and potential future ones in a better way than the current policy without creating new or more serious evils.

Whether the affirmative team chooses to argue the traditional case or the comparative advantages one, and whatever the breakdown of responsibilities, the same basic issues are being addressed. Although the responsibilities of each speaker change, the same issues are argued. The affirmative team always (1) demonstrates a rationale for change,[6] (2) presents a plan, and (3) delineates the benefits to be derived from the solution it has proposed.

Negative Case Options

In the right-to-privacy example at the beginning of this section, we sketched a type of negative case that is called the *adjustment and repairs case.* Its central theme is that by making minor adjustments, the *status quo* can be repaired to solve the minor problems that exist. It consists of a defense of the *status quo* as being inherently sound and an attack on the affirmative's plan for change.

Other options are open to the negative side. A more traditional approach might be to deny that anything is wrong with the present situation. In this scheme, the negative side makes no concessions. It denies that any need exists for a change.

The negative side has two additional options. Neither defends the *status quo;* that is, no attempt is made to deny that a need for a change exists.

DIRECT REFUTATION CASE

One option is called the *direct refutation* case. It consists of an in-depth attack on the plan proposed by the affirmative. The negative side does not deny that a problem needs to be solved. Nor does it propose a solution to the problem. Instead, it concentrates on pointing out the inadequacies and disadvantages of the plan that the affirmative side is supporting.

---

[6] The *need* issue in the traditional affirmative case is critical and must be fully developed. If the affirmative side chooses to argue the comparative advantages case, it must show the desirability of the plan being proposed. Thus the need is not the same as in the traditional affirmative case. Put another way, the affirmative team arguing a traditional affirmative case must demonstrate inherency; the affirmative team arguing a comparative advantages case need not. See note on p. 68.

Some judges dislike this type of case because it reduces the responsibility of the negative team. The negative side can waive all arguments about need and not argue in defense of anything. Instead, they can concentrate their efforts on attacking the affirmative plan.

COUNTERPLAN CASE

The second option not involving a defense of the *status quo* is called the *counterplan* case. Simply put, the negative team advancing a counterplan case concedes that a problem exists but presents its own plan for solving the problem.

If this option is selected, the negative side may go along with the affirmative's analysis of need. They may agree that a need for change exists; they may even agree for precisely the reasons pointed out by their opponents.

But there is a risk in the negative side's accepting the affirmative's analysis of need. The negative side must make it very clear that the plan it is proposing is essentially different from that of their opponents. Otherwise the negative side will probably lose the debate.

Let us consider what happens when the negative team chooses to make its own "need" case. Suppose you are a member of the negative team and, along with your partner, decide to accept part but not all of your opponents' analysis of need. Why would you make such a decision and what are its merits? One reason is that your counterplan might address itself to some of the needs advanced by your opponents. Your position would be strengthened if you could simultaneously justify your ignoring those needs posited by the affirmative side that you consider to be irrelevant. If those needs were left outstanding and your opponents could show that your plan does not meet them, it would be apparent to a judge or an audience that the affirmative plan is superior to yours. As an illustration, suppose an auto salesman wanted to sell you an electric-powered car that traveled two hundred miles before it needed recharging. He would certainly emphasize the number of places you could go without worrying about running out of power. He would be foolish to begin by pointing out the places you could not go. If your best friend were with you and began pointing out all the interesting places located more than a hundred miles away, don't you think the salesman might try to play down the appeal of those places? Wouldn't he try to affirm the desirability of those places located within the range of the car? In much the same way, the negative team who advances a counterplan case would have to refute those areas of need to which its plan is not geared.

For a brief look at the responsibilities of the negative speakers in a counterplan case, we shall assume that some of the affirmative's analysis of need is accepted. Here is what each negative speaker might do.

First Negative Speaker:

The first negative speaker would address himself to the definitions of disputed terms (if any exist) in the proposition. Next, he would admit that certain needs pointed out by his opponents are real. He would also directly refute those areas of need that he and his partner disagree with. And finally he would introduce the counterplan he and his partner are proposing. He would identify the benefits to be derived from its adoption and application. (Note that the negative team must assume the burden of proof in arguing in favor of its plan.)

Second Negative Speaker:

The task of the second negative speaker would be to defend his team's analysis of need—that is, to show once again that the needs the affirmative side is concerned with are insignificant. He would then answer questions posed by the second affirmative about the counterplan and defend it as a better alternative than the affirmative plan.

OTHER FORMATS

To familiarize you with other debate formats you are likely to encounter, we will examine a few of the more common frameworks. Whatever the format, bear in mind that each side in a debate must (1) analyze the proposition and prepare a case, (2) be prepared for the arguments to be delivered by the opposite side, and (3) stand ready to defend its own arguments against the attacks of the opposition.

CROSS-EXAMINATION DEBATE

The cross-examination debate, as distinguished from the traditional format, conforms to these general rules, with one exception. As its name implies, the cross-examination debate provides the members of each team with an opportunity to question one another directly. This can serve to point out weaknesses in your opponents' analysis of the proposition, their case, and the arguments they have advanced. Skillfully used, the question period can be the pivotal point on which the outcome of an entire debate hinges.

The order of speakers in a cross-examination debate is neither arbitrary nor capricious. The sequence that follows is designed to afford each team an equal opportunity to strengthen its position by asking and answering cleverly worded and penetrating questions. The outline will be followed by some tips on asking and answering questions.

Constructive Speeches

First affirmative (constructive speech)	(8 minutes)
Second negative questions First affirmative	(4 minutes)
First negative (constructive speech)	(8 minutes)
First affirmative questions First negative	(4 minutes)
Second affirmative (constructive speech)	(8 minutes)
First negative questions Second affirmative	(4 minutes)
Second negative (constructive speech)	(8 minutes)
Second affirmative questions Second negative	(4 minutes)

(Note that during the question-and-answer period, neither the questioner nor the answerer may consult with his partner. The questioner works alone. The respondent works alone.)

Rebuttal Speeches

Negative (either speaker)	(5 minutes)
Affirmative (either speaker)	(5 minutes)

In preparing for and participating in a cross-examination debate, these points should be borne in mind. First, the question-and-answer period is designed to advance the debate. It is not meant as an opportunity for *ad hominem* argument, sarcasm, childish outburst, or discourtesy. Neither is it a time for long, complex questions or speech-making. Some debaters use their four-minute question time to continue their constructive speech or to begin the constructive speech they are about to deliver. *This is incorrect.* The time allotted to the question-and-answer period is meant exclusively for that purpose. Again, bear in mind that your audience must be able to hear and understand your questions or your answers.

Sometimes, beginning debaters make the mistake of asking a great many questions, each of which bears no relation to the one preceding it. The effect created is chaotic. It is like trying to scramble eggs, make toast, brew coffee, and set the kitchen table—all at the same time. It is better to prepare a series of organized questions that pursue one line of thought. Avoid the helter-skelter disorder of the overly ambitious breakfast maker.

Another common mistake is to ask a question without having a clear idea of the answer you can expect. As a questioner, you should familiarize yourself with the answers your opponent is likely to give. When you are taken by surprise, it is due to your lack of preparation. There is no more disheartening experience for a cross-examination debater than seeing the tables turned on him by his opponent. This happens when a poorly prepared questioner makes a query that his opponent is able to use for his own purposes. Consider the following exchange:

John (first negative):	You have argued that any attempt to link trade agreements with the Soviet Union to human rights legislation is doomed to failure. How do you support that claim?
Roberta (first affirmative):	I make that statement on the basis of these facts reported in *The New York Times Magazine* of September 25, 1977, p. 111: In 1971 approximately 15,000 Jews were allowed to emigrate from the Soviet Union, according to both Soviet and United States figures. By 1972 the figure jumped to 30,000; and in 1973 the figure rose to approximately 35,000. In 1974 Senators Jackson and Vanick proposed an amendment to a bill regulating trade arrangements with the Soviet Union. The amendment tied future trade arrangements with the Soviets to freer emigration of Soviet Jews. Following the introduction of debate on the eventual passage of the amendment, two things happened. First, the Soviets abrogated the United States-Soviet Trade Agreement of 1972, bringing to a halt what had been a growing trend toward increased economic cooperation. Second, the number of Jews allowed to emigrate from the Soviet Union actually began to *decline* to approximately 20,000 in 1974 and 15,000 in 1975. Thus, any attempts to link trade arrangements with human rights legislation is not only ineffective, it is counterproductive. Incidentally, the source of these statistics is Samuel Piscar, author of *Coexistence and Commerce,* former adviser to the State Department and to the Joint Economic Committee of Congress.

In this instance, the questioner, due to inadequate preparation, has left himself wide open. His opponent used his query to her own advantage. Still another common error in cross-examination debating is the failure to use information acquired during the question period in your constructive speech. The novice debater frequently fails to use important admissions made by his opponent. Remember, you ask and answer questions for only one purpose: to strengthen your case. Whether the questions deal with reasoning, evidence, needs, or benefits, they should be directed—as your answers should—to strengthening the case your side has prepared and to weakening the case of your opponents.

One last point. In answering questions, be as brief and forthright as possible. Laying smoke screens, hiding behind ambiguities, and talking quickly in order to be misunderstood will usually work against you. A keen opponent will perceive your hedging and will point it out to the audience. Ultimately, such evasive ploys serve your opponents' purpose and not yours.

TWO-SPEAKER DEBATES

Two additional formats both designed for two speakers can also be employed:

Debate Format 1

Affirmative	(8 minutes)
Negative	(10 minutes)
Affirmative	(2 minutes)

Debate Format 2

First affirmative	(5 minutes)
First negative	(5 minutes)
Second affirmative	(5 minutes)
Second negative	(5 minutes)

As you can see, the number of format options is extensive. But, keep this important principle in mind: Whatever the format used in a debate, both sides must have equal opportunity to argue their cases and defend them against the attack. Fairness is the key.

DEBATE JUDGING

We now turn to the standards by which debates are judged. These standards are both logical and qualitative. The outcome of a debate may be determined by the logical adequacy of the cases presented by each side. Judges who base their decisions on logical adequacy are concerned with such questions as these: Has the affirmative team presented a *prima facie* case? Did the affirmative win all the issues? Did the negative team defeat the affirmative team on at least one issue?

By the term, *qualitative standards,* we mean the criteria having to do with the debating skill displayed by each side. Judges who base their decision on the quality of the debating are concerned with such questions as these: Did the negative team recognize the weaknesses in the affirmative team's case? Did the affirmative team offer convincing and adequate proofs for the contentions it advanced, regardless of whether or not the negative team saw the weaknesses in the affirmative team's case?

This distinction warrants a brief discussion because, occasionally, inconsistencies in judgments arise. The distinction between qualitative and logical standards, helps to explain why there are disagreements even among professional debate judges as to which team should win or lose a given debate.

Consider this example: Jane and Roberta are the affirmative team. They are arguing for the proposition: RESOLVED, That a system of direct election of the president of the United States should be established. The negative team consists of Bob and Mark. The proposition being debated is proposition of policy.

Let us assume that Jane and Roberta decide to argue a traditional affirmative case; that is, they will maintain that there is a need for a change in the way the president is elected and that this need arises out of conditions inherent in the existing state of affairs. No mere alterations of the electoral college system can solve the problem. Rather, a complete and radical change in our method of electing the president is required.

Let us further assume that the negative team elects to argue a traditional case. Bob and Mark will argue that there is no need for the proposed change. In fact, no alteration in the *status quo* is necessary.

There are two other issues to be argued in the debate. First, would a direct system of presidential election remedy the inequities in our present electoral methodology? Second, would a direct system of election solve these inequities without creating new and more serious problems?

In our hypothetical debate, imagine that Jane and Roberta fail to demonstrate a need for the change they propose. Although they advance all kinds of proofs demonstrating the inadequacies of the electoral college system, they do not prove a need growing out of conditions inherent in the *status quo*. Perhaps they show that it would be nice or that it would make people feel better. (John Q. Citizen likes to feel he has a direct voice in government.) Perhaps, they even show that it would save time and money to switch to a direct election system. However, they fail to answer the need issue satisfactorily.

Next, let us suppose that Bob and Mark spend most of their time attacking their opponents' plan. Due to inexperience, the two men do not realize that the affirmative team has failed to demonstrate need. In their enthusiasm, the negative team ignores the issue of need and simply tears apart the plan the affirmative team has proposed.

If a decision on this debate were to be made on purely logical grounds, the negative team would win. By failing to demonstrate the need for a change, the affirmative side has failed to present a *prima facie* case. Even though the negative team did not detect this flaw in the affirmative team's case, the decision would still have to go to the negative team. Whereas the negative team's debating may have been inferior, the affirmative team must lose on purely logical grounds. The presumption, being in favor of the negative team, warrants its receiving the decision.

Now, let us look at the situation from the point of view of proficiency.

The judge sits and listens to the entire debate, recognizing that the affirmative team has failed to demonstrate a need for a change and that the negative team has failed to pick up this flaw. Further, the judge recognizes that Jane and Roberta have done a superior job in their arguments and Bob and Mark have been careless. The documentation of their proofs has been poor and they have not taken the affirmative team to task on the issue of need.

The judge renders the decision on the basis of debating proficiency and awards the victory to Jane and Roberta. Although logically they must lose the debate because they failed to show a need for change, they have nevertheless done the better job of debating.

We tend to side with the judge in this instance. School debates are not intended to resolve real world questions of fact, value, or policy; they are exercises in critical thinking, proposition analysis, and argument. The application of logical criteria alone fails to take into account the value of the debate as a learning experience and as an exercise in argumentation. Therefore, the question we ask as debate judges is this: Which side did the better debating, regardless of which would win on the basis of logic alone?

A word of caution is appropriate here. A debater should strive to win the debate on the basis of both the logical strength of the case and the overall quality of debating. Do not rest content to present a logically inadequate case because you are confident that your team's overall performance will be superior to that of the opposing team. The debate must work toward the perfection of logical adequacy and consummate argumentative skill.

There are specific criteria with which to evaluate a team's performance. We will discuss six: analysis, reasoning, evidence, organization, refutation, and delivery. See Figure 3-1 for a sample debate ballot.

Listed below is a series of questions debate judges will consider in deciding which team will be declared the winner of the debate.

Analysis

1. Does the debater demonstrate an awareness of the kind of proposition he is arguing?
2. Does the debater give insight into the origins of the present controversy?
3. How are the key terms in the proposition defined? Are the definitions adequate? Are the definitions consistent with the arguments?
4. Is an awareness of the issues to which the proposition gives rise demonstrated?
5. What sort of case has the advocate prepared?
6. Is an understanding of the proof requirements to be satisfied revealed?
7. Is the case the debater prepared logically adequate?[7]

[7]For additional information on proposition analysis, see Chapter 2, Rules of the Game, and the discussion of case construction in this chapter.

American Forensic Association Debate Ballot   FORM C

Division_____ Round_____ Room_____ Date_____ Judge_____

Affirmative_____ Negative_____

Check the column on each item which, on the following scale, best describes your evaluation of the speaker's effectiveness:

| 1—poor | 2—fair | 3—average | 4—excellent | 5—superior |

1st Affirmative					2nd Affirmative						1st Negative					2nd Negative				
1	2	3	4	5	1	2	3	4	5		1	2	3	4	5	1	2	3	4	5
										Analysis										
										Reasoning										
										Evidence										
										Organization										
										Refutation										
										Delivery										

Total_____   Total_____   Total_____   Total_____

Team Ratings: AFFIRMATIVE: poor   fair   average   excellent   superior

NEGATIVE: poor   fair   average   excellent   superior

Rank each debater in order of excellence (1st for best, 2nd for next best, etc.).

COMMENTS: COMMENTS:

1st Aff. (name)_____Rank (   )   1st Neg. (name)_____Rank (   )

2nd Aff. (name)_____Rank (   )   2nd Neg. (name)_____Rank (   )

In my opinion, the better debating was done by the _____
                                                        (AFFIRMATIVE OR NEGATIVE)

_____   _____
JUDGE'S SIGNATURE   SCHOOL

This form reproduced by permission of the American Forensic Association. Copies may be purchased from the treasurer of the Association. The name of the current treasurer can always be found in the *Journal of the American Forensic Association.*

FIGURE 3-1

Reasoning

1. Is the line of argument reasonable?
2. Are the proofs free of logical flaws?
3. Do the proofs rely on logical fallacies?
4. How probable are the conclusions advanced, given the facts and evidence accumulated?[8]

Evidence

1. Does the advocate offer adequate evidence for the assertions made?
2. Does the evidence stand up under scrutiny?
3. What sort of evidence is employed? Are better types of evidence available? Could they have been used?[9]

Organization

1. Are the speeches outlined logically?
2. Is the case outline logically adequate?
3. Does the advocate demonstrate an adequate appraisal of his case?
4. Do subpoints support main contentions?[10]

Refutation

1. Does the debater demonstrate skill in attacking the arguments of the opposition?
2. Does the debater demonstrate critical listening skills?
3. How successful is the debater at attacking the central weaknesses of the opponents' case?
4. How well does the debater defend his own case and proofs against the attacks of the opposition?
5. Can the debater support his contentions after they have been called into question by the opposition?[11]

---

[8] For additional information on reasoning, see Chapter 2, Rules of the Game, and 4, Exposing a Fallacy.

[9] For additional information on evidence, see Chapter 2.

[10] For additional information on organization, see Chapter 2 and discussion of case construction in this chapter.

[11] For additional information on refutation, see Chapters 2, 4, 5, and the first part of this chapter.

Delivery

1. Does the debater demonstrate an awareness of the audience?
2. Does the debater reveal an ability to make himself heard and understood?
3. Does the debater use both voice and body to enhance the presentation of the proofs?
4. Is the debater courteous, respectful, and committed?

These questions are not intended to provide you with an exhaustive list of everything a debate judge will consider; however, they may alert you to the kind of criteria to be employed. Thoughtful preparation and critical listening, coupled with sincere effort and attention to presentation skills, will greatly enhance your chances of winning debates. Consider the criteria specified here. Ask your teacher or coach about others.

Before concluding this discussion about judging debates, a word of advice regarding the acceptance of the judge's decision is in order. Whether or not you agree with the judge's decision, accept it graciously and, by so doing, demonstrate your respect for the art of debate. If you should have any inquiries concerning the basis on which the decision was reached, they should be made in the spirit of sincerity and good will. Antagonistic questioning of a judge, snide commentaries, and disrespectful innuendoes are to be avoided. Try to come away from every debate with the feeling that you have learned something that has a positive application for future debates.

WRAP-UP

In this chapter, designed with the school debater in mind, we have surveyed the typical debate formats encountered in school debates. First we discussed the various kinds of affirmative and negative cases. Next we examined the two bases for judging a debate: *logical adequacy* of a case and *the skill with which it is argued.* Also mentioned were other criteria used in judging a debate: *analysis, reasoning, evidence, refutation, organization,* and *presentation.* We concluded with the admonition that an appropriate attitude toward the outcome of a debate is essential to ethical and meaningful exchanges of ideas on any collegiate debate circuit.

PROBES, PRODS, AND PROJECTS

What is the difference between a constructive and a rebuttal speech?

What are the usual duties of a first affirmative speaker in a traditional affirmative case?

Name two affirmative case options. How do they differ?

What is meant by the comparative advantages case? What are the responsibilities of the affirmative team if they elect this option?

What is meant by the direct refutation case? the counterplan case? How do they differ?

List four common errors made by inexperienced cross-examination debaters.

Explain the two points of view with respect to judging debates. Which do you support? Why?

Attend a school debate and report to the class on such matters as (1) the kind of proposition debated, (2) the kind of case argued by the affirmative team, (3) the kind of case argued by the negative team, (4) the extent to which each team fulfilled the responsibilities outlined in this chapter.

With the guidance of your instructor, conduct a debate in your class.

4

EXPOSING A FALLACY

BEHAVIORAL OBJECTIVES:

After reading this chapter, you should have a better understanding of

1. the nature of a fallacy
2. why it is so important for a debater to be able to detect fallacious arguments
3. the kinds of personal and public situations capable of generating fallacious reasoning
4. how to uncover fallacies
5. why an argument, stripped of its fallacious content, loses its false air of legitimacy
6. why merely reading about fallcies and how to expose them is not enough if one seeks to become a successful debater

The art of knowing how to expose a fallacy in your opponent's case is the *piece de resistance* of argumentation. The success of any encounter is often commensurate with this ability. However, a word of warning: Merely reading about fallacies and how they are exposed is not enough. All it produces is a false sense of security. Exposing fallacies is a delicate art requiring keen observation, infallible timing, and indefatigable effort. To prepare you, we tell what a *fallacy* is and present twenty-six of the more common ones, with discussion. In Chapter 6, your skill at detecting fallacies *in context* will be tested.

THE NATURE OF A FALLACY

A fallacy is defined as a deceptive or misleading tactic used intentionally or accidentally by an advocate, which may have the effect of deluding an opponent or an onlooker. This is a broad definition, and it includes two kinds of practices: (1) the use of wrong reasoning or faulty evidence to support conclusions; and (2) the employment of dishonest strategies such as ignoring the issue or asking loaded questions. The first broad category is made up of fallacies that are bound to a particular proof unit and that grow out of a faulty handling of the reasoning or evidence used. The second category includes strategies that are not intrinsic to any particular proof unit but that appear in a variety of situations.

Whatever the nature of the fallacy and whether it be intentionally or accidentally committed, its effect is the same: It creates an illusion based on deception. Unless fallacies are detected and exposed, the arguments in which they occur assume a *false air of legitimacy*. Once the inner workings of a fallacy are revealed, the illusion of proof and the false air of legitimacy vanish. What's left is an argument destined to stand or fall on its intrinsic merits alone. And it is *this* that should provide the basis for rational decision making.

On the following pages, we present fallacies in their most familiar setting: one-to-one conversations. Following each dialogue is a discussion in which we point out the nature of the fallacy and the argumental dynamics from which it originates. You are encouraged to attempt your own analysis of the dialogue before reading the discussion. You may then compare your diagnosis with that of the authors.

FALLACIES
OF REASONING AND EVIDENCE

ARGUMENT 1

Father: I think they should close the colleges for a few years.
Son: Why?
Father: Because all these students are radical leftists, plotting violent revolution.
Son: But how can you say that? Not *all* students are like that!
Father: Nonsense! Seen one, seen them all!

Discussion: This dialogue harbors the *fallacy of composition,* which holds that *what is true of the parts of a thing is true of the whole.* The inference made by the father was that because certain students are radical leftist revolutionaries, all of them are. This kind of wrong reasoning is the root of prejudice and stereotyping. The colloquial expression, "seen one, seen them all," is the essence of this fallacy. Minority groups have had to bear such unjust accusations too long. The best remedy for this kind of sloppy reasoning is exposure on sight!

ARGUMENT 2

Lynn: I am surprised to learn that George is now teaching on the college level.

Hector: Why?

Lynn: Because he's certainly no serious intellectual.

Hector: So what makes you think that every college teacher is an intellectual?

Lynn: Well, as a group they are, so each of them must be!

Discussion: This is one of the easiest fallacies to detect. It is called the *fallacy of division: what is true of the whole is true of the parts.* It may be that *in general* college teachers are serious intellectuals; but it does not follow that every college teacher fits that description. This fallacy overlooks the differences and variations within a class of things.

Stereotyping is, in a sense, a double fallacy. It forms a "seen one, seen them all" judgment about a whole group of people on the basis of a few particular instances *(fallacy of composition),* and then it applies that faulty generalization to every individual who falls within that group *(fallacy of division).*[1]

ARGUMENT 3

Political science student A: It sure looks like America is heading for another depression.

Political science student B: What makes you say that?

Political science student A: The recent instability of the stock market. If it should take a dive like it did in 1929, we're going to have another one.

Political science student B: Are you saying that the *cause* of the depression in the early 1930s was the stock market crash?

Political science student A: Sure! If the market hadn't crashed, we wouldn't have had a depression.

[1] For a very interesting discussion of stereotyping, see Henry Clay Smith, *Sensitivity to People* (New York: McGraw-Hill Book Co., 1966), pp. 133-51.

Discussion: The dialogue illustrates the *fallacy of mistaken causation.* In it student A establishes a one-to-one causal relationship between the stock market crash and the depression that followed. He refuses to consider (1) whether the crash was a symptom or a sign rather than a cause of the depression and (2) the existence of any other possible causes of the depression (for example, business cycles, world economy, or international affairs). The reluctance to consider such alternatives justifies labeling of this kind of reasoning as fallacious. To protect oneself against it, always inquire into the relationship between the alleged cause and its effect.[2]

ARGUMENT 4

Husband:	You know, dear, I couldn't start my car this morning.
Wife:	Why are you telling me?
Husband:	Because you used it last, honey.
Wife:	And just what is that supposed to mean?
Husband:	Nothing, except that it was okay until you drove it.
Wife:	Are you insinuating that because I used your old car yesterday and it wouldn't start for you this morning, *I* was responsible?
Husband:	It certainly makes sense, darling. You were the last one to use it, therefore. . . .

Discussion: The fallacy committed in this argument is a common variety of faulty causal reasoning. It is called *post hoc ergo propter hoc* (after the fact therefore because of the fact). The fallacy consists of arguing that because one thing precedes another in time and space, it causes the second to occur. The church bells rang, and ten minutes later it rained. *Conclusion:* The ringing of the church bells caused the rain. In many primitive societies, an eclipse of the moon followed by the death of their leader might provide ample proof that the eclipse *caused* his death. In short, any attempt to establish a causal relationship solely on the basis of sequentiality warrants the label of *post hoc ergo propter hoc.*

ARGUMENT 5

Joe:	So, you're saying that the use of artificial means of birth control is wrong.
Jim:	Yes, I am.
Joe:	Why is it wrong?
Jim:	Because my church says it is.
Joe:	And why do you think your church says that?
Jim:	Because the use of artificial means of birth control is wrong, and it's the church's job to guide its members on moral matters.

[2] For tests of causal reasoning, see Chapter 2, Rules of the Game.

Discussion: This fallacy, which is called *arguing in a circle* (because it goes nowhere, like a dog chasing its tail), is characterized by the presence of two or more unsupported claims, each of which supposedly *proves* the other. In our example, Jim's argument runs as follows:

Assertion 1 (claim):	The use of artificial means of birth control is wrong, *because*
Assertion 2 (support):	My church says so.
and	
Assertion 2 (claim):	My church says that the use of artificial means of birth control is wrong, *because*
Assertion 1 (support):	The use of artificial means of birth control is wrong.

The redundancy and logical weakness of the argument becomes evident when it is analyzed closely, using our *proof unit* formula presented in Chapter 2. You can test for this fallacy by determining (1) the conclusion or claim of the argument, and (2) the support or backing for the claim, remembering that *the same statement cannot be both the claim and its support.* The two must remain separate and distinct. When they do not—when they overlap or when each statement supports the other—the fallacy of *arguing in a circle* has occurred.

Hence, you can point out to the next employer who refuses to give you a job because you lack experience that he is guilty of arguing in a circle. "You can't get the job because you lack experience; and you can't get experience without having the job." (We doubt whether this will get you hired, but it might start him thinking.)

ARGUMENT 6

Scene: the front office of a large industrial firm

Alice:	Did you hear about Helen?
Harriet:	No, what happened to her?
Alice:	The police found out that she's addicted to hard drugs.
Harriet:	That's impossible; she's not the type! She's a good girl. She just wouldn't do such a thing!

Discussion: This is an example of the *genetic fallacy*—a form of *a priori* reasoning in which it is assumed that "good" people do good things, and "bad" people do bad things. The remark, "I would expect that of her!" typifies this fallacy. We make judgments about people, then we estimate the probability of their behaving in a certain way on the basis of our prior judgments. "My aunt is honest, so these charges against her cannot be accurate." This reasoning begins with principles or beliefs that we hold dear and proceeds to the evaluation of facts and evidence *in the light of our prior convictions.* To guard against this fallacy, you must challenge the assumption that people and their deeds are inseparable.

ARGUMENT 7

Scene: a dentist's office

Dentist:	Mr. Jones, did you know that the incidence of cavities in the borough of Manhattan is sixty-four percent?
Patient:	So what?
Dentist:	So what! That's a lot of people with cavities!

Discussion: The dentist in this argument committed the *fallacy of significance*. The figure of sixty-four percent in itself tells very little, unless certain questions are answered—for example, what is the incidence of cavities in other boroughs and in other urban areas? Without answers to such questions as these, the figure of sixty-four percent has no meaning. In the light of this discussion, a question like "How's your husband?" could justifiably be answered, "Compared to what?"

ARGUMENT 8

Deist:	There is no doubt in my mind that God exists.
Atheist:	Do you have any proof that God exists?
Deist:	Yes, personal proof. He has made His presence known to me.
Atheist:	That is not proof to me. Do you have any other more persuasive evidence?
Deist:	Yes, the fact that millions of people all over the world agree with me that God exists.

Discussion: Here, the fallacy resides in the contention that something is true because so many people believe it. This *argumentum ad populum* (appeal to popular opinions and prejudices) is captured by the phrase, "a hundred thousand Frenchmen can't be wrong." History is frought with instances in which new ideas were attacked because most people held older ones. Original thinkers like Sister Kenny, Freud, Martin Luther King, and Pasteur incurred the wrath of their peers, who cried, "Everyone knows that such a notion is absurd!" An advocate who seeks support for his view solely because it is supported by popular opinion stands on very shaky ground.

ARGUMENT 9

Mother:	Steven, you are not to go out tonight.
Teen-ager:	But, Mom, I have to go out.

Mother:	I'm sorry, I think it best that you don't go out tonight.
Teen-ager:	Please, Mom, I'll stay in all day tomorrow. Let me go out tonight.
Mother:	Steven, my job is like the captain of a ship. It is my responsibility to protect you in spite of yourself. *You are not going out tonight!*

Discussion: Steven's mother drew a *faulty analogy* between her role as a mother and that of a ship's captain. This analogy does not hold up for the following reasons:

1. The captain of a ship is trained for command whereas the mother of a household is not.
2. The captain's ship is governed by naval law whereas the mother's household is not.
3. The number of people under a captain's command is substantially greater than the few usually supervised by the mother—hence the captain's need for more rules and regulations.
4. The goals of a naval captain are essentially different from those of a mother.

Although it is not too difficult to see certain similarities between the two roles, there are sufficient differences to justify rejecting them as being analogous at every level. The problem here is that the two things compared are not sufficiently similar to warrant the conclusion drawn.[3]

ARGUMENT 10

Leigh:	So you approve of the "spare the rod, spoil the child" approach?
Gertrude:	Yes—without reservation!
Leigh:	Well, I certainly respect your opinion, but let me ask you this: where were you born?
Gertrude:	In Chicago.
Leigh:	In the city proper?
Gertrude:	Yes.
Leigh:	Well, that explains it.
Gertrude:	Explains what?
Leigh:	Why you believe what you do!

Discussion: The fallacy in this dialogue is called a *non sequitur,* meaning *it does not follow.* In her last two remarks, Leigh implies a relationship between discipline and urban upbringing that is, at best, illusory. The charge of *non*

---

[3] For tests of reasoning from analogy, see Chapter 2, Rules of the Game.

sequitur, then, can rightfully be applied when an advocate states a relationship that appears to have little or no basis in fact or when she draws conclusions that lack support. Seek out possible "missing links" in her chain of reasoning to determine its validity.

Successful argumentation is not a science but an art. Simply knowing its principles will not guarantee competence as an advocate. One must learn through experiences where, when, how, and why these principles are applied. This, of course, takes time, patience, and practice. May we suggest an excellent method of achieving proficiency at exposing fallacious arguments? Using daily private conversations, radio and television programs, and the local newspapers, make a concerted effort to expose at least one fallacy a day. This one-a-day technique, if seriously pursued, can produce a noticeable difference in your ability to shoot down spurious arguments.

OTHER FALLACIES

ARGUMENT 11

Conservative: Well, the way I see it, the situation is summed up in the slogan:
America—love it or leave it!
Radical: And I say: America—change it or lose it!

Discussion: Both parties are guilty of the same fallacy—*false dilemma.* Here, two and only two alternatives are presented when, in fact, there may be others. Simplistic thinking such as the kind underlying slogans and rallying cries often leads to the fallacy of the false dilemma.

The best way to deal with this fallacy is to point out that more than two alternatives exist. In our example, we recommend that the radical tell his opponent that "love it or leave it" overlooks the possibility of changing or improving it. The conservative should remind his opponent that "change it or lose it" reflects an alarmist mentality: It might be possible to bring about desired changes gradually, without the fear of losing it because reform is not drastic and immediate.

ARGUMENT 12

Scene: father and eight-year old son.

Son: Dad, can I have a dollar?
Father: What for, son?
Son: I want to buy something, Dad.

Father:	A dollar is a lot of money. I'd like to know if you're going to spend it wisely.
Son:	It's a secret, Dad, and if you don't give me a dollar, I'll steal one. If I steal one, then I'll get caught by the police; and they'll put me in jail and if they put me in jail, I'll try to escape; and might kill a guard; and if I kill a guard, they'll try me for murder; and I'll get the gas chamber. *All because you won't give me a dollar!*

Discussion: This example illustrates the *fallacy of reductio ad absurdum* (reduction to the absurd). It consists of carrying a rational argument to an absurd conclusion. The fallacy of reduction to the absurd occurred recently when a politician argued against abortion reform on the grounds that it would ultimately destroy the country by fostering prostitution, promiscuity, venereal disease, and moral decay. Should your opponent reduce an argument to the absurd, demand that he show you exactly *how* and *why* the conclusions advanced would follow from the original premise.

ARGUMENT 13

Chris:	I say when a government spends fifty-five percent of its income on weapons of war, it's spending too much!
Leroy:	But look at North Ereheron. They spend almost seventy percent of their income on weapons.
Chris:	Really? Seventy percent? I guess I shouldn't complain. . . .

Discussion: This is a *fallacy of false consolation,* otherwise known as the *count your blessings fallacy.* A wife complains about a lazy husband, and he reminds her of Charlie, a neighbor, who is not only lazy but is an alcoholic and is unfaithful. The implied conclusion is, "Well, see how lucky you are after all!" If the user of this fallacy could have his way, his opponent would feel ashamed of his complaining attitude and actually be grateful for the state of affairs about which he complains.

This kind of argument can always be applied because certain people are invariably better off than others. But this does not justify the continuance of an evil situation. In our example above, we must make clear that the wife *isn't* married to neighbor Charlie. And so the introduction of a hypothetical "what if you were" doesn't prove anything. The best rejoinder to this fallacy is to explain emphatically that you are talking about the issues immediately at hand and nothing else.

ARGUMENT 14

Scene: a political rally

Senator A:	My worthy opponent professes to support better education for our children. But his voting record proves otherwise.

Senator B:	The Senator has been guilty of many similar baldfaced lies about me; I call him a liar to his face.
Senator A:	It is indeed unfortunate that my opponent must resort to such language to make his point.
Senator B:	What language are you talking about, you fat-faced, Fascist pig?

Discussion: When an argument is embellished with colorful and flowery language like this, the *fallacy of psychological language* has occurred. When it is used against you, identify it, and inform your opponent that if he insists on functioning at that level, you cannot continue to argue. Explain that emotionally loaded words often force conclusions before the appropriate evidence can be presented, heard, and thought through. In short, indicate that you are interested in rational, rather than ridiculous, disagreement.

ARGUMENT 15

Hustler:	Hey, Mac, ya wanna buy a watch?
Mark:	What kind is it?
Hustler:	It got seventeen jewels, an it runs unda water.
Mark:	What brand is it?
Hustler:	It also got da date, an it winds audamatically.
Mark:	Who makes it?

Discussion: This is an example of the *fallacy of ignoring the issue.* The hustler's reluctance to answer the man's question stems from a desire to sell a probably inferior product. Since it was not in the hustler's best interest to identify the brand of watch, he repeatedly ignored the question as though it had never been asked. This popular argumentative technique once recognized must never be tolerated. If the answer to a question is important to your argument, you must pursue the matter relentlessly until an answer is obtained. If your opponent rigidly avoids the question, his avoidance must be openly exposed and registered clearly as an attempt on his part to evade the issue.

ARGUMENT 16

Scene: an exchange of words at a sensitivity group session

John:	You're full of crap, Frank; man is not a monogamous creature.
Frank:	How the hell do you know that?
John:	Because I've lived a little—I've been around—I know what life is all about.
Frank:	And you seriously think that because a man is faithful to his wife he's a fool, eh?
John:	Come on, Frank—you're a fine one to talk. When did *you* stop cheating on your wife?

Discussion: This is the *fallacy of the loaded question.* No matter how (or even whether) you answer it, you lose! This technique is often used in court to influence the jury. The moment the question is asked, the other attorney objects and, almost without exception, the judge sustains the objection. *But the jury has already been influenced by the remark.* The best course to follow when someone hurls a loaded question at you is this: Announce emphatically that you are fully aware of the nature of his question and its purpose. Better still, throw the question—or something like it—back at him. In our case, we might recommend that Frank ask John when *he* stopped cheating on *his* wife; or, if he doesn't have a wife, something similar—"I stopped cheating on my wife about the time you stopped stealing money from the poor box at church."

ARGUMENT 17

Pearl: Did you give your little Audrey that polio vaccine?
Ruth: No, Pearl, I don't think it's any good.
Pearl: What do you mean, Ruth? It's wiped out polio completely!
Ruth: Yes, but it's absolutely worthless against measles, cancer, smallpox, and malaria.

Discussion: If you identified this one as the *fallacy of extension,* you are correct. While Ruth appears to have accepted the fact that polio has been wiped out by the vaccine, she extends its purpose beyond reasonable bounds and uses that extension as a basis for arguing against the vaccine. The same sort of fallacious reasoning occurs when Shakespeare's plays are criticized for being factually inaccurate (they are not intended to be accurate histories); or when a popular songstress is criticized because she lacks the ability to sing opera (she does not claim the ability; she has been trained to sing popular songs). Careful determination of the proof requirements of a contention can prevent your being duped by the fallacy of extension. Insist that your opponent address himself to the relevant issues of the case; do not allow him to dredge up irrelevant or immaterial issues.

ARGUMENT 18

Karen: Do you really believe that a teacher should allow students to grade themselves?
Janine: Yes, I'm convinced it's the best way to grade.
Karen: I suppose you support the abdication of all responsibility on the part of people in authority. Should policemen let criminals arrest themselves? Should parents let children raise themselves?

Discussion: This is the *fallacy of the straw man,* in which an advocate brings up a point that is only indirectly relevant to his opponent's position and refutes the weaker point. He thereby appears to have refuted his opponent's main thesis. Karen, in our example, introduces straw men by bringing up the absurd notions of criminals arresting themselves and children raising themselves. Both are easily refuted and, therefore, seem to counter the practice of student self-evaluations. However, the various situations are not parallel. The best defense against straw men fallacies is the careful analysis of the parallel theses raised, in search of faulty analogies and reduction to the absurd. Bear in mind that the destruction of straw men does not weaken your original position.

ARGUMENT 19

Older Musician:	I can't understand how you can say that the clarinets they are manufacturing today are superior to those made fifty years ago.
Young Musician:	Come now, you know perfectly well that the key work is better on the clarinets made today.
Older Musician:	Perhaps, but you must admit that the way they seasoned the wood years ago stands head and shoulders over these quick modern methods.
Young Musician:	No, I don't think so. The modern methods are superior! Modern technology has obviously raised the quality of goods—you can't deny that, can you?
Older Musician:	Are you saying that just because something is new, it's necessarily better?
Young Musician:	Of course!

Discussion: This infraction of the rules is called *argumentum ad novarum,* which occurs when an arguer insists that simply because something is new, it is better than that which is old. People guilty of this fallacy typically base their convictions entirely on newness rather than evidence.

This popular fallacy manifests itself in many areas of everyday life. There are people who will go only to a young physician. Their reasoning is that the newly graduated doctor has the advantage of modernity and is surely more competent. Others extol the virtues of owning new things (from automobiles to can openers) rather than older ones.[4] Although there is little doubt that newness does possess certain undeniably attractive elements, rational decision-making should include a broader spectrum of considerations before a judgment is rendered.

---

[4]The converse of this fallacy is embodied in the statement, "They just don't make 'em like they used to!"

ARGUMENT 20

Scene: a lawyer summing up his case to the jury

Lawyer:　　　Ladies and gentlemen of the jury, you have heard the evidence against my client, who is charged with first degree murder of seven women. Before considering his fate, I beg you to take full notice of his history and personal reputation. He is a devout Christian who goes to church every Sunday without fail. He is a loyal husband and devoted father of three lovely children (each an honor student in school). He is respected by his neighbors and an active member on the local school board. . . .

Discussion: If the *fallacy of argumentum ad miseracordiam* (appeal to pity) entered your mind, you are on target. In this case, the attorney attempts to evoke the sympathy of the jury by pointing up those conventionally admirable traits possessed by his client. Although these attributes in no way negate the fact that the defendant did murder seven women, they may evoke compassion in the minds and hearts of some jurors. Be on the alert for such a technique in an argument, and expose it where necessary.

ARGUMENT 21

Congressman:　　I'm strenuously opposed to unilateral disarmament.
Constituent:　　Why?
Congressman:　　Because it's too radical a departure from our time-honored tradition of military preparedness as a deterrent to aggression.
Constituent:　　But don't you think that military preparedness encourages rather than discourages violence?
Congressman:　　That may be so, but I am still reminded of our honored ancestors, who, in their wisdom, did not see fit to be caught with their defenses down. And it is to our founding fathers I turn for guidance and direction.

Discussion: Arguments based on blatant appeals to time-honored traditions and precedents fall under the category of *ad verecundium fallacies.* All progress comes about through changes—breaks with the past. Yet man's natural desire to cling to the past results in the commission of this fallacy. When an opponent seems to be approaching this argumental bog, remind him that you respect his right to support the *status quo,* but request that he be willing to change his stand if your arguments are reasonable and convincing. As added spice, you might toss in the following two remarks. The first is by the English philosopher Jeremy Bentham, the founder of Utilitarianism: (1) "It is from the folly, not from the wisdom, of our ancestors that we have so much to learn; and yet it is to their supposed wisdom, and not to their folly, that the fallacy in question would send us for instruction."[5] The second is by Woodrow Wilson: "I have often said that the use of a university is to make young gentlemen as unlike their fathers as possible."[6]

ARGUMENT 22

Customer:	I would like to return this blouse, please.
Clerk:	I'm sorry, madam; it cannot be returned after it has been worn.
Customer:	But I haven't worn it!
Clerk:	There seems to be some dirt around the collar.
Customer:	What dirt? I don't see any dirt.
Clerk:	Really madam, I don't intend to argue with you. By the way, haven't you been in here before trying to return dirty blouses?
Customer:	Young man, I will not stand here and have you insult me by suggesting that I habitually return dirty blouses. You have absolutely no right to talk to me that way. I would like to see the manager.

Discussion: This altercation raises the *argumentum ad hominem (damning the origin* or *character assassination)* fallacy. It is characterized by an attack upon the individual rather than an examination of the issues involved. In this situation, the argument began with the blouse as the focus. In a few seconds, rather than attempting to establish whether or not the blouse in fact was dirty, the clerk shifted his attack to the woman personally, accusing her of habitually returning dirty blouses. Whenever you are in an argument in which the focus shifts from the issues to you or to the source of an idea, object immediately and demand that your opponent address himself to the subject at hand rather than the person. In the final analysis, two plus two equal four, regardless of whether the statement is made by a genius or a moron.

ARGUMENT 23

Actor:	Say, Marge, I heard you were great in your new play last week up in Boston.
Actress:	Thanks, Mark. You are very kind to mention it. But how did you hear about it?

---

[5] Jeremy Bentham, *Bentham's Handbook of Political Fallacies,* ed. by Harold A. Larrabee (Baltimore: Johns Hopkins Press, 1952), p. 51.

[6] Woodrow Wilson, *The Public Papers of Woodrow Wilson, Authorized Edition,* ed. by Ray S. Baker and William E. Dodd. *The New Democracy* (New York: Harper and Row, Publishers, Inc., 1927), I, p. 199.

Actor:	I read it in one of the Boston papers, I think.
Actress:	Oh, what did it say, Mark?
Actor:	Let me see . . . it read "Marge Brissavour's . . . comeback shocked Boston audiences last week. Her performance left them standing in the aisles. . . .
Actress:	You're a real gentleman to say that, Mark, but I happen to have that particular quote here in my purse.

Discussion: In this situation, Mark *quoted out of context.* The entire quote actually read: "Marge Brissavour's pathetic comeback shocked Boston audiences last week. Her performance left them standing in the aisles *shouting 'boo! boo! go home!' and hissing loudly.''* The tendency to quote things out of context is very common. Although often unintentional, this fallacy is sometimes perpetrated with malice of forethought when an advocate selects from a larger text only those things that strengthen his position. Awareness of the context from which a remark comes is the best defense against this fallacy. Short of that, a common-sensical analysis of the remark and its source can sometimes expose the fallacy.

ARGUMENT 24

Commuter A:	(Reading from the evening paper.) Are you going to listen to Senator Fudd on the TV tonight, Harry?
Commuter B:	No, I'd rather listen to the Secretary of State.
Commuter A:	Oh, is he going to be on, too?
Commuter B:	It says so right here in the paper, The Secretary of State, said the senator, will issue a statement tonight.
Commuter A:	Wait a minute Harry, I have the same quote right here in *my* paper. Mine says: The Secretary of State said the senator will issue a statement tonight.

Discussion: Here we have the *fallacy of ambiguous grammatical structure.* The entire meaning of the quote changed with the presence or absence of the *commas* after the words "state" and "senator." Commuter B, reading it with the commas in, concludes that the Secretary of State will issue a statement tonight. Commuter A, reading it *without* the commas, concludes that the senator will issue a statement. Punctuation can be critical to a statement's meaning and can decide the fate of an argument. In doubtful cases, it is best to cross-check the accuracy of punctuation before accepting a written report as evidence.

ARGUMENT 25

Danya:	Did you see the president on TV last night?
Eric:	Yes. Did you?

Danya:	Sure. But I'll tell you one thing—I'm beginning to worry about the free air time given to presidents in office.
Eric:	Why should that worry you?
Danya:	Because free time gives the president a lot of influence over American public opinion. Yet the opposition party leaders almost always have to pay for air time to present their views. And if they can't pay, they don't get the opportunity to present their side of the story. I think the Federal Communications Commission should establish clearer rulings that guarantee free and equal time to the opposition.
Eric:	What's the matter, don't you trust the president? He's a good, honest man. The kind of law you suggest would be an insult to him. We have nothing to fear.

Discussion: This is the *fallacy of laudatory personalities.* There can never be too many laws to protect the public good, yet the user of this fallacy argues *against* such measures *on the grounds that the people in office are trustworthy and of good character.* That may be true, but it's no guarantee that future office-holders will be. Hence, it is best to take the necessary precautions and pass the protective measures.

If you think this fallacy is restricted to national politicians alone, think back to club meetings you've attended. This fallacy emerges when people argue against proposals that protect the organization but seem to impinge on the character of the leader.

ARGUMENT 26

Ray:	Have you heard the *Daily Journal's* charges of corruption against the police commissioner?
Don:	Yes. I think it's a disgrace!
Ray:	A disgrace? Why?
Don:	Because by charging him with corruption the *Journal* is casting aspersions on the character of the whole police force. A breakdown of respect for the department is sure to follow.

Discussion: This is called the *fallacy of untouchable authority.* When people in official positions do dishonest things, they should be punished. Yet there are many who are opposed to criticizing officials, because it tends to lessen the public's respect for the agency in question. This is a somewhat backward approach to respect for authority. Generally, respect should follow the establishment of honesty and integrity. False criticisms often lend themselves to refutation by honest men. Hence, we ought to allow all reasonable criticisms against such established agencies as the government, the church, and the university to be made. The false ones will be disposed of and the valid ones, we would hope, will bring about reform.

WRAP-UP

In this chapter we have presented an expanded analysis of twenty-six fallacies. Each has been illustrated in dialogue form and followed by a discussion designed to explain its nature. If you enjoy participating in or listening to arguments, you must have recognized some of them at once. The frequency with which one encounters fallacies is virtually unlimited. The problem is their detection and remedy. In this age of mass communication, the number of words heard daily by members of the general public is beyond estimation. In this deluge of verbiage are countless well-disguised fallacies, suitably dressed up to deceive even the more sophisticated among us. A moment's careful scrutiny can make the difference between being needlessly duped and exposing a fallacy.

PROBES, PRODS, AND PROJECTS

What would result if the advertising industry were prohibited by law from using any of the fallacies in this chapter?

What fallacies do you encounter most often?

What fallacies are you guilty of committing?

If someone were to catch you using a fallacy, what would you do or say? Why?

Can you conceive of a circumstance in which not exposing a fallacy would be the wiser course?

Invite a guest advocate into your group and ask her to make a presentation heavily loaded with fallacies of reasoning and evidence. See how many you can detect. Group competition may be arranged using this format.

Select any five fallacies discussed in this chapter. For each of them, prepare your own dialogue to illustrate that fallacy.

5

APPLIED ARGUMENTATION

BEHAVIORAL OBJECTIVES

After reading this chapter, you should have a better understanding of

1. the distinctions between arguments that are controlled, static, and simplified and those that are uncontrolled, fluid, and dynamic
2. the practical sense of arguments as they emerge in their natural state
3. the strengths and weaknesses of an argument
4. the development of a systematic and analytical approach to an argument or a series of arguments
5. how to use the Toulmin Model more effectively

Some years ago, a professor of biology decided to take his anatomy class to the Museum of Natural History in New York City. There, the class was to view one of the world's largest collections of human skulls. Shortly after the students began to examine the various types of skulls, one of them quietly moved to the professor's side and whispered, "Professor, why aren't the frontal bones in these specimens blue?"

Somewhat surprised by the question, the professor asked, "Why do you think they should be, Roger?"

"Well," he replied, "in the illustrations in the course text, the frontal bone of the human skull is colored blue, so I just thought. . . ."

The student's confusion raises an important point. When one's knowledge of reality is gleaned solely from books, it is at best of limited use and at worst downright misleading. The student may be accustomed to descriptions of reality that are static and oversimplified. He may be accustomed to color-keyed diagrams, neatly labeled photographs, and carefully constructed flow charts. But the real world is far more complex than such descriptions would imply. It is a phantasmagoria of dynamic events and processes.

Just as the student of biology needed to learn that the frontal bone of the human skull is *not* blue, the student of argumentation must realize that such things as propositions, issues, evidence, fallacies, and various kinds of proof do not come in neatly arranged little packages with clearly marked tags, reading: *this is a fallacy, this is a proposition, this is an example of reasoning from effect to cause,* and so on. Instead, they come in complex packages.

Within a written essay or during a brief segment of conversation, you may encounter both logical and illogical arguments. Some points may be supported with appropriate evidence, others with inappropriate evidence, and still others with none at all. In any event, these utterances come at you all at once. They are complex and uncontrolled. It is your task, as an advocate in the real world, to decipher what you hear or read: to identify the proposition being argued, to determine the kinds of reasoning and evidence used by your opponent, to identify fallacies when they appear, and to uncover the strengths and weaknesses of your opponent's arguments.

In this chapter we present arguments as you will encounter them in the real world. We have made no attempt to ensure that each argument includes only one type of reasoning, or one type of evidence, or anything of the kind. On the contrary, we have intentionally sought to avoid these artificial limitations. You will read arguments in their natural state. Your task is to pick them apart and to identify the critical elements in each.

The chapter is divided into two sections. In the first we present "pro" and "con" arguments, prepared by students, on a variety of topics. You are to analyze each argument. For your convenience we have included an Argument Analysis Inventory after each passage. There you will find questions to guide your analysis.

In the second section, we provide you with an opportunity to develop your skill in using the Toulmin Model.[1] You should analyze the content of each argument, then construct three individual Toulmin Models.[2]

---

[1] See Chapter 2, pages 68-69, for a review of the Toulmin Model.

[2] On pages 126-127 you will find completed models with which to compare your own. Naturally, a sense of honesty and fair play should keep you from peeking at these models before you have completed yours.

PROS AND CONS

To Have Children or Not to Have Children: That is the Question

PRO

Every couple who plans to marry should plan to have children. This makes sense spiritually, practically, and psychologically.

It is God's will that couples procreate. In Genesis 2:24 it is written that in order to form a procreative bond with a woman, a man "leaves his father and mother and clings to his wife, and the two of them become one body." And in Genesis 1:28, God says that man is to "be fertile and multiply; fill the earth and subdue it."

From a practical standpoint, procreation makes sense. Children carry on the family name. They provide company and perhaps financial aid in one's old age. They represent an heir to one's financial, intellectual, and professional resources. They often provide the cement to hold together a failing marriage. And let us not forget that child-bearing is mankind's only hope for the future of the human race.

Psychologically, procreation is sensible. Many couples find that the creation of a child provides a unique expression of their love. Children give one's life meaning. They allow parents to relive the pleasures of their own childhood. Often they satisfy a husband's and wife's own parents by making them grandparents. Perhaps most important, procreation is the most valid evidence that a man is a man and a woman is a woman.

Argument Analysis Inventory

1. What proposition is being argued in this passage? What kind of proposition is it? _____

_____

_____

_____

_____

_____

_____

_____

_____

2. What are the three main contentions advanced in this passage? How many reasons are given for accepting each contention? _____

_____

_____

_____

_____

_____

3. Outline the case advanced in this passage. Determine which assertions are supported and which are unsupported. _____

_____

_____

_____

_____

_____

_____

4. What kind(s) of evidence, if any, does the advocate use? _____

_____

_____

_____

_____

_____

CON

To the amazement of the more tradition-minded among us, recent times have ushered in a wave of young men and women who have expressed a preference *not* to have children. In the past there was never any question as to whether one should or should not procreate; it was expected. Today things are different. According to Claudia Dreifus in an article entitled, "Do I Want A Baby?" which appeared in the November 1977 issue of McCall's magazine, modern technology and the mass media have created situations in which an individual can discover means of achieving satisfaction other than by having children. People have more buying power and, because they have higher incomes, they spend more. This activity, in turn, sparks a surge of mass production that gives rise to a higher standard of living. People's lives have become filled with sources of meaning that challenge the fulfillment previously supplied by childbearing. The feminist movement has rescued many women from the heretofore inescapable role of housewife; it has made it possible for many of them to enter the job market on practically equal footing with men. At this very moment, an enormous number of women are successfully enjoying careers that afford them a great deal more satisfaction than they would have enjoyed had they elected to be baby-makers.

Another good reason for not having children in today's society is the spiraling cost of living. Countless married men cannot support their families adequately by working one job; many must work two jobs to make ends meet. If it is impossible for the husband to work a second job, the wife must often go out and work. This, naturally, raises the problem of baby-sitting expenses. All around, the problem of supporting a family is strained in an accentuated number of cases. Many couples start out their marriages planning to have children, but by the time they finish buying furniture and paying off the house, they have become so adjusted to a child-free lifestyle that children seem out of the question.

This society has also proved not to be one of the best societies in which to rear children. Too many things aside from the family, affect the way children grow up. Often children give their parents a lot of heartache when they get older, and that is one thing most people would definitely be glad to do without.

There is still an additional complication that might arise. A couple could, in their enthusiasm, want a child desperately at the outset of their marriage. After having it, they might come to realize that they were too young, too unprepared both psychologically and economically. What are they to do then? A child could ruin the marriage. If a marriage where there were no children went sour, the couple walk away without disadvantaging the innocent life of a helpless child. Children often create emotional and legal ties that tend to compound an already foundering marriage.

Argument Analysis Inventory

1. Outline the case advanced by this advocate. Indicate which contentions and assertions are supported and which are unsupported. _____

_____

_____

_____

_____

_____

2. Compared to the affirmative argument, does this argument represent a broader or a narrower perspective? Why? _____

_____

_____

_____

_____

_____

3. According to this advocate, what factors have detracted from the popularity of having children? How persuasive are the arguments presented on this point? Why? _____

_____

_____

_____

_____

_____

4. How would you evaluate the quality of the evidence presented by this advocate? Why would you rate it as you do? _____

_____

_____

_____

_____

_____

_____

Is Divorce An Acceptable Remedy For a Failing Marriage?

PRO

Divorce is no longer considered an extreme remedy for unsuccessful marital relationships. In past times marriage was considered an unbreakable bond; but it is no longer viewed that way. Today's society is more permissive;

even when marriage vows are grossly violated, there is no such thing as a guilty party. In short, the stigma has been removed from both divorce and the divorced individual.

With the change in current economic structure, it is no longer necessary for anyone to maintain an unhappy marriage. At one time, before industrialization and in some rural communities, the family was the main production unit and source of income. Under those circumstances, it was necessary for the family to remain together for the benefit of the family as a whole. This situation no longer exists; hence, the process of industrialization and urbanization has contributed markedly to the spiraling incidence of divorce in this country.

Today, a greater number of educated women earn a good living; they are far less willing to remain married for an outdated moral reason. Many are now finding self-support and personal independence extremely attractive as a life style. Current divorce laws and procedures are now favoring women, enabling them to obtain a divorce more easily.

A growing number of men and women have come to the realization that marriage should not be a punishment; if it is not working out—if it is failing to provide for the basic needs for each member—it should be terminated. One of the most unforgivable myths associated with the continuance of a marriage that has gone sour is that it is in the best interest of the children (if there are any). Nothing could be further from the truth. Responsible persons from welfare agencies across the country encourage the dissolution of bad marriages as being in the best interests of any children involved. Evidence of this trend is provided by the growing number of religious denominations who now argue for and not against divorce in special cases. Overall, there is currently a much greater social acceptance of divorce as a means of resolving marriage difficulties.

Argument Analysis Inventory

1. What is the proposition being argued in this passage? What kind of proposition is it? _____

_____

_____

_____

_____

_____

_____

_____

_____

2. According to the advocate, what changing circumstances have resulted in changing attitudes toward divorce? Do you find the advocate's arguments on these points persuasive? Why or why not? _____

_____

_____

_____

_____

_____

_____

3. What fallacies, if any, appear in this passage? _____

_____

_____

_____

_____

_____

4. Examine the final paragraph. Would you press for additional information if you were debating this advocate? Specifically, what information would you want? _____

_____

_____

_____

_____

_____

CON

In the past hundred years while it has become increasingly easy for couples to get divorced, we have witnessed a marked deterioration of our society. Moral values have been cast to the wind. Unbridled sexual freedom has resulted in the creation of blatantly pornographic magazines, films, books, and the like. Fornication has reached epidemic proportions. Children are increasingly unmanageable. Homosexuality is on the rise. A host of evils has followed from the liberalization of divorce laws. It is time to call a halt to the process. It is obvious to the intelligent layman that liberalized divorce laws can only destroy our society, for divorce is the enemy of accountability. Without accountability, can society survive?

Argument Analysis Inventory

1. What fallacies, if any, occur in this passage? _____

_____

_____

_____

_____

_____

_____

2. What sort of reasoning is used in this passage? How would you evaluate the reasoning? Why? _____

_____

_____

_____

_____

_____

3. Outline the case advanced by the advocate. Indicate those statements requiring support. Can they be supported? If so, how? _____

_____

_____

_____

_____

_____

_____

4. Read the last two sentences of the passage. An argument appears there, though it is in abbreviated form. Flesh it out (that is, write it out completely in logical form), and determine its strengths and weaknesses. _____

_____

_____

_____

_____

_____

_____

Should Homosexuality Be Tolerated In Today's Society?

PRO

More than fifteen million Americans are homosexual. Although most of the statistics on homosexuality are drawn from the records of those homosexuals who have come into conflict with the law and from those who present themselves for psychotherapy, the majority of homosexuals in this country do not run afoul of the law, nor do they seek psychiatric help. On the contrary, according to W. Dwight Oberholtzer the vast majority of gays "live relatively discreet, stable, law-abiding, constructive, and socially useful lives" (*Is Gay Good?* Philadelphia, Pa.: The Westminster Press, 1971, page 80). Who gives anyone the right to lump these people together and treat them as if they were all diseased?

Being gay is a sexual preference. It is no one's business but the persons' involved whether they engage in homosexual or heterosexual relations, whether their ties represent one-night stands or long-lasting love relationships. The contention of certain heterosexuals that all homosexuals are promiscuous is absurd. According to Oberholtzer, "many homosexuals [are] intelligent, sensitive, hardworking, serious-minded, [and] loyal in their interpersonal relationships. . . ."

Homosexuality is more often an extension of love between two people than is generally recognized. Although most heterosexuals focus on the *sexuality* in a homosexual relationship, these ties possess important emotional and spiritual dimensions as well. Even if one were to believe that the homosexual act is abnormal, it is difficult to believe that the emotional and spiritual satisfaction shared between the two individuals is not a beautiful and worthwhile experience.

Some fundamentalist churches condemn homosexuality to the point of embarrassment, using bible stories to support their claims. Curiously, those who condemn the homosexual act of sodomy say very little or nothing about the supposed sins of incest, fornication, or lust. If we truly believe in the ideal Christian society and the teachings of Jesus, can we not accept homosexuals as being still other children of God and accept them whether or not we approve of them?

In a democratic spirit, each of us should have the privilege of choosing whatever form of sexual relationship will give our lives meaning. Wanting to be close to another person is a human variable; to want to love and be loved is a human factor. To have sexual urges and responses is part of being human. It is essential that we respect these rights in one another.

Argument Analysis Inventory

1. What is the proposition being argued in this passage? Is there more than one? Identify each as to type. _____

_____

_____

_____

_____

_____

_____

2. Before accepting the expert testimony of W. Dwight Oberholtzer, what information, if any, would you like to have? Why? How would it have bearing on the controversy? _____

_____

_____

_____

_____

_____

_____

3. What fallacy, if any, appears in the fourth paragraph? _____

_____

_____

_____

_____

_____

4. Outline the case offered by the advocate here. How would you evaluate it? Why? _____

_____

_____

_____

_____

_____

CON

Homosexual behavior is repulsive to the normal male or female. Homosexuals range from men in chiffon to men in leather—the former being overtly effeminate, the latter drifting into worlds of Nazism and strange interpretations of such masculine models as motorcyle policemen or drill sargents. Obsessions with these extreme roles of masculinity suggest an impaired sexual identity. Gays seem to be striving for something they cannot become and, as a substitute, get whatever satisfaction they can from the world of fantasy and make-believe. Generally, they live promiscuous lives trying to get what they need by having as many sex partners and as much sex as they can. Those relationships into which they do enter are, as a rule, both shallow and impermanent.

The single most common objection leveled at the homosexual community is that it ends with the individual. Since homosexual relationships, whether long- or short-term in nature, never end in procreation, they make no contribution to the perpetuation of the race. Although homosexuals may, as individuals, make contributions to society, they fail to make the one form of contribution enabling the evolutionary process to continue. This is a shortcoming that cannot be tolerated if life on this planet is to go on.

Many "gays" claim to be able to separate their homosexuality from their work. This is extremely questionable. The homosexual teacher, for example, cannot help but see the world differently from the heterosexual teacher. This difference in viewpoint can influence the psychological development of susceptible young children during the formative years. In whatever occupation or profession one finds the homosexual, there will be a preoccupation with sexual encounters. They are always "on the prowl," always seeking new physical releases.

If the homosexual act were not evil, why would the religious teachings of every faith condemn it? In Leviticus 20:13, it is written: "If a man lies with a male as with a woman, both of them shall be put to death for their abominable deed; they have forfeited their lives." And in Romans 1:26-28 there is a distinct condemnation of the gay life style. Says the apostle Paul, homosexual behavior represents not a form of pleasure but a form of punishment. "Disgraceful passions," he calls them, "inflicted on perverse people."

The cross-section of opinion on the question of homosexuality is clear. If learned scholars in the fields of religion, philosophy, psychiatry, and sociology all agree that it is a deviant form of behavior, then it must be just that—a deviant form of behavior.

Argument Analysis Inventory

1. What fallacies, if any, appear in the first, third, fourth, and fifth paragraphs? _____

_____

_____

_____

_____

2. The final paragraph reads as though it were a summary of the entire passages. Is it? Why or why not? _____

_____

_____

_____

_____

3. What evidence would be required to buttress the contention advanced in the first four sentences of the first paragraph? _____

_____

_____

_____

_____

_____

4. Overall, how persuasive do you find this passage? Why?   _____

_____

_____

_____

_____

Is Euthanasia (mercy killing) Ever Justified?

PRO

There is a steadily growing interest in euthanasia, a phenomenon by which terminally ill patients are allowed to die with dignity. Modern technology has made a great many advances, including machines that will sustain the life of a dying person. However, along with the problem of how to save life comes the problem of when to stop it.

The question I want to raise is this: Is euthanasia ever justifiable? I believe it is. Under exceptional circumstances, one or more of the following three parties ought to have the right to withdraw life-support equipment and thereby allow the patient to die. Ideally, the *patient* himself should make the decision. If he is incapable of doing so, then the *family*, in consultation with the *doctor*, should be permitted to make that choice for him.

What are the exceptional circumstances that would justify euthanasia? I see two: (1) if the disease or illness is truly terminal and there exists no hope for recovery or return to normal life; and (2) if the continued use of the life support equipment yields only agonized, lonely, or dehumanized death.

Unfortunately, a great many doctors and families equate euthanasia with murder. But according to O. Ruth Russwell, author of *Freedom to Die* (New York: Human Sciences Press, 1975, page 224), "the epithets of murderer or executioner, often hurled freely by the opponents of euthanasia, are patently inapplicable to the act of mercifully ending a painful and meaningless life."

Society has a responsibility to treat its members with kindness. According to Marvin Kohl and Paul Kurtz, authors of "A Plea of Beneficient Euthanasia", which appeared in the book, *Beneficent Euthanasia* (New York: Prometheus Books, 1975, page 135), this means that in certain circumstances, we have a moral obligation to induce death, that it is not only virtuous to help most where help is most needed, but it is often a duty to do so. Our first commitment, according to the authors of this essay, is to preserve, to fulfill, and to enhance life. "But," they add, "when a meaningful or significant life may no longer be possible, we should be able to die with dignity."

If a person can live with pride, then why should he not be able to die with it?

Argument Analysis Inventory

1. What is the proposition being advanced in this passage? What kind of proposition is it? _____

_____

_____

_____

_____

_____

2. What kind(s) of evidence does the advocate use? Are you satisfied with the evidence he presents? Why or why not? _____

_____

_____

_____

_____

_____

_____

3. Reread the last sentence of the second paragraph. What is the weakness of that sentence with respect to the case the advocate is advancing? _____

_____

_____

_____

_____

_____

_____

CON

Rational-minded people all agree that euthanasia is immoral and to take an innocent life is murder. I want to show that for two verifiable reasons, euthanasia cannot and should not be allowed. The first reason is religious, the second is human.

Among those of the Jewish faith, euthanasia is considered immoral, even when the patient asks to be put out of his misery. According to Jewish law, a dying individual is regarded as a living person in all respects. The Christian faith is also against euthanasia because it is the direct taking of an innocent life. It is the belief of Catholics, according to Joseph V. Sullivan, author of "The Immorality of Euthanasia," which appeared in the book *Beneficial Euthanasia* (New York: Prometheus Books, 1975, page 16), that, "man does not have direct dominion over human life, either his own life or the life of another man."

So much for the religious reasons for opposing euthanasia. Next we examine the human ones.

If euthanasia were legalized, it would most certainly be abused. Dishonesty and graft would certainly find their way into decision-making about life termination. Just as a person may now go to court to seek the administration of property by having the real owner declared insane, in the same way euthanasia would be abused. Children would seek to have their parents and sibling rivals destroyed in order to gain control of their estates. Politicians would use euthanasia against those who oppose them.

Without question, the most chilling possibility of the abuse of euthanasia was provided during World War II in Germany. Millions of people were put to death by the Nazis with the flimsy excuse that their continued survival was necessary for the common good. Joseph Sullivan, cited earlier, has cautioned that many present-day advocates of euthanasia might accept mass extermination as within reason, since the unfit and the undesirable are of no benefit to society. Any government could use euthanasia for its own selfish purposes.

In short, euthanasia cannot and should not be tolerated in any form whatsoever.

Argument Analysis Inventory

1. What fallacies, if any, appear in the first and fifth paragraphs of this passage? _____

_____

_____

_____

_____

2. What sort of reasoning is used in the fourth paragraph? Evaluate the argument advanced. _____

_____

_____

_____

_____

_____

3. Apply the Toulmin Model to the arguments advanced in the fourth and fifth paragraphs. Pay special attention to the rebuttal section of the model. What would be required to guard against possible abuse in the event that euthanasia were legalized? _____

_____

_____

_____

_____

_____

_____

_____

_____

_____

_____

_____

Should IQ Tests Be Used in Schools?

PRO

As long as they are approached with an understanding of their limitations, IQ test scores constitute a reliable and valid means of determining an individual's functional ability. Any failure in IQ testing lies not in the tests themselves, but in the minds of the people who interpret them. Holding IQ tests responsible for errors arising from misinterpretation and misuse is irrational. By this mode of reasoning, the airplane would have been banned as soon as it was first used in warfare. Atomic energy would have been condemned after Hiroshima and Nagasaki. Any instrument, any man-made tool or technique, can be misused. But the misuse of a potentially useful tool does not render it useless or harmful.

Argument Analysis Inventory

1. What sort of reasoning is used in this passage? Do you accept the conclusion advanced? Why or why not? _____

_____

_____

_____

_____

_____

_____

2. The advocate claims that IQ test scores constitute a reliable and valid means of determining an individual's functional ability. What support is offered for his claim? _____

_____

_____

_____

_____

_____

3. Do any terms used by the advocate require definition? If so, which ones? _____

_____

_____

_____

_____

_____

CON

IQ tests are invalid, unfair, and harmful. They are invalid because they do not measure intelligence or the ability to learn, as their supporters claim. Rather, these tests measure a child's performance on a specific exam at a particular time. This performance is necessarily a function of more than innate intellectual endowment. It is affected (as was recognized by one of the originators of the

IQ test, German psychologist Wilhelm Stern) by all the influences to which a child has been subjected up to the moment he takes the test. Thus, IQ tests are measures not of intelligence, but of the interplay of such factors as innate intellectual endowment, cultural heritage, intellectual stimulation provided by the family, physical and psychological health, and reading ability.

IQ tests are unfair because they are culturally biased. As Ronald J. Samuda has pointed out in his book, *Psychological Testing of American Minorities* (New York: Dodd, Mead & Co., 1975, pages 31-32) IQ tests are standardized. That means that everyone's scores are compared with everyone else's. Test norms are determined, then each examinee's test results are compared with these norms. It is widely and mistakenly assumed that IQ test norms are fair, since they are based on a representative national sampling of children. But, as Samuda points out, this assumption does not take into account the fact that the national sample is weighted heavily by average, middle-class, white children.

IQ tests are harmful because they destroy incentive and cause teachers to give up on students. When a person believes he is "stupid," he is disinclined to expend energy to learn. "Why bother trying?" he may say to himself. "I'm a dummy anyway!" Also, it is commonly known that most teachers—rightly or wrongly—see IQ scores as absolute indicators of a child's ability to learn. And then they proceed to teach that child accordingly. Hence little children are pigeon-holed early in life. They are classified and stigmatized for their school careers and perhaps for the rest of their lives.

Argument Analysis Inventory

1. What sort of proposition is being argued in this passage? _____

_____

_____

_____

_____

_____

_____

2. Do you find the advocate's claims persuasive? _____

_____

_____

_____

_____

_____

3. Should the advocate have cited a source for the viewpoint he attributes to German psychologist Wilhelm Stern in paragraph one? Why or why not?

_____

_____

_____

_____

_____

_____

4. Outline the case advanced by the advocate in this passage. What contentions or subpoints require additional support? What would be the best forms of support the advocate could offer? _____

_____

_____

_____

_____

_____

_____

Is The Death Penalty Ever Justified?

PRO

Capital punishment is necessary for the safety and protection of good citizens from the most dangerous and hardened criminals. Our right as good citizens is to have our lives and property protected, and anyone who takes these rights away from us should be severely punished.

Murder against an innocent victim has always been the strongest motivation for the death penalty. The famous expression from the bible "an eye for an eye and a tooth for a tooth," expresses the justification for capital punishment as the only just punishment that can be given to a person who has taken the life of another. There has been much written in the bible that has shown that God is in favor of capital punishment. Here are two examples: "Genesis 9:6: Whoso sheddeth man's blood, by man shall his blood be shed; for in the image of God made He man." Exodus 21:12 says the same thing: "He that smiteth a man, so that he die, shall be surely put to death."

The death penalty is a deterrent to murder. It would make a prospective murderer think many times before committing a crime. No crime is worth the penalty of his own life, which is precious to him. Death is the most feared form of punishment there is. In order for the death penalty to deter crime more effectively it is necessary for more states in the United States to have and use capital punishment more frequently. Since 1935 there has been a trend in the United States to use the death penalty less and less.

The death penalty is also needed after the crime has been committed. When a person has committed a serious crime, it is necessary for the public to be protected from that person. With the death penalty such a person could never again be free to commit these crimes; it is a final solution to the problem. Once a person is eliminated he can never again hurt society. Without the death penalty a criminal can be paroled and freed to kill again.

The death penalty also protects those living and working inside the prison: the inmates themselves and the security officers. If an inmate is serving a life sentence, what is to prevent him from killing other inmates and officers? He can be given no further punishment if he murders and will continue to do so if he pleases. The death penalty is therefore necessary to protect security officers and criminals who have committed less serious crimes.

As taxpayers, we should not have to feed and support someone who has damaged a part of society. We should not have to give our money to someone who will never contribute to society again. The limited funds we now have should go to helping society, rather than to maintaining some criminal who will continue to collect our desperately needed money until the day he dies.

Last, we must take the humanitarian point of view. If we give a criminal life imprisonment with no probation, we give him no hope and the absence of hope is a cruel and terrible thing. It is lifelong suffering for the criminal. Swift and painless death is a better punishment for the criminal and a better solution for society.

Argument Analysis Inventory

1. What contentions are advanced by the advocate in support of capital punishment? _____

_____

_____

_____

_____

_____

2. The advocate claims that the death penalty is a deterrent to murder. What support does he offer for the claim? What would be the most effective proof he could offer? _____

_____

_____

_____

_____

_____

3. If you were to argue in favor of capital punishment, would you argue your case differently? What changes would you make? _____

_____

_____

_____

_____

_____

4. If you were the opponent of the advocate who prepared this passage, what strategy would you employ? (In answering this, consider the strengths and weaknesses of the arguments advanced here.) _____

_____

_____

_____

_____

_____

CON

Capital punishment is a barbarous form of punishment; our society should have outgrown it. It is a form of punishment the civilized world should have left behind long ago. If no person has the right to take the life or another, what gives society the right to take the life of a criminal? The state's execution is legalized murder. What has become of the Christian concept of mercy and redemption? We should try to rehabilitate the criminal and give him just punishment and nothing more. Murder should not be punished by the death penalty, because "two wrongs don't make a right." One murder (the victim's) is not justified by another (the murderer's). Human life should be considered sacred no matter who's life it is.

The death penalty is not a deterrent to murder. In most cases the murderer does not think a great deal about the penalty while committing the murder. According to Thorsten Sellin, *Capital Punishment* (New York: Harper & Row, 1967, page 245), there is little difference between the number of murders committed in the states that have capital punishment and the ones that don't. Sellin suggests that a long prison sentence is more likely to deter a person from murder than is the death penalty.

Taxpayers often complain about the cost of putting a murderer in jail for a lifetime. What they don't realize, though, is that enormous costs go into a trial for someone accused of a capital crime. Taxes would also go to the equipment and people who execute anyone guilty of a capital crime.

Perhaps the greatest tragedy of capital punishment is the fact that execution is irreversible. People are not infallible beings; we have made mistakes in the past and will continue to do so. How many innocent people have been executed because they were labeled guilty? People who have been executed in the past have continued claiming they were innocent until the moment of execution. It is bad enough to execute somebody who is guilty of the crime he is accused of, but it is horrible to even imagine an innocent person being executed for a crime he did not commit. Although it is probably rare, that kind of a mistake should never have a chance to occur. Substituting a prison sentence for capital punishment protects both the criminal and the public. Even if this criminal is paroled after serving a part of his original sentence, it has been shown (See *Capital Punishment*, previously cited, page 252) that paroled murderers have the best record of all parolees. Capital punishment should be abolished because it is unnecessary and uncivilized.

Argument Analysis Inventory

1. Would you rate this passage as better than or worse than, the preceding one? Why? _____

_____

_____

_____

_____

2. In the second paragraph, the advocate cites Thorsten Sellin's book, *Capital Punishment*—once to support the claim that capital punishment is no deterrent to murder, and once to buttress his stand on the deterrent power of a long prison sentence. What is the difference between the two types of testimony offered here? To which of the statements attributed to Sellin would you give more weight? Why? _____

_____

_____

_____

_____

_____

3. Do you consider the argument developed in the third paragraph satisfactory? If not, what additional information might the advocate have included to strengthen his position? _____

_____

_____

_____

_____

_____

4. In your judgment, what are the strengths and weaknesses of the case developed in this passage? _____

_____

_____

_____

_____

_____

USING THE TOULMIN MODEL

Chiropractic vs. Medicine

For the past eighty-one years the medical and chiropractic professions have been engaged in an uninterrupted confrontation with one another. Although they are both members of the healing arts, there is a fundamental difference in their ideologies: The practice of medicine is predicated upon the use of drugs; chiropractic is a drugless profession. In addition to this basic difference in premise, there are other areas of disagreement. The three areas to be presented in this unit are: (1) chiropractic education, (2) public regulation, and (3) theory of disease. Here, now, is one argument advanced by the medical profession against the chiropractic profession in each of these areas. Read each argument, then construct a Toulmin Model in the space provided:

CHIROPRACTIC EDUCATION

The three recognized educational bodies that accredit institutions of higher education in the United States are the Federation of Regional Accrediting Commissions of Higher Education, the National Commission of Accrediting, and the Office of Education of the Federal Government. The Federations of Regional Accrediting Commissions of Higher Education accredits colleges and universities through its member regional associations. The National Commission on Accrediting and the Office of Education list approved accrediting agencies for the professions. Chiropractic schools are not recognized or listed by any of these accrediting organizations. [3]

[3] Source: "Did You Know That....?", American Medical Association (Chicago, 1965).

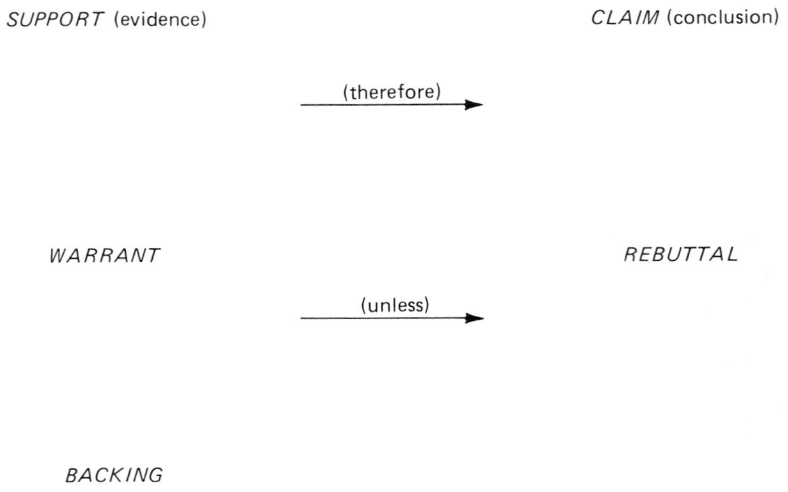

SUPPORT (evidence)   CLAIM (conclusion)

                        ―――――(therefore)――――▶

WARRANT   REBUTTAL

                        ―――――(unless)――――▶

BACKING

FIGURE 5-1   Toulmin Model

PUBLIC REGULATION

> *Chiropractors endanger the public health
> because they do not believe in the well
> established and scientifically proven Germ
> Theory of disease. Chiropractors do not
> believe in vaccination even though the
> vaccine protection against typhoid fever,
> lockjaw and diphtheria saved thousands of
> lives during the wars and has reduced civil
> incidence to a minimum occurrence.*[4]

[4] Source: Morris Weintrob, "Why Chiropractors Should Not Be Licensed," Medical Society of the State of New York, n.d.

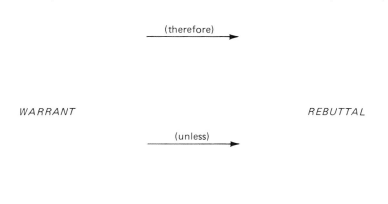

SUPPORT (evidence)   CLAIM (conclusion)

(therefore)

WARRANT   REBUTTAL

(unless)

BACKING

FIGURE 5-2   Toulmin Model

THEORY OF DISEASE

> *Chiropractors claim that subluxations, or partial displacements of the vertebrae, can cause a perturbation of the distribution of nervous impulses to tissues and cells. Neurophysiologists have developed methods of recording the passage of nerve impulses in nerves. Exceptionally sensitive apparatus is available to anyone wishing to use it. No scientific study has been published on the subject by a chiropractor. No chiropractor has ever defined, either quantitatively or qualitatively, what chiropractic means by perturbation of nerve impulses. Is it their number, their amplitude, their frequency, the speed of their propagation, or their wave patterns which are affected? All of these qualities can be identified, recorded, and studied. It is no longer permissible to accept empirical statements. Proof should have preceded practical application. With the first point untenable, the rest crumbles. In pure scientific logic, the argument should not need to go further than this.[5]*

[5] Source: "The Scientific Brief Against Chiropractic," *The New Physician,* XV (September 1966), p. 227.

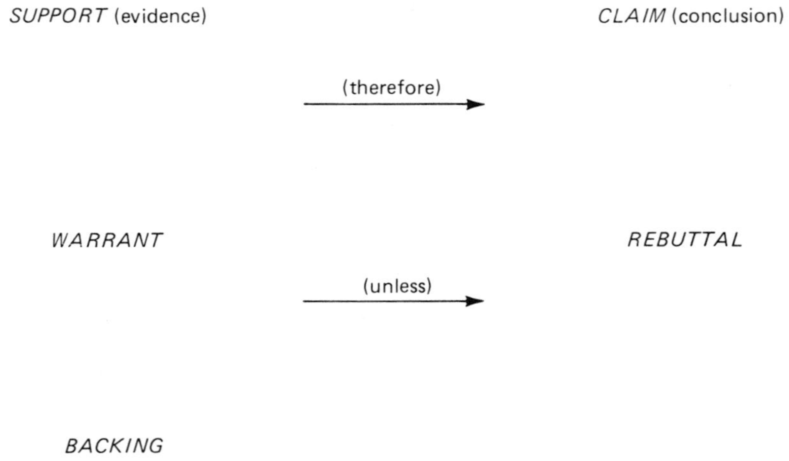

SUPPORT (evidence)   CLAIM (conclusion)

                        (therefore)
                        ─────────────▶

WARRANT   REBUTTAL

                        (unless)
                        ─────────────▶

BACKING

FIGURE 5-3   Toulmin Model

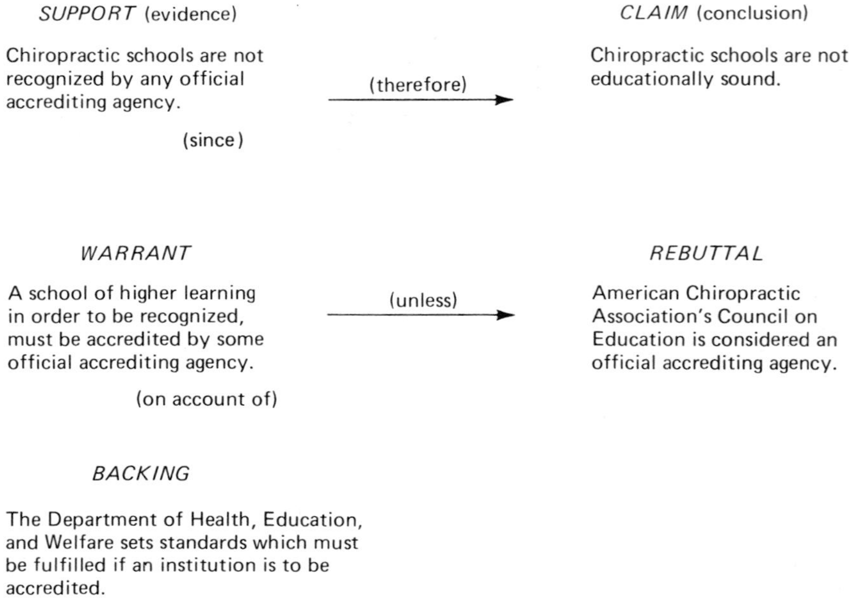

SUPPORT (evidence)   CLAIM (conclusion)

Chiropractic schools are not   Chiropractic schools are not
recognized by any official   (therefore)   educationally sound.
accrediting agency.   ─────────────▶

            (since)

WARRANT   REBUTTAL

A school of higher learning   (unless)   American Chiropractic
in order to be recognized,   ─────────────▶   Association's Council on
must be accredited by some   Education is considered an
official accrediting agency.   official accrediting agency.

        (on account of)

BACKING

The Department of Health, Education,
and Welfare sets standards which must
be fulfilled if an institution is to be
accredited.

FIGURE 5-4.   Completed Toulmin Model: Chiropractic Education

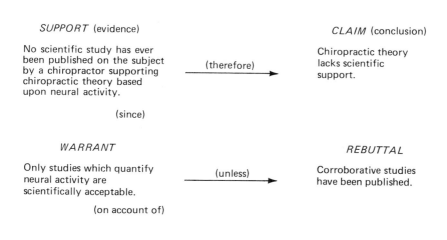

SUPPORT (evidence)

Chiropractors do not believe in
the germ theory of disease.

(since)

(therefore)

CLAIM (conclusion)

Chiropractors endanger the
public health.

WARRANT

The validity of the germ theory
has been well-established by the
medical profession and its acceptance
is necessary for the proper treatment
of disease.

(unless)

REBUTTAL

There are scientific data which
challenge the correctness of
the germ theory; alternate
hypotheses of disease causation
exist.

BACKING

The medical profession has proved
the germ theory by scientific
methods.

FIGURE 5-5.   Completed Toulmin Model: Public Regulation

SUPPORT (evidence)

No scientific study has ever
been published on the subject
by a chiropractor supporting
chiropractic theory based
upon neural activity.

(since)

(therefore)

CLAIM (conclusion)

Chiropractic theory
lacks scientific
support.

WARRANT

Only studies which quantify
neural activity are
scientifically acceptable.

(on account of)

(unless)

REBUTTAL

Corroborative studies
have been published.

BACKING

The basis for the acceptance of
any theory is that it be confirmed
by a scientific study.

FIGURE 5-6.   Completed Toulmin Model: Theory of Disease

WRAP-UP

In this chapter we have emphasized the importance of recognizing that arguments, as they occur in the real world, are complex and fluid communication events. Their parts are not neatly labeled. Weak and strong arguments frequently occur in juxtaposition. The kinds of reasoning and evidence offered by an advocate must be discovered by an opponent before the appropriate tests can be applied. We have given you the opportunity to study arguments in their natural state and to analyze them systematically and intelligently. We have offered for analysis a total of fifteen passages containing anywhere from one to several arguments. Some of these passages were designed to improve your use of the Toulmin Model. Others were offered to sensitize you to the subtle factors which so often operate in an argument. We are confident that the diligent use of the principles applied in this chapter will make a significant improvement in your performance as an advocate.

PROBES, PRODS, AND PROJECTS

Do certain arguments lend themselves to the use of the Toulmin Model? When does the model seem to be of particular usefulness?

Construct an argument, or a series of arguments, that contain various fallacies, erroneous modes of reasoning, or faulty evidence. Ask a friend who has read this book to evaluate your work. Ask someone who has not read this book to do the same. See who does better.

The next time you read a newspaper editorial, an opinionated pamphlet, or a political broadside, try subjecting it to the kind of scrutiny we have been applying to arguments in this chapter. Make a judgment as to its logical cogency.

If you had to prepare an Argument Analysis Inventory that would be appropriate to an unlimited range of arguments, what elements would you include? What form would your inventory take?

Part Two

Interpersonal Aspects
of Argument

6

WHY PEOPLE ARGUE

BEHAVIORAL OBJECTIVES

After reading this chapter, you should have a better understanding of

1. the reasons why people argue
2. the kinds of people who argue
3. how arguments get started
4. the things people usually argue about
5. the difference between an aggressor, instigator, and victim
6. those physical traits capable of leading to an argument
7. yourself as an advocate
8. gesture as a source of insult and precursor to argument
9. the meaning and relevance of such terms as stimulus hunger and recognition hunger
10. how Goffman's use of the designation "personal front" can be applied to argumentation

Idealists often bemoan the fact that of all animal species, humans alone go to war, inflict pain on their own kind, and delight in killing others in the name of politics, religion, and ethnicity. "Why?" asks the idealist. "Why can't humans live in peace?"

The idealistic position can be overstated. We know, for example, that animals fight with their own kind over such things as food, females, and territory. Humans, however, seem to have a unique talent for organizing and systematizing their hostility.

Perhaps light can be shed on this curious phenomenon by studying why people argue. After all, what is war but a large-scale, violent argument?

In this chapter, we consider the reasons why people argue (the *why* of argument), the people who argue (the *who* of argument), the ways an argument can get started (the *how* of argument), and the things people argue about (the *what* of argument).

The application of this knowledge will help you to better understand the origins of humankind's tendency toward organized strife. More specifically, it will help you (1) avoid unwanted arguments, (2) judge the motivation of your opponent, (3) detect conflict-prone individuals, (4) recognize the things you are apt to argue about, and (5) help you avoid antagonizing your opponent needlessly.

REASONS WHY PEOPLE ARGUE

We are concerned here with the short-term *motivation* of the people who argue. What makes them argue? What's in it for them? What good can they derive from arguing? Knowing the possible motivations of an adversary can alert you to dangers and can make for a more constructuve and productive exchange.

Some of the more popular reasons for arguing are these: (1) arguments provide an opportunity to express opinions and prove a point; (2) they give us a chance to test our ideas; (3) they provide an opportunity to test our argumental skills; (4) they can help us satisfy psychological needs; and (5) they provide an outlet for foul moods.

Arguments Provide an Opportunity
to Express Opinions and Prove a Point

Most people have opinions on nearly every subject, and they seek ways of expressing them. The enthusiastic response to sidewalk interviewers bears witness to this fact. Many people have a compulsive need to tell others what they think. Informal opinion exchange centers such as London's Hyde Park, Los Angeles' Pershing Square, and New York's Union Square were designed specifically to meet this human need. In fact, in the democratic tradition free speech is crucial. Our Founding Fathers recognized that by utilizing the human tendency to argue, important decisions of state could be made. In our society, free speech is a cherished and indispensable tradition. From our point of view, it represents a constructive application of the human tendency toward arguing to express opinions and prove a point.

One of the positive features of informal oral argument is that it requires no special equipment, time, or place. As an advocate, you may meet an opponent over a cup of coffee, on a cross-town bus, or in an elevator. The exchange may be completely spontaneous or planned beforehand. In any event, once the two of you are together, you need only talk!

We recognize that some arguments are carefully planned and are governed by many rules and conventions.[1] We know, too, that preparation for arguments can vary from extremely casual to meticulous. It seems that the more weight we assign to an argumental exchange, the more preparation we demand and the more formal the exchange becomes. Thus, a debate in the U.S. Senate is likely to be characterized by a high degree of peparation by the participants. Furthermore, the exchange will be governed by many rules; plans (including strategies to be employed by each side) will be elaborate and detailed.

To repeat, the roots of argument are in people's desire to express opinions and to prove a point.

Arguments Give Us a Chance to Test Our Ideas

Have you ever had a pet theory? Perhaps you once believed that a certain make of car was accident-prone because of the shape of the front fenders, or that the sex of an infant was determined by physical positioning during intercourse. Some have maintained that criminal behavior is determined by the shape and contours of the skull. Others argue that the stars determine one's fate. There is no end to the variety of beliefs people hold. Not surprisingly, many persons argue with others in order to test such theories. Lacking confidence in their cherished beliefs, they corner others and attempt to impose their bizarre ideas on their listeners. "Perhaps, if she will believe me," say such advocates to themselves, "I will be more firmly convinced." Or again, "There may be some truth to this notion. Let me try it out on Alex and see what he has to say about it."

Schools encourage such behavior. Students who can think on their feet are often admired by both teachers and peers. Perhaps your own instructor has asked you to give impromptu speeches. Such assignments can be invaluable, for

---

[1] Review the section on Kinds of Arguments in Chapter 1, Orientation to Argument.

they can help you to formulate ideas, organize them, and present them with conviction. At the root of such assignments is the recognition that people tend to argue to test their ideas.

A great teacher of public speaking once remarked that three things were required to learn to speak effectively: (1) natural talent, (2) a knowledge of the theories and techniques of speech-making, and (3) practice. We are concerned here with practice. No advocate, regardless of his natural talent or his knowledge of the principles of argumentation, can consider himself accomplished until he has had the opportunity to apply what he has leaned. Practice and more practice is required to hone one's skills to a razor-sharp edge. Without practice, knowledge is valueless, skills deteriorate, and competencies evaporate into thin air. Advocates who know this avail themselves of every opportunity to argue. Some join a debate club, others a toastmaster club, and still others sororities and fraternities in order to participate in decision-making debates. Whatever outlet they elect, practice is the watchword.

Joining your school's debate club provides an excellent opportunity to learn the fine points of argumentation. You will be coached by an experienced, knowledgeable expert in the field. You will be given many opportunities to ply your skills. You will argue against many different opponents. (This, of course, will require that you adapt to many different styles of advocacy.) In addition, you will discover your strong and weak points as an advocate. You will be given a chance to participate in many different kinds of debates: two-person, four-person, cross-examination, and so forth. You may argue the affirmative side of an issue one week, the negative side the next.[2] You will learn by observing. And, all the while, you will be encouraged to do your best by a climate of competition. There can be no finer opportunity for you to learn the techniques of argument! (A suggestion: If your school doesn't have a debate squad, *start one!*)

Not all arguers have the opportunity to join a debate team or a club designed to give its members a chance to argue. Such individuals wander around picking arguments with others in order to test their argumental skills. The legendary urban taxi driver, eager to engage in debate about any topic from international politics to child care is a prime example. He cruises the streets of a busy metropolis and engages in a variety of short-lived exchanges of opinion.

In your next argument, consider the possibility that your opponent is merely texting his argumental skills.

---

[2] The advantages of arguing both sides are many. Some, however, object to the practice, since they maintain it encourages sophistry. For a classic discussion on the topic, see Richard Murphy, "The Ethics of Debating Both Sides," *The Speech Teacher,* VI (January 1957), pp. 1-9.

Arguments Can Help Us
Satisfy Psychological Needs

Have you ever had the feeling that the person you were arguing with didn't really give a damn about the subject under discussion? All he cared about was winning, or impressing you favorably, or embarrassing you. If so, you know what we mean when we say that people sometimes argue to satisfy psychological needs.

Consider those who argue to nourish a hungry ego. Whether or not they are right is unimportant. Their primary objective is get into a heated argument—the hotter the better. One thing is sure: Their actions will provide them with some much-wanted attention. What provokes an argument better than being contrary? Picture the following scene: Some friends are sitting around talking about what they're going to do next Saturday night. Just about everyone agrees that they would like to go to a particular theatre. But one member of the group says no. At once he becomes the center of attention. His contrariness, perhaps brought on by a desire to be the focal point of attention, is the *means* he uses to attain his end. We all satisfy our ego needs in various ways. For many, one of the most popular ways is by engaging in or starting arguments!

Others argue to satisfy the need for psychological contact.[3] As infants, we enjoy physical intimacies with parents. We are hugged, kissed, tickled, fondled, and caressed. Studies have found that babies deprived of such intimacies show signs of ill health. Their physical and psychological development can be impaired. In extreme cases, they die. As we grow older, the opportunities for physical intimacies diminish. As a result, we learn to get the same emotional satisfaction from psychological (as opposed to physical) contact. A nod or a smile becomes equivalent to a pat or a hug. Communication, interaction, or words provide the necessary stimulation. Deprived of this, many persons drop into depression or lethargy. For some, the telephone's failure to ring at least twice within any given hour may be enough to spark intense anxiety.

Verification for the point of view advanced here is readily available. Some persons never quite overcome their need for physical intimacies. They may grow up to become Don Juans or nymphomaniacs. Others may satisfy their need for physical contact by habitually standing close to others and touching them when they talk. A few probably become boxers. Watch people walking on crowded streets or sitting on buses and trains. Some deliberately bump into others, carelessly push or pull, or force themselves into seats between people.

It's an interesting coincidence that those who crowd others often wind up arguing over being crowded themselves. This, too, satisfies a need for *contact.*

---

[3] See Eric Berne, *Games People Play* (New York: Grove Press, Inc., 1964), pp. 13-20. We have drawn on his discussions of *stimulus hunger* and *structure hunger.*

Many people start arguments because they're bored or lonely. Arguments are a way of making contact with people—sometimes total strangers.

Some people are motivated to argue because of structure hunger. This term refers to the need to pattern our time. "What are we going to do *now?*" is a question often asked by children and adults alike. "Argue!" is one answer. Ask any husband or wife. Nothing fills a dull Saturday night like a good, lively argument! That may sound silly, but it's true. Many an argument is begun just to fill time and give the arguers something to do. But it's the skilled arguer who *knows* the purpose of the argument. He is careful not to overstep the bounds of propriety and risk changing the complexion of the disagreement. Knowing your own motivation and that of your opponent can save you much anxiety, aggravation, and needless bungling.

Another reason why people argue is to save face. Everyone likes to think he's the best. No one enjoys being told (either in words or silently) that he's stupid, uninformed, or shallow. It is the rare person who can admit any of these things to himself—let alone stand being told about them by someone else. The average person will be strongly motivated to save face under such circumstances. In fact, a sure way to make a confrontation deteriorate (that is, go from discussion to debate, debate to altercation, and so on) is to insinuate that your opponent is stupid. You may do it with a glance, a gesture, or with the tone of your voice. No matter how you do it, if he receives your message, your opponent will struggle to save face using any and all means at his disposal. Continued prodding and goading will usually result in a fight or discontinuance of the confrontation.

One of the most interesting psychological roots of arguments was hinted at by Gestalt psychologist Fritz Perls. At the heart of his Gestalt therapy is the notion that people invariably project parts of themselves onto others.[4] By this we mean that people attribute to others, qualities, emotions, or tendencies that they themselves possess. Take this example: Not long ago, one of the authors was riding an elevator in a New York skyscraper along with several other passengers. Suddenly, the machine ground to a halt between floors. All attempts to get it started failed. Within several minutes, it became apparent that they were destined to remain in a stuffy, dimly lit elevator until help arrived. There was some nervous shuffling, a few feeble smiles, and a great deal of tension in the air. One of the passengers, obviously frightened, looked around at the rest of us and said, "Hey! I bet you people are getting scared. Don't worry! It will be all right!" In saying those words, he was projecting his fear on to us. It was *he* who was terribly frightened; he sought to reassure himself. But because he could not consciously cope with his own fear, he projected it onto the rest of us and then dealt with it as "our" fear.

[4]See, for example, Fritz Perls, *Gestalt Therapy Verbatim* (New York: Bantam Books, Inc., 1971), especially pp. 220-31.

Projection is an everyday phenomenon. We believe it operates in interpersonal argument to a great extent. When people disagree with others, especially when they disagree violently, they may really be talking to themselves.

Projection is at work when husbands fault their wives for being timid and backward when they themselves are timid and backward. Projection is at work when boyfriends argue with their girlfriends about being sexually frigid when they themselves are frightened to death at the prospect of sexual intercourse. Projection is at work when white racists project onto black people traits such as aggressiveness, sexual potency, and mental slowness when it is they themselves who own those qualities. Projection operates when young people argue with their parents about the need to go to church, whereas, in fact, the argument is within themselves.

Our discussion of projection may seem paradoxical. But, to summarize and highlight the most important point, we maintain that *many individuals, in arguing with others, are actually externalizing their own inner conflicts.* It is easier and less of a psychological risk to find an opponent who personifies that aspect of yourself that you find uncomfortable. The hope, of course, is that by defeating your opponent, you will overcome the tendency within yourself. (Just as the passenger in the elevator was allaying his own fears by reassuring the others.)

What strategy can we suggest to the advocate who is the repository of another's projections? Without going into depth, here are a few recommendations: If you do not possess the attitude, belief, or feeling being attributed to you (if, for example, you are a passenger on the elevator and are *not* afraid), you *m*ight want to make your own attitude or feeling clear. Anything you can do to help the projector assume responsibility for his own feeling or belief is desirable.

Interestingly, Perls used this technique relentlessly. In therapy, he insisted that clients recognize that they were *always* and *only* talking about themselves. When he dealt with dreams, he urged clients to recognize that everything in their dreams (other people, inanimate objects, animals) represented a part of themselves. He asked clients to act out the parts of everything in their dreams. If it rained in a dream, the client was told to be rain and talk from its vantage point. Perls also used the "empty chair" technique, asking the client to carry on a conversation with himself. For instance, a frightened man might be asked to carry on a conversation with his fearful self. A woman concerned about her promiscuity might be asked to have a talk with her promiscuous self. The whole idea was to bring about a resolution of the internal conflict by bringing it to the fore and dealing with it consciously.

Other strategies are available to the advocate upon whom an opponent is projecting unwanted beliefs or attitudes. If you, in fact, do not believe the point of view being attributed to you, you really have no choice but to argue your position. However, you should recognize that, in all likelihood, you will not be able to convince your adversary. We suggest you not even try to convince him. Recognize that the conflict is his own, that until he confronts it and works it through, nothing you say will convince him.

Arguments Provide an Outlet for Foul Moods

Our final motivation involves an argument as a means of "letting off steam." Everyday language bears out the fact that many people argue because they're in a foul mood: "Watch out! He's in one of those moods again!" "Don't cross her now; she's on the warpath!" Every so often, we all get into a bad mood. Perhaps we get up on the wrong side of the bed, or things just go wrong during the day. We wind up out of sorts. When we feel that way, we tend to get involved in arguments—perhaps to try to make others feel sorry for us or because we want company in our misery. The point is, we argue. As the recipient in such situations, it is important to know how to respond. A careful analysis of your opponent's motivation may dictate the proper course of action.

PEOPLE WHO ARGUE

We can study the people who argue from two perspectives—the *psychological* and the *physical*. Although these characteristics are closely related, let's first look at the psychological traits of people who argue.

Psychological Characteristics

Since we all know that it takes two to make an argument, we probably believe that it is impossible for an argument to develop unless *both* parties want to argue. This is not so. From a psychological point of view, three kinds of people inhabit the world of argument: *aggressors, victims,* and *instigators.* There is some of each in all of us. Different people and situations bring out one or the other. Usually, one of the three is dominant at any given time. The timid man who bullies his wife is an aggressor at home, a victim elsewhere. The big, brave, masculine football player whose wife wraps him around her little finger is a victim at home, an aggressor elsewhere. The snide little salesman who delights in instigating arguments between fellow workers but who is intimidated by his boss is a victim in the boss's office, an instigator on the floor. In the paragraphs to follow, the authors sketch the broad character-types of aggressors, victims, and instigators. These people, we suggest, seldom exist in a pure form. But for the purposes of this discussion, we consider each separately distinct from the others.

The aggressor enjoys arguing. For various reasons, he enjoys pushing people around—physically or verbally. He carries around on his shoulder the proverbial chip, constantly searching for someone to knock it off. He has a particular talent for steering conversations in disagreeable ways toward disagreeable outcomes. Such people often prompt questions like: "How come I can never talk to Herbie without it ending up in a fight?"[5]

Another inhabitant of the argumental arena is the victim. He is a necessary foil for the aggressor. The victim is the person who is always involved in arguments without knowing why. If he is not asking himself "What'd I say?" he is feeling sorry for himself by musing "Why me? Why is it always me?" A closer study of the victim's personality may reveal some deeper reason for his being in the midst of arguments wherever he goes. Most victims feel bad after they are victimized. Others get some sort of masochistic kick out of the experience. However, we are not concerned with people of the latter inclination. It is enough to say that unwilling victims can avoid their fate by adopting the appropriate strategy.[6]

In addition to the aggressor and his victim, there is one other character type involved in argument. He is the instigator—the troublemaker who starts the argument but who does not himself become involved. Recall the restaurant scene in which a wife urges her husband to reprimand an obnoxious waiter. Here, while she sits quietly on the sideline, her poor spouse falls prey to the experienced rhetoric of the waiter.

Physical Characteristics

Along with psychological characteristics, there are certain physical traits that can lead to arguments. Erving Goffman has written about an individual's "personal front," which includes both variable and fixed elements of his appearance.[7] A person's clothing and hairstyle are variable and clearly capable of triggering altercations: *hippie, freak, baldy, afro,* and *straight* are a few argument-provoking labels relating to a person's hairstyle and dress. Skin color *(nigger, whitey, coolie)*, ethnic characteristics *(spic, wop, kike, kraut)*, and body types are relatively fixed aspects of an individual's personal front. Much has been said about the manner in which these can influence interactions; we need not repeat the obvious. However, we would like to say this about body type: first, *a person's body type might dictate the role he is conditioned to play in an argument.* The big, burly longshoreman has probably become accustomed to

[5] We shall meet the aggressor again in Chapter 10, Argument in a Group.

[6] See Chapters 4, Exposing a Fallacy, and 8, Know Your Opponent.

[7] Erving Goffman, *The Presentation of Self in Everyday Life* (New York: Doubleday & Co., Inc., 1959), pp. 24-26.

commanding respect because of his size and strength, even though he might be a victim inside. Along similar lines, the slight person may have become conditioned to withstanding abuse. He may be a seasoned victim. Second, *body type can tempt potential opponents.* Such insensitive remarks as "fat slob" and "little shrimp" often are intended to provoke arguments. Persons with specific physical characteristics might be argument-prone simply because of *how they look.*

Knowing that it is risky to generalize, and aware of the dangers of oversimplification, what advice can we give? We recommend that you evaluate your opponent by considering what sort of a person he is likely to be and what kind of expriences he might have had in the past. Does he impress you as aggressive and assertive? Does he seem to be easily led? Adapt to your opponent. Put yourself in *his* shoes! It's amazing how many people overlook this simple principle when they argue. For various reasons (for example, emotional involvement, impatience) advocates often neglect to adjust their remarks to their audience. But it is exactly this basic strategy that can make a significant difference in the fate of an argument.

WAYS AN ARGUMENT CAN GET STARTED

To our knowledge, no systematic study has ever been made concerning the way arguments get started. As a preliminary generalization, we offer this: The more sophisticated the argumental exchange, the more likely it is the result of careful planning. Debates are carefully planned. Growing out of public controversy on some topic of social significance, debates tend to be a result of carefully orchestrated preparations. When two candidates for public office debate during their campaign, both sides do a great deal of planning and preparation.

The same holds true of discussions and dialogues. Public forums on such issues as social security and welfare reform most ofen involve diligent planning by all interested parties. A time and place is prearranged, representatives are selected, and the event is publicized.

In cases like these, arguments get started as a result of careful work and planning. By contrast, most informal arguments arise spontaneously.

Sometimes a disagreement can arise spontaneously when two people unintentionally come upon some genuine difference of opinion. You may be casually chatting with a friend when something comes up that is very dear to both of you—say, conservation. Suppose you are an avid conservationist, and suppose your friend owns stock in a company that has a reputation for deliberately polluting our environment. Your friend regards conservation propaganda as alarmist nonsense. You consider the conservation issue crucial to man's survival. Here, a subject that came up quite by accident sparks a disagreement.

People can provoke arguments intentionally. Your friend might bring up the subject of conservation purposely—hoping to lure you into an argument. Or again, someone on a bus might poke you in the ribs for no other reason than to start trouble.

Finally, some third party can instigate an argument without becoming involved himself. Gossip often causes friction among friends while the gossipers themselves do not become involved in the feud. Such people are examples of instigators.

We don't pretend for a moment that the convenient formulation just presented totally covers how arguments start. Many other factors operate, sometimes simultaneously. Let's consider the most obvious.

At times, arguments start because one party invalidates the feelings of another.[8] Consider the aggressor who invalidates the feelings and opinions of his opponent: "How could you say that? That's the most ridiculous thing I've ever heard!" Such invalidation of another's feelings occurs whenever one person denies another the right to his feelings or beliefs.

It is the rare person who can tolerate invalidation. Few people know what to do when their feelings have been invalidated. Instead of simply asserting their right to feel the way they do (the course we recommend), most advocates become threatened and angry. They sense a need to fight back. Thus, invalidation breeds counterinvalidation: "I'm sure you find my opinion ridiculous, but I think you're an idiot for feeling the way you do!" As you can see, when invalidation occurs, it provokes a response in kind. The result is almost always an altercation or fight.

Closely related to invalidation is judgment-making. When others make judgments about us (who we are, what we do, how we feel, or what we believe) most of us become defensive. Such remarks as "You're stupid!" and "That's ridiculous!" are likely to nurture the growth of arguments. These remarks (personal judgments) translate as, "I disagree with what you said," or "I find that hard to accept." Notice that in the last two cases, the one who judges assumes the responsibility for the judgment. (Psychologists call this "owning one's feelings and judgments.") His words reveal that it is he who feels a certain way. He doesn't attribute the quality of stupidness to the object or statement about which he is speaking. Instead, he expresses a personal opinion that does not label or stigmatize the remark or person he is responding to.

Judgment-making invites arguments. If you want to discuss rather than fight, avoid making judgments and form the habit of owning feelings.

So far, we have been talking about intentionally offensive things people do. But we can also invite disagreement unintentionally.

Sometimes, arguments get started because of the words people use. Ac-

---

[8] For our discussion of invalidation, we have drawn on Claude Steiner, *Scripts People Live* (New York: Grove Press, Inc., 1974), especially pp. 119-38.

customed to putting themselves down, they might begin a statement or a series of statements with the phrase, "This may sound silly, but . . . ," or "You probably wont't agree, but . . . " Such statements put the listener into a contrary frame of mind and can convert a friendly listener into a hostile one.

Some speakers feel a need to apologize for what they think, particularly when they assume an unpopular position. Unwilling to assume the responsibility for their convictions, they undercut them or play them down in the hope that others will forgive them for feeling as they do. They are likely to open their remarks with such disclaimers as, "I'm sure you're better informed than I am, but I think. . . ."

Such psychological indulgence serves no useful purpose. Rarely is there a need to apologize for what you believe. If you don't know what you're talking about, be quiet. If you do, don't apologize. Free speech is a basic right. Each of us is entitled to our opinion. When we speak with self-assurance, others listen. When we put ourselves down and undercut what we say, we invite arguments.

Still another behavior invites disagreement. Many people habitually respond to others with such phrases as, "I understand what you mean, but . . ." The word *but* in that phrase is a divisive one. It creates a climate of conflict. As a result, cooperation is replaced by disagreement. People fall into camps—those in favor and those against, the pros and the cons.

"I know what you're saying, but . . ." and similar phrases suggest a mind that sees things in *either/or* terms. The users of such phrases divide the world into separate and mutually exclusive categories: Either John is smart or he is stupid; either Betty is attractive or she is ugly; either the president is doing a good job or he isn't. You are to be commended if you recognize that this kind of thinking constitutes the fallacy of the false dilemma discussed in Chapter 4. The world doesn't divide itself up that neatly. John may be smart in math but ignorant when it comes to repairing his car. Betty may not have a beautiful body, but perhaps she possesses personality traits such as generosity and faithfulness that make her beautiful in other respects. The president may be doing a terrible job in foreign policy, but an admirable one in welfare reform.

The *either/or* frame or reference oversimplifies reality. It is a divisive way of conceptualizing the world. We prefer a *both/and* frame of reference, which is incorporative rather than divisive. People who see things in terms of *both/and* recognize that there is a bit of truth in all things, no matter how contradictory they appear. During a discussion, they are likely to recognize that there is right on both sides of every issue. If they are patient and skilled, they can nurture cooperative effort, despite apparent conflicts.

If you have developed the habit of seeing things in terms of *either/or*, we urge you to reconsider. At minimum, whenever possible, avoid such phrases as "you're partly right, but . . ."

THINGS PEOPLE ARGUE ABOUT

It is difficult to separate *what* people argue about from *why* they argue. But we must. The two are distinct, although often intimately related. We will deal here not with the motivations of the arguers but with the things they argue about.

It may also seem difficult to separate *what* people argue about from *how* arguments get started. But if you have ever unintentionally offended someone—caused an argument you didn't intend to start—then you know what we mean when we say that *how* an argument gets started is different from *what* people argue about.

We cannot possibly list or categorize all the topics people argue about, nor will we try. Our purpose is to suggest some of the more common areas of disagreement.

All arguments deal with either *matter*—beliefs, convictions, values—or *manner*—ways of doing things that stem from beliefs, convictions, and values.[9] Included in manner are threats, challenges, insults, offenses, and violations as well as clothing, posture, and bearing. Manner is more superficial than matter. What a person wears may trigger certain responses in us, so we argue. But a person's clothing is a superficial thing, and we may find, as we come to know the person better, that "he's really a nice guy—beneath the surface."

Let's first look at insults and offenses. It is possible to offend or insult someone in different ways, such as by talking down to him or by mocking him. But perhaps the most blatant way of doing so is by gesturing or behaving in an offensive way. Certain antisocial movements and gestures can provoke an argument from susceptible individuals. In the United States, thumbing one's nose at someone or holding up a hand with the middle finger extended could and frequently does induce offense. Every country has its national repertoire of insulting gestures and movements. Their use is sure to provoke an argument.

As we said earlier, what you wear can also make waves. Many industrial concerns have strict rules regarding appropriate dress. In some instances breaking these rules means immediate dismissal. Modes of dress worn by members of certain religious sects, avant-garde movements, and revolutionary organizations often provoke hostility. Many restaurants refuse to serve people who wear their affiliation insignias on their backs, heads, arms, or legs. A refusal to be dressed according to the norm or standard of the establishment is to invite trouble.

The way you sit, stand, or hold yourself may also be considered argumentative. Some people stand so very tall that their posture and bearing give the impression of snobbery. The lad who sits slumped on a bus or train with his long

---

[9] For a discussion of the matter of argument, see Chapters 8, Know Your Opponent, and 10, Argument in a Group.

legs extending well out into the aisle also invites arguments from the people passing by. Surely someone will refuse to ignore his obstructive legs and take issue with him.

A final potential cause of arguments concerns threats and challenges arising from violations of a person's *territoriality*. As the word implies, *territoriality* refers to the space a person occupies. We are all familiar with the signs NO TRESPASSING and STAY OUT. In addition to the boundaries prescribed by law, there are those prescribed by tradition. As pointed out in Chapter 1, society lives by unwritten rules as well as written ones. A towel and slippers on a beach chair suggest occupancy. If you ignore such signposts, your actions will almost always be taken as a threat or a challenge. Since man is a territory-oriented animal, he will defend the space he claims as his own.[10]

WRAP-UP

We have considered some of the more common reasons why people argue. They included the need to express opinions, to prove a point, to test ideas, to satisfy psychological needs, and to air a foul mood. We found that people who argue can be classified as *aggressors, victims,* and *instigators.* Invalidation (discounting another's feelings) and judgment-making were advanced as sources of arguments, along with habits of speech that serve to invite disagreement. Finally, the things people argue about seemed to distribute themselves into one of the two classes: *matter* and *manner.*

With insight into why people argue, you are better prepared to plan your disagreements effectively and to manage them successfully.

PROBES, PRODS, AND PROJECTS

Why do educated people seem to argue more effectively than uneducated people? Or do they?

Prepare a list of topics for impromptu speeches, or ask your instructor to do so. (Some suggestions: the advantages or disadvantages of being an only child, a woman, an older or younger sibling; the best or worst thing about this class; the trouble with parents.) Give each speaker five minutes to prepare. Speakers are judged on the basis of the strength of the arguments

[10] For a discussion of territoriality, see Edward T. Hall, *The Silent Language* (Garden City, N.Y.: Doubleday & Co., Inc., 1959), and his *The Hidden Dimension* (Garden City, N.Y.: Anchor Books, Doubleday & Co., Inc., 1969).

they advance. As a variation, try impromptu debates, speeches with heckling allowed, cross-examination debate.

When does having an open mind help you in an argument? When does it hurt?

Are you inclined to be an aggressor, a victim, or an instigator in most arguments? Why?

Is there such a thing as an "argumentative look"? Describe it in physical terms.

Observe people who tend to crowd into tight spaces between others, who touch others while talking, and who are physical in their interpersonal communication behavior. Do they have any traits in common? How would you characterize them? Why?

Are men or women more argument-prone?

Complete the following self-evaluation quiz. Bring it into class and discuss your answers with a small group of classmates. (Note: The purpose of this quiz is to emphasize that people, not computers, argue. Personality and character traits play an important role in any argument. Therefore, it is essential that you expand your awareness of self.)

SELF-EVALUATION QUIZ*†
(Profile of an Advocate)

NAME _____

COURSE _____

SECTION _____

Physical characteristics:

1. Somatotype:
   ectomorph ☐   mesomorph ☐   endomorph ☐
2. Manner of dress:
   high style ☐   average ☐   unconcerned ☐
3. Voice volume:
   loud ☐   average ☐   soft ☐
4. Speech speed:
   fast ☐   medium ☐   slow ☐
5. Haptic behavior (touching):
   a toucher ☐   a touchee ☐   untouchable ☐

*Since all responses elicited by this quiz will depend upon whatever circumstances prevail at a given time, only answers of a general nature are expected from the reader.

†Abne M. Eisenberg, *Living Communication* (Englewood Cliffs, N.J.: Prentice-Hall, Inc., 1975), pp. 203-4.

6. Eye-contact behavior:
   extensive ☐   moderate ☐   minimal ☐   none ☐
7. Kinesic behavior:
   hyperkinetic ☐   hypokinetic ☐   average ☐
8. Postural attitude preferred:
   upright ☐   seated ☐   recumbent ☐

Psychological characteristics:

9. Personality type:
   introvert ☐   extrovert ☐   ambivert ☐
10. Intelligence:
    high ☐   average ☐   low ☐
11. Open-mindedness:
    high ☐   average ☐   low ☐
12. Perception of SELF as an:
    instigator ☐   aggressor ☐   victim ☐
13. Ability to stay on subject:
    high ☐   average ☐   low ☐
14. Pleasure derived from arguing:
    high ☐   average ☐   low ☐   none ☐
15. Tendency to argue:
    high ☐   average ☐   low ☐   none ☐
16. Lifespan of arguments:
    short-lived ☐   average ☐   long-lived ☐
17. Frequency of arguments:
    high ☐   average ☐   low ☐   none ☐
18. Tendency to alienate an opponent:
    high ☐   average ☐   low ☐   none ☐
19. Type of opponents:
    same ☐   different ☐   unimportant ☐
20. Subjects argued:
    same ☐   different ☐   unimportant ☐

Environmental characteristics:

21. Proxemic status (interpersonal distance during an argument):
    less than 6 inches ☐   between 6 and 12 inches ☐
    between 12 and 24 inches ☐   over 24 inches ☐
22. Location of most arguments:
    Home:
    kitchen ☐   bedroom ☐   living room ☐   bathroom ☐
    Office:
    your office ☐   someone else's office ☐   hall ☐
    School:
    in class ☐   cafeteria ☐   halls ☐   outdoors ☐
23. Time most arguments occur:
    early morning ☐   forenoon ☐   afternoon ☐
    evening ☐   middle of night ☐
24. Relationship of arguments to meals:
    before meals ☐   during meals ☐   after meals ☐
25. Climatic relationship to arguing:
    rainy days ☐   sunny days ☐   cloudy days ☐   any days ☐

7

FATE OF AN ARGUMENT

BEHAVIORAL OBJECTIVES

After reading this chapter, you should have a better understanding of

1. the ways an argument can end
2. why winning an argument through violence generally results in a hollow victory
3. why so many people have a tendency to elect alienation as a means of resolving their conflicts
4. the premise that compromise is a positive rather than a negative course of action
5. the false contention that the arguer who succeeds in effecting a conversion is necessarily the winner
6. why arriving at a stalemate in an argument is so frustrating
7. what the term *win* means
8. how knowing the personality of your opponent can help you set goals for yourself in an argument
9. the preferred role that ethics plays in any given argument

10. how to go about "following through" on an argument
11. how to use your arguments as learning tools by analyzing rather than rationalizing
12. the psychology of a winner as compared to that of a loser

A disquieting thing about most arguments, especially with strangers, is that you're never sure how they will turn out. What begins as a simple disagreement may escalate into a violent confrontation. Or your most ambitious efforts may be wasted on an opponent with a closed mind.

In this chapter we describe the various ways arguments end: physical violence, alienation, compromise, conversion, and stalemate. By being alert to the course and direction of your arguments, you may choose suitable end products, and avoid undesirable ones. In the second part of the chapter, we talk about what it means to *win* an argument. Contrary to popular belief, winning isn't simply a matter of defeating an opponent. There are degrees and kinds of victories.

The skilled advocate is aware of the subtle variations that fall under the category of winning. In the third part of the chapter, we go beyond argument, suggesting that a disagreement does not end when the talking stops. We point out how you can apply what you have learned from past arguments to those in the future.

WAYS AN ARGUMENT CAN END

Scene 1: a bar where two men are standing and having a drink after work.

1st Man:	Boy, this city is certainly going to the dogs.
2nd Man:	Then why don't you move somewhere else?
1st Man:	Why should I?
2nd Man:	Didn't you just say you were fed up with this place?
1st Man:	No, I said that it was going to the dogs!
2nd Man:	As far as I'm concerned, it means that you don't like it here. It sure doesn't mean that you're happy here, does it?
1st Man:	Listen, why don't you mind your own damn business.
2nd Man:	Now hold on there, Charlie; I didn't start this conversation—you did. If you didn't want my opinion, you should have just kept your mouth shut.
1st Man:	Who do you think you're telling to shut up?
2nd Man:	You, you stupid *@*%!!

This is one of the typical ways an argument can progress. How did it end? Probably in a fist fight!

Physical violence is a common method of resolving differences because it is usually quick and to the point. Discussion or debate takes time, an understanding of the issues, and an ability to express one's self with words. There are many people who either lack these prerequisites or who for other reasons, simply take the line of least resistance and punch you in the mouth.

Of course, this kind of behavior seldom solves the problem. In an extreme case, you might literally beat someone into submission. But would that change his mind? Probably not—at least not for long. History teaches us that victory is seldom lasting. Instead, it tends to intensify the hostility of the defeated party. Given the right support and encouragement, the person you have put down through the use of violence would turn on you with redoubled fury.

As mentioned in Chapter 1, it is generally true that as an individual becomes more learned and able to manipulate ideas more efficiently, he is less inclined to use physical means of resolving his conflicts with others. But we must not overlook man's psychobiological nature. With or without an education, man still has a good measure of animal in him, and, if pushed far enough, he will react like one. We assume that a highly educated person involved in an argument would use language rather than muscle as a tool to win. But with or without an education, a person's response under stress can go either way. Just as words are not the only recourse of the educated person, so violence is not the only alternative open to the uneducated person.

Scene 2: a living room. Husband is silent.

Wife:	What's the matter dear?
Husband:	Nothing.
Wife:	What do you mean nothing?
Husband:	Just what I said, nothing.
Wife:	You look upset about something.
Husband:	Do I?
Wife:	Yes.
Husband:	Come to think of it, I am a little annoyed.
Wife:	Over what, dear?
Husband:	You.
Wife:	But why?
Husband:	Because your nagging is driving me nuts!
Wife:	When do I ever nag you?
Husband:	Damn it, you're doing it right now!
Wife:	I was just concerned because you were so quiet.
Husband:	Martha, please go away and leave me alone.
Wife:	George, you give me a pain. If I don't ask you what's wrong, you accuse me of not giving a damn whether you live or die. If I do ask, you bitch that I'm nagging. As far as I'm concerned, you can drop dead. I'm going out. Good night!

Another way an argument can end is with *alienation*. Martha, in our scene, was alienated by her husband. We tend to react as Martha did when we are thoroughly fed up with someone's attitude, misguided point of view, or insulting and offensive manner. At such times we may vow not to say another word and perhaps never to talk to our adversary again. This, like physical violence, may be a rather immature but expedient way of bringing an argument to a screeching halt. Doubtless there are situations, such as the one above, in which the choice of such an option is the wisest choice we can make. In some situations, however, it suggests a lack of experience and ability to cope with conflicts. Many a fine relationship or marriage has fallen by the wayside because the parties were unable to face up to a problem. Instead, they ran away from it, and each became the object of the other's hostility. Alienation, then, is one fate that may befall an argument.

Scene 3: a kitchen. Two boys have just run to their father to settle an argument.

Little Brother:	Daddy, Jimmy won't let me watch the Space Avenger on television!
Jimmy:	Yeah, but he's been watching TV for an hour. Now it's *my* turn to pick a show!
Father:	*(To the little brother):* Have you been watching TV for as long as Jimmy says?
Little Brother:	Yeah, but Jimmy wasn't even watching it then!
Jimmy:	I was so! I wanted to . . .
Father:	Well, Bobby, I think it's about time for Jimmy to pick a show. After all, it's his TV as much as yours!
Little Brother:	But he always picks old movies, and I hate old movies!
Father:	That may be so, but it's time for Jimmy to pick. If you don't like what he watches, you can play with your toys, or you can go out and play. You've got to learn to share.
Little Brother:	Oh, all right.

Sometimes *compromise* is the outcome of a disagreement. Compromise results when both parties (or some third party) recognize that each side has presented an argument that has some merit. This can only happen when the arguers are open-minded—willing to listen to reason and to one another's point of view. In the light of our discussion in Chapter 1, we can say that compromise is more likely to be the end product of a dialogue or a discussion than any other type of disagreement. In addition to open-mindedness, compromise requires some maturity on the part of the arguers. It is far more difficult to reach a compromise than to resort to violence. Compromise requires self-discipline as well as a willingness to "swallow your pride" and admit that you were at least partly wrong.

A word of advice: the best way to bring about a compromise is to argue the *ideas* you're talking about, not the personality of your opponent. As we say in a later chapter, people are strongly inclined to save face in an argumental situation. If you insinuate that by yielding, your opponent is admitting his stupidity or bias, you can be almost certain he'll never give in. Rather, you should *avoid* making an opponent feel that he has to save face if he capitulates. In persuasion theory, it has been shown that if you want to change a person's mind, you've got to provide an "out"—a reason for rejecting what he's believed until now. Make him feel *good* about it, not ashamed of it.[1]

The same thing applies directly to an argumental situation.

Scene 4: a counter in a neighborhood store. A customer has just walked up to a salesman.

Customer:	I'd like to buy these shirts, please.
Salesman:	Oh surely, Sir. Let's see, that'll be $24.50.
Customer:	You'll take a check, won't you?
Salesman:	I'm sorry, we're not allowed to take checks.
Customer:	Not allowed? Why, that's an insult.
Salesman:	It's store policy, Sir. You know, we have had some people who tried to pass bad checks.
Customer:	Bad checks! Are you insinuating that I'm going to give you a bad check?
Salesman:	No, I wasn't implying...
Customer:	You weren't implying! Well, you just listen to me, young man. I've been shopping here for fifteen years, and I've never been accused of passing bad checks before. I don't have to stand for your insults.
Salesman:	Well, you see, today is Saturday, and the banks aren't open....
Customer:	I'll pay for these shirts right now, and I'll pay by check. If you won't take the check, then get the manager. Mr. Fuller is an old friend and a gentleman!
Salesman:	*(Hesitating a moment)* I'm sorry, Sir. Very well, I'll take the check.

Although compromise is a desirable outcome of a disagreement, there is another consequence that, from one point of view, may be even more desirable—namely, *conversion*. The reason this may seem better is that it requires no con-

---

[1] This principle finds expression in the nonviolent persuasion carried on by Mahatma Ghandi and Martin Luther King. The Indian word *Satyagraha* refers to the requirement that both sides in a confrontation coerce and injure one another as little as possible. Each side must give the other the courage to change by not placing him in a position in which he must react defensively. See Erik Erikson, *Ghandi's Truth* (New York: W. W. Norton & Co., Inc., 1970).

cession on your part. It doesn't require you to give in at all. When conversion is effected, your adversary is the only one to give ground. In this instance, you have either made your point convincingly or your opponent has seen fit to concede for other reasons. In either case, his concession may be your greatest prize.

It is very important to mention that the individual who is the object of conversion is not necessarily the weaker advocate. It may be that because of a superior intellect or a more complete understanding of the issues, he or she has seen fit to yield on purely rational grounds. Moreover, the reader should not assume that the arguer who succeeds in effecting a conversion is necessarily the winner. There is such a thing as *apparent conversion.* Your opponent might *say* he's persuaded, while really he's not. He just doesn't want to go on arguing. Often, apparent conversion goes hand-in-hand with alienation. Take the following example:

Scene 5: a coffee shop. Two women are sitting at a counter, talking politics.

1st Woman:	I think all politicans are bums.
2nd Woman:	Really? Why?
1st Woman:	What do you mean why? Because they are, that's all!
2nd Woman:	But how do you know? I mean, what evidence do you have?
1st Woman:	Don't give me that evidence stuff. Politicans are bums. Period!
2nd Woman:	But how can you. . .
1st Woman:	Look. Did you ever know an honest politican? Huh? I've never known an honest one in my life!
2nd Woman:	*(Convinced she can't reason with her adversary)* You know something? You're right! You're absolutely right! Well . . . ah . . . you'll have to excuse me now. I've got to . . . ah . . . catch a train. *(She walks off quickly.)*
1st Woman:	Hey! Aren't you even going to finish your coffee?

In this case it is obvious that the second woman was alientated by her adversary. Although it may look as though the second woman was converted, in fact, she was not. She simply gave in because she knew it would have been futile to go on. We've all had this experience at one time or another. We just give up rather than waste our time batting our heads against a brick wall. In a case like this, the question of what it means to *win* an argument comes up. The first woman—although she is the apparent victor—didn't really win at all. Later we will discuss exactly what it means to win an argument.

Scene 6: a local department store. Two cashiers on a coffee break.

1st Woman:	This religion stuff is a lot of nonsense.
2nd Woman:	Yeah? How do you figure that?
1st Woman:	If there were a God, there wouldn't be so many innocent children getting killed and so many really wonderful people dying before they've even had a chance to live.
2nd Woman:	God works in mysterious ways. A lot of things that happen seem strange because we don't understand.
1st Woman:	Understand what?
2nd Woman:	Why, the meaning of it all—the Master Plan.
1st Woman:	Who says there's a master plan?
2nd Woman:	God does.
1st Woman:	How do you know that?
2nd Woman:	I read it in the Bible.
1st Woman:	You mean you actually believe what's in the Bible?
2nd Woman:	I sure do!
1st Woman:	How can you believe all that stuff?
2nd Woman:	Because it's the word of God.
1st Woman:	Who says so?
2nd Woman:	My pastor.
1st Woman:	How does he know?
2nd Woman:	The Pope told him, wise guy! Now do you believe me?
1st Woman:	Nope!

Stalemate is probably the most frustrating way for an argument to end. In the preceding case, it's unlikely that either disputant felt much satisfaction. Even if the argument had been continued, it is doubtful that either could have changed the other's mind.

Paradoxically, an argument that results in a stalemate does not actually end; it becomes stalled and fails to continue. Neither opponent is able to persuade the other to accept a point of view, either in part or completely. As a result, a stalemate, which may easily last from minutes or hours to years, occurs. Some such arguments never end. They continue on for a lifetime, ending only with the death of one of the advocates. Legendary frontier feuds are examples of family arguments that were never resolved and that were passed on from parent to child.

The stalemate may happen as a result of stubbornness on the part of one or both of the participants, of very ineffective and distorted communication of ideas, or of a failure on the part of both sides to share values about what constitutes *proof.* In the preceding case, it's very unlikely that either side would convince the other, because the two people didn't agree on what proof would justify each other's claims. The second woman could cite the Bible, her pastor, and even the Pope until she was exhausted, and she would not convince her adversary. The first woman could discuss war, injustice, and wrongdoing all she wanted, but she would not change her opponent's mind; the second woman would see it all as part of God's Master Plan. In a case like this, the advocates would be wise to examine not each other's assertions, but each other's reasoning, evidence, and values. In other words, they would probably have to go beneath what they're saying and determine *why* they're saying it. Possibly, such an approach would result in a resolution of the conflict. Rarely does an argument exist in which common ground cannot be found on which to work out some kind of mutually satisfactory solution—providing both advocates are willing to listen and each has a genuine desire to solve the problem.

WHAT DOES *WIN* MEAN?

Until now we have been talking about the ways an argument can end. We used the word *win* very sparingly, because *winning* is a much more involved concept than it seems to be at first glance. Sometimes we concede an argument and still win. Other times we can emerge the apparent victor but really lose. How can this be?

To answer this question, we have to determine the arguer's goal. If he succeeds in achieving it, then he has *won*—whether or not he seems to have come out best. Take the following example: A customer, arguing with a salesperson for a refund, has a definite goal; he wants his money back. He doesn't care what the salesman thinks of him; he just wants his money. If he gets it, he has won. The situation is very different when an employee argues with his boss for a raise or a special assignment. Here, the worker must be persuasive but polite and tactful at the same time. His main goal may be the raise or the special assignment. However, he may have other goals as well; he may want to impress the boss favorably, for example. In fact, he might regard impressing the boss favorably as *more* important than the particular request he's making. If the worker got the raise but was fired two months later, do you think he would consider the victory worth the price? On the other hand, if he failed to get what he wanted immediately, but he did succeed in getting it at some later date, then didn't he really *win?* There are short-term and long-term victories. As an observer, you need to know which kind of a victory an advocate wants—or if his goal is victory—before you can label him a winner or a loser. More important to you as a reader of this book, as an advocate, you need to decide on a definite goal. You should make a choice about exactly what it is you want out of an argument. As we said before, there are short-term and long-term victories. You must decide yourself what you want to achieve. However, we *will* say this: There's not much consolation in winning the battle and losing the war.

Here are some of the things that can help you decide the goal(s) you should set for yourself in an argument: (1) the nature of the confrontation; (2) the personality of your opponent; (3) the number of times you will argue this issue with your opponent; and (4) the facts of the case.

The Nature of the Confrontation

The kind of confrontation you find yourself involved in, strongly influences the goals you can reasonably set. If, for example, you're screaming at somebody and he's screaming back at you, then it's unlikely that either one of you will succeed in changing the other's mind.

In distinguishing among dialogues, discussions, debates, altercations, and fights in Chapter 1, we listed, among other criteria, *level of emotionality, open-mindedness* and *physical and psychological setting.* These are important determinants of the goals you can expect in a disagreement. Let's assume you want to change your opponent's mind. The chances of your doing so *decrease* as you move from dialogue to fight. In other words, as his level of emotionality increases, his reluctance to change his mind also increases. The relationships can be seen in Figure 7-1.

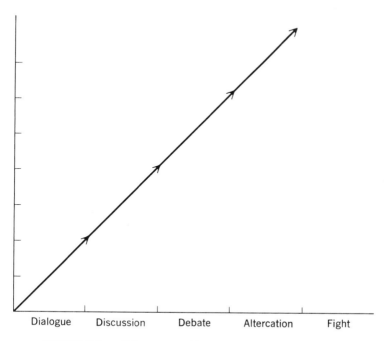

FIGURE 7-1   Reluctance to Change One's Mind as Related to
Level of Emotionality

The same applies to open-mindedness; obviously, the more closed-minded a person becomes, the less willing he is to change. Finally, the more unpleasant the atmosphere, the less inclined a person will be to capitulate. Prisoners of war, because of their hostility toward their captors and their subhuman living conditions, often display a profound resistance to "mind-bending."

In an altercation or fight, you have these three things working against you: The level of emotionality is high; the participants are relatively closed-minded; the setting is often unfavorable. Hence, you are unlikely to succeed in bringing about a major change in your opponent's attitude. Thus, determining the kind of confrontation can help you establish your desired goal or modify the goal you started out with.

Sometimes a disagreement deteriorates into a debate, altercation, or fight. This can force you to abandon or modify your original goal (as we've suggested). If an argument is going downhill, you can try to soften the tone of the argument or channel it into less turbulent waters. You might say, "Look, Joe, we're not getting anywhere. Let's take a break, have a cup of coffee, and see exactly where we stand." This strategy can work for you by clearing the air and reestablishing a climate of cooperation. However, what we're suggesting here does presuppose a measure of maturity and objectivity.

The Personality of Your Opponent

The personality of your opponent can help you set goals for yourself. Some people are, by nature, more open-minded than others. (And a person who is open-minded on one subject can be closed-minded on another.) Some are more intelligent than others, some are more independent. The list could go on endlessly. The point is, your opponent may determine, unintentionally, how far you can go in a particular argument.

Have you ever argued with a bigoted or prejudiced person? If you have, try to recall what he was like. Was he intelligent? fair? objective? Probably not. How would you describe his psychological make-up? Why did he cling to ridiculous beliefs that were contradicted by the facts? Why was he too stupid or lazy to open his eyes and his mind? What needs were fulfilled by his self-sustained ignorance? Is it possible he felt inferior? Only a qualified psychotherapist could tell us. But, as an arguer, it's a good idea to try to judge the motivation of your opponent and to adjust your remarks to him. This may influence your choice of goal or require you to adjust your goal in an argument.[2]

Suppose you were arguing with a bigot who believed that women are mentally inferior to men. This prejudiced fool has probably held his belief for years. Do you think his mind could be changed in just one or two arguments?

[2] For additional information on adapting to your opponent, see Chapter 8, Know Your Opponent.

Probably not. In fact, by trying too hard, by attempting to do too much too soon, you might strengthen his initial belief! What do you do in a case like this? Perhaps the best thing would be to set a more limited goal for yourself. Try to open this man's mind just a little. Shake his castle-on-sand a bit. Make him doubt. Make him think. If you succeed, you may well have *won* the argument, although the effects of your persuasion may not be felt for some time.

The Number of Encounters

Consider this: How many chances will you have to change your opponent's mind? Should you try to do it all at once or in stages? In this context, we can report that persuasion theorists have found that it almost always takes more than one encounter to change a person's mind. Advertisers take this fact into consideration when planning not single ads but *ad campaigns*—months and sometimes years of advertisement for a single product. The results have shown that the campaign approach works. It is far more successful than the single advertisement. As an arguer, you can apply this same principle to your day-to-day discussions. In setting down goals for yourself, then, consider carefully the number of encounters you anticipate.

The Facts of the Case

The facts of the case can help you set goals for yourself in an argument. For instance, you get a speeding ticket on the day you're rushing your pregnant girlfriend to the hospital. The policeman issuing the ticket was correct in calling you a speeder; you were going eighty-five miles per hour in a thirty-five-mile zone. But because of the extenuating circumstances, you decided to go to court to contest the fifty-dollar fine. What should your goal be? Would you try to convince the judge that you weren't speeding? No. That would be impossible; the facts of the case are against you. But you *could* legitimately set a more limited goal. You could argue that you were "guilty with an explanation." The chances are that the judge, after hearing your story, would at least reduce your fine and perhaps let you off with no fine. In this case, you have let the *facts* help you decide on your goal.

The subject of ethics comes up here. Is it legitimate to behave unethically in order to win an argument? Should you lie or distort the facts in order to emerge triumphant? Does the end justify the means? Or should you go only as far as the facts of the case will allow?

Our position is clear: It is never justifiable to lie in order to win an argument. You may *not* lie or behave unethically in order to win. Like our speeder, you should examine the facts of the case and let them help you set goals for yourself.

This is not to say that your opponent won't lie. We're not naive enough to believe that everyone is honest. But if you know your facts and are trained to recognize the more common fallacies and inadequate proofs, you should be able to put down your opponent in grand style.

BEYOND ARGUMENT

Arguments don't end when the last word is spoken. The fate of an argument may well be determined by what happens after the advocates have finished talking. This can be readily seen in jury trials. Deliberations follow the oral arguments advanced by attorneys for both sides. Similarly, in your arguments the aftermath may profoundly affect the ultimate outcome. For this reason we urge you to form the habit of thinking beyond the arguments you engage in. Ask yourself such questions as these: (1) *What, exactly, has been agreed upon?* (When you and your opponent reach an agreement on any important matter, it should be written down.) (2) *What is to be done next?* (3) *Who is responsible for carrying through on the decision?* (4) *What are my responsibilities? My adversary's?* (5) *How can potential problems be both anticipated and avoided?*

If other people are needed to facilitate a resolution, you should ask yourself these further questions: (6) *To whom else must I speak, in order to ensure that the agreement is acted upon?* (7) *What is his most likely response?* (8) *How can I prepare myself to counter his objections?* (9) *Can I enlist my adversary's support in winning over the third party?*

By weighing such questions, you prepare a follow-through on the results of your arguments. Failure to follow through is a frequent and crucial error. We cannot recommend too strenuously that you form the habit of thinking beyond argument!

A second topic to consider is the advocate's personal response to winning or losing. Arguments do not occur in a psychological vacuum. Because each interaction affects the advocate's attitudes, it has the potential for a positive, negative, or mixed impact on subsequent confrontations. Winners, for instance, generally emerge from their encounters looking and feeling different from losers. Do you remember some of your own reactions to winning or losing? Compare them with the ones that follow.

Portrait of a Loser

The traditional portrait of a loser is a familiar one: a dull, far-away look in the eyes, head slightly pitched forward, arms dangling at sides or hands limply folded in lap, an unwillingness to discuss what happened, and a feeble smile that invites sympathetic consolation from teammates and well-meaning friends. These are some of the physical characteristics displayed by a great many losers. There are, however, some far more important psychological manifestations.

Losers often equate failing at a particular task with *being* a failure. They may think of themselves as inadequate or incompetent. They may feel sorry for themselves. Some consider themselves unlucky.

Losers are also inclined to rationalize. They find excuses for their failures. For example, they might say "That study the affirmative cited was so old, it had a long gray beard," or "I'm convinced the judge was prejudiced against me because I wasn't wearing a jacket and tie." Immature losers desperately try to save face. Often, they make light of their opponent's strengths. They may deny their own weaknesses. Occasionally, they refuse to face up to their failure, contending that they didn't really lose!

Such reactions, resulting from the ego-involvement that occurs in all competition, overemphasize the emotional at the expense of the rational. Rather than licking their emotional wounds or rationalizing their defeat away, losers would be well advised to think about what happened. What errors did they make? How did their debating contribute to their defeat? What did they fail to do adequately during the exchange? Which of their opponents' strengths were they unable to handle? By analyzing their performance rationally, losers can learn from their mistakes.

Portrait of a Winner

How do winners differ from losers? Do most winners exhibit common traits? Do bright eyes that engage others directly, a head held high, a generous smile, and a rich and outgoing voice characterize a winner? These physical behaviors contrast with those previously assigned to losers. Are they, in themselves, reliable barometers? How important are psychological factors?

A winner cannot be identified on the basis of any single physical or psychological trait. The portrait of a winner is a matter of chemistry, an elusive mixture of essences. To say that winners are made, not born, is a statement open to argument. A less assertive claim would be that, in most cases, the "potential to win" can be significantly increased in those willing to make the effort.

Winners come away from arguments with positive and constructive thoughts. Rather than rationalize, they analyze; they attempt to build new "rights" on old "wrongs." Once an argument is over, the winner thinks forward, not backward.

If, as this book suggests, most people are woefully unprepared to cope with the disagreements that punctuate their lives, they must make an effort to remedy the situation. One method of doing this is to think beyond the argument at hand. Past arguments and debates have a great deal to teach those who have experienced them. As teaching tools, they are invaluable and indispensable to the growth and maturation of any advocate.

WRAP-UP

This chapter was divided into three parts. In the first, we noted some of the ways an argument can end. These included: *physical violence, alienation, compromise, conversion,* and *stalemate.* In the second part, we talked about what it means to *win* an argument. We looked at the paradox that results when the person who comes out on top in an argument is labeled a loser and when the person who seems to be defeated emerges the real winner. In explaining what it means to win an argument, we found that it was necessary to look at the arguer's *goal.* If an arguer succeeds in achieving his goal, then he can be called the winner, regardless of how he seems to fare in an argument.

We listed the considerations that can help you set goals for yourself, including the kind of disagreement you're involved in, the personality of your opponent, the number of times you have argued this issue with him, and the facts of the case. In the third part of this chapter, the reader was encouraged to think beyond an argument, to think about implementing its outcome. Specifically, questions were recommended to help the advocate facilitate the ultimate resolution of a disagreement. As an additional source of assistance, advice was given on the psychology of winning and losing, and on the importance of analyzing rather than rationalizing.

We are confident that the careful application of the topics and strategies discussed in this chapter will assist you in carrying your disagreements to a satisfactory outcome.

PROBES, PRODS, AND PROJECTS

In this chapter, the authors imply, "History teaches us that victory by violence is seldom lasting." Why is such a statement absurd?

How do most of your arguments generally end?

Wouldn't you consider compromising in an argument tantamount to "copping out"? Isn't it a sign of weakness?

Should parents force children to "make up" after an argument, regardless of the circumstances?

The authors list five ways an argument can end: physical violence, alienation, compromise, conversion, and stalemate. Can you think of any other ways?

Describe three arguments you have had in the past. How did each of them end? Based on what you have learned in this chapter, speculate about what circumstance would have had to prevail in order for them to have ended differently.

Reflect on arguments you have won. Tell why you think you emerged a winner.

8

KNOW YOUR OPPONENT

BEHAVIORAL OBJECTIVES

After reading this chapter, you should have a better understanding of

1. why, in any interpersonal or rhetorical disagreement, knowing one's opponent can be an invaluable asset
2. how, in an argument or debate, it is possible for an advocate to infer his opponent's beliefs by what he says or does
3. the difference between attitudes and beliefs
4. why debaters who have a keen insight into their own values tend to have an advantage over those who do not
5. what it means to *upset someone's psychological balance*
6. the distinctions between such terms as *bias, prejudice,* and *open-mindedness*
7. why it is unwise to use the words *knowledge* and *intelligence* interchangeably
8. the possible consequence of allowing yourself to enter into an argument or debate with someone who employs illogical means or who is unwilling to acknowledge logical proof

9. how to use external indicators as guides to your opponent's internal state

10. what techniques can be used against the more difficult opponent

In Chapter 2 we defined proof as "whatever rhetorical methods are used to convince your listener(s)." We recognized also that when an opponent says, "Prove it!" he means, "Use the kind of proof that I will accept." To do this, the advocate, acting as a persuader, must learn enough about his opponent to determine what will make him change his mind. Professional persuaders such as national advertisers spend millions of dollars each year testing television commercials to determine their effect upon audiences. Unfortunately, the average advocate has neither the facilities nor the funds to pretest his arguments in this grand fashion. He can, however, evaluate his opponent carefully and project the kinds of arguments he thinks will work most effectively. This chapter is designed to help accomplish such a predetermination. The first part deals with your opponent's internal state: his beliefs, values, attitudes, biases, level of intelligence, and so on. The second part examines several external signs of your opponent's internal state: his age, occupation, language, and so on. Should these cues be inadequate, we recommend the tactics found in the third part of the chapter. Our strategies are especially useful when ordinary observation of telltale external characteristics fails to reveal enough about your opponent's internal state.

YOUR OPPONENT'S INTERNAL STATE

Beliefs, Attitudes, and Values: An Introductory Overview

We are all walking storehouses of experience, knowledge, and feelings, the products of everything that happened to us since childhood. These experiences vary from person to person and are revealed in the beliefs, attitudes, and values we hold.

Beliefs: Descriptive, Evaluative, and Prescriptive

A belief is a simple proposition that is held consciously or unconsciously and that is capable of being inferred from what a person says or does.[1] Example: "I believe that leprechauns actually do exist." There are three kinds of beliefs:

---

[1] Milton Rokeach, *Beliefs, Attitudes, and Values: A Theory of Organization and Change* (San Francisco: Jossey-Bass, Inc., Publishers, 1968), p. 113.

descriptive, evaluation, and prescriptive. Definitions and points of difference appear in the narrative below.

Recently, the authors were involved in an argument with a thirty-five-year-old father of three. The subject was the rearing of children, and our friend argued this way: "I do not discipline my children; I think it stifles creativity." The discussion that followed shed a great deal of light on the subject of beliefs. We found that our friend's remark contained three kinds of beliefs. First, it contained a *descriptive* belief statement: "I do not discipline my children. I think it stifles creativity." Belief statements such as this have a purely factual ring to them in that they assert an objectively verifiable relationship between two things ("Group sports discourage individuality" or "Strenuous dieting is harmful"). When our friend said, "I do not discipline my children; I think it stifles creativity," he didn't evaluate either *discipline* or *creativity*. He simply told us that he believes an objectively verifiable relationship exists between them.

Further examination revealed that his remark was based upon still another belief, an *evaluation belief:* "Creativity is preferable to habits of self-discipline." Evaluate beliefs state personal preferences, and because of the intimate nature of our values, we seldom think about them unless they are challenged. Hence, the evaluative beliefs beneath our arguments are often implied rather than explicitly stated. An advocate should train himself to pick up these *implied* value statements; knowing them facilitates a strategic response. More will be said about values later in the chapter.

The third element implied by our friend's remark was a *prescriptive belief statement.* We suspect that, if he were asked to recommend a course of action, he would probably say, "discipline should be given less emphasis in raising children than encouragement of creativity." Like propositions of policy, prescriptive beliefs dictate courses of action that should be taken.

Belief-Position Sequence

Earlier, we indicated that it was possible to infer the beliefs a person holds from what he says or does. One might guess that our friend's home is a rather loosely structured place where the children are permitted the run of the house, given much freedom, and encouraged to say what they think and feel. A visit to such a home would probably reveal the parents' attitude toward discipline.

In an argument, it is important that an advocate develop the ability to infer basic beliefs from what an opponent says or does. Because beliefs frequently dictate the positions taken in controversy, an ability to expose them from beneath an opponent's superficial position is essential. Consider the following illustration:

The positions taken in an argument about smoking marijuana may be determined by each advocate's beliefs about the drug. If I believe that marijuana is physically addictive, I will probably oppose its use. My *belief-position sequence* looks like this (Figure 8-1):

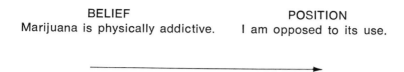

BELIEF

Marijuana is physically addictive.

POSITION

I am opposed to its use.

The other person's *belief-position sequence* looks like this:

BELIEF

Marijuana is not physically addictive

POSITION

I am not opposed to its use.

FIGURE 8-1   Belief-Position Sequence

You can now see how much our beliefs influence the positions we take. Finding out your opponent's beliefs will give you an indication of what you must do to change his mind. In the above case, an opponent would have to convince me that marijuana is not physically addictive. Then, assuming that this were my only reservation, I might withdraw my opposition to its use.

Attitudes

An attitude is a relatively long-lasting cluster of beliefs organized around some object or situation. Beliefs and attitudes, according to recent theorists, are related to one another like construction materials and the finished product. Fundamentally, beliefs are the building blocks of attitudes. The relationship between the two can be seen in Figure 8-2.

As shown, beliefs lie beneath attitudes. Our beliefs determine the attitudes we hold. The belief that peace is a desirable goal will probably determine attitudes toward such things as international conflicts, family interrelationships, and so on. Attitudes, then, are composed of an interrelated set of beliefs, organized around a particular focus. We possess attitudes toward things, never attitudes in the abstract. We have attitudes toward money, sex, people, government—our attitudes are always directed *toward* something. What purpose or functions do attitudes serve? They predispose us toward a particular response. Our attitude toward sex will predispose us to behave in a particular way. Again, as an advocate you must penetrate your opponent's attitudes and, from a

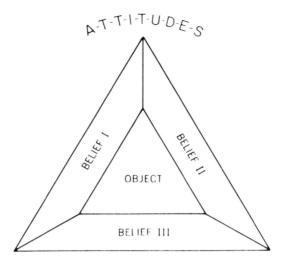

FIGURE 8-2   Relationship Between Beliefs and Attitudes

knowledge of them, determine the building blocks from which they were constructed. *You can never argue conclusions, only the reasons for them; similarly, you can never change attitudes, only the beliefs comprising them.*

	A	You value pursuit and discovery of truth – the intellectual life.
	B	You value what is useful, practical.
	C	You value form, harmony, and beauty.
	D	You value love, sympathy, warmth, and sensity in relationships with people.
	E	You value competition, influence, personal power.
	F	You value unity, wholeness, a sense of purpose above man.

FIGURE 8-3   Value Analysis

Values

As a means of introducing the topic of values, it might be useful to spend a few minutes in self-analysis. In Figure 8-3, we have described six types of people.[2] Read over the descriptions, then mark in the spaces on the left of the box the numbers one through six. Put the number six next to the type of person that best describes you. Put the number five next to the description that seems to typify you second best, and so on down to number one, which will be the description that fits you *least*.

Now look at the graph in Figure 8-4:

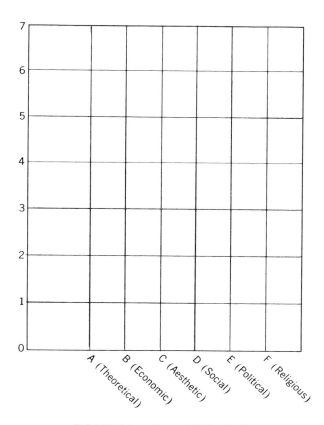

FIGURE 8-4   Personal Value Profile

[2] The categories are adapted from Eduard Spranger, *Types of Men*, translated by P. Prigors from the 5th German ed. (Halle: M. Niemeyer, 1928). Adapted from Thomas M. Scheidel, *Persuasive Speaking* (Glenview, Ill.: Scott, Foresman and Co., Inc., 1967), p. 42.

Take the numbers you wrote in Figure 8-3, and plot them in the appropriate place on the graph. Connect the dots, and what you have is your *personal value chart*—a visual representation of six dimensions of your personal system of values. Although this quiz is certainly far from scientific, it does permit an approximation of where some of your preferences lie, and it can perhaps serve to predict the decisions you are likely to make when faced with certain choices. Such information could be helpful to an opponent in an argument; it would tell him how to best approach changing your mind.

Assume you are arguing with a man whose values are primarily political and secondarily economic. You are urging him to buy a new automobile. Would you encourage him to buy it primarily because of its aesthetic beauty or would you emphasize its ability to enhance his status, his prestige? In the light of his values, the second alternative is probably the better one. The point here is to adapt your persuasive appeal to your opponent.

Psychological Balance[3]

Beliefs, attitudes, and values are reciprocal. Together, they form a dynamic network of psychological stuff that constitutes a "self" or a personality. This network is an *open system.* In biology, an open system refers to a structure that is capable of maintaining itself and developing in a changing environment: An open system is continually interacting with its environment, taking in and giving out, all the while maintaining structural and functional integrity in the process. We eat, excrete, breathe in, breathe out, and yet maintain our biological selves. Another term used to describe a state of well-being in the body is *homeostasis:* the condition preserved in the face of a changing environment. A physiological example of a homeostatic function is heat regulation. We perspire to maintain our proper body temperature when external factors are inclined to raise it.

What does all this have to do with argument? Consider the following analogy. Each of us is biologically and psychologically an open system. *Homeostasis is both a biological and psychological phenomenon.* Our intricate network of beliefs, attitudes, and values maintains itself by continually responding to environmental changes. Just as our bodies resist adverse changes in temperature, our minds also resist changes in set.[4] In short, we exist in a state of *psycholog-*

---

[3] In this section we have adapted and simplified the concept of psychological-cognitive balance as presented in the theories of Heider and Newcomb. The reader who is interested in a more detailed exposition of the theories should consult the work of the original authors or such a book as Chester A. Insko, *Theories of Attitude Change* (Englewood Cliffs, N.J.: Prentice-Hall, Inc., 1967), pp. 161-76.

[4] "One of the best established findings of social psychology is that individuals who have well-established attitudes and beliefs act so as to maintain them; the more extreme the attitudes, the more difficult they are to change." Gary Cronkhite, *Persuasion: Speech and Behavioral Change* (Indianapolis: Bobbs-Merrill Co., Inc., 1969), p. 139.

ical balance—resisting those things that threaten it. Suppose I respect and admire a politician named Senator Fudd. My attitude toward him is based on the belief that he is honest. One day, in a speech by one of his opponents, Fudd is accused of being corrupt. Would I be inclined to believe the charge? No! I would be unwilling to abandon my belief about Fudd because of one hostile speech by a political rival. It would take much more to change my mind about him. In this way, we tend to resist changes in our inner psychological states. Imagine the incredible number of changes that would be necessary were we to believe all that we heard or read. We would be like leaves blowing in the wind without direction or consistency. People can't exist that way. *Psychological balance* must be preserved at all costs, lest one invite the possibility of mental breakdown. Thus, in an effort to maintain such a state, people resist messages that tend to upset their *psychological balance*. The Fudd situation can be looked at this way (see Figure 8-5):

FIGURE 8-5   Maintenance of Psychological Balance in the Case of Senator Fudd

A persuader can create imbalance in his opponent through the use of *proof*, which consists of reasoning and evidence. Fudd's rival would have to *prove* the charge of corruption by producing evidence capable of changing my mind. Only after the submission of conclusive proof would I change my belief, but perhaps not my attitude, toward Fudd. What I might do is reexamine my tolerance level of honesty and see whether or not the other fine qualities possessed by Fudd outweigh the dishonesty charge. The object in situations like these is to create an imbalance in an opponent, then seek to create a new balance (see Figure 8-6).

Bias, Prejudice, and Open-Mindedness

Remarks such as "You're prejudiced" or "You're biased" are not uncommon in arguments. Biases and prejudices should be explored for five reasons: (1) Knowing your opponent's biases and prejudices will help you change his mind by enabling you to select arguments appropriate to his value system. (2) The

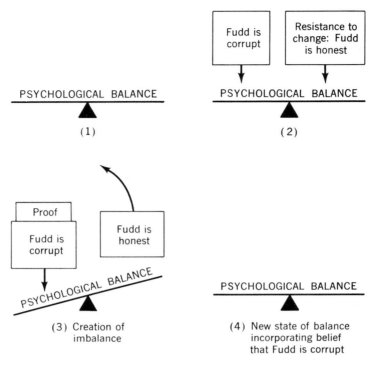

FIGURE 8-6 Balance-Imbalance-Balance Progression in Persuasion

knowledge will help you to avoid antagonizing him by contradicting his basic convictions without proof. (3) Knowing why your opponent is biased makes it possible for you to bring the reasons for his bias to his attention. (4) Understanding an opponent's prejudices can at times suggest particular strategies. It might, in certain cases, be expedient to demonstrate the irrationality of a particular prejudice before proceeding with an argument.[5] (5) Last, an awareness of your own prejudices and biases can alert you to pitfalls, fallacies, and errors in your own thinking.

A distinction should be made here between bias and prejudice. Although these terms are often used interchangeably, they are not synonymous. To be biased is to "have an ax to grind" Bias is a quality of emotional/cognitive processes that is based on some underlying motive. We may be biased for or against something, but we have a reason or a motive. If, in an argument, your opponent

---

[5] Research has shown that it may sometimes be more useful to help authoritarian or closed-minded individuals recognize the motives underlying their beliefs, attitudes, and values than to attack their beliefs with factual data. *Ibid.,* p. 133.

expresses enthusiasm for legalized gambling and you learn that he owns two or three gambling casinos, rest assured that he is biased in favor of gambling.

The word prejudice, broken down, means to prejudge,[6] to form an opinion or make a judgment before examining all available facts.

A prejudiced person is like a jury that renders its verdict without having heard the evidence. Whereas the biased person has access to the necessary facts but chooses to either ignore or distort them according to his motive, the prejudiced person seldom has the necessary facts at his disposal and thus forms judgments out of ignorance. Although prejudice is usually directed toward people, recent research suggests that differing value systems are more often the target from the standpoint of the person who is prejudiced.[7]

Open-mindedness is related to bias and prejudice in that the more biased and prejudiced a person is the less inclined he is to be *open-minded.* We are all biased and prejudiced toward some things; hence, we are both open- and closed-minded with regard to certain things under certain circumstances. One of the keys to success in argument is the ability to discern the degree of your opponent's open- or closed-mindedness.

Knowledge and Intelligence

Let us distinguish between a person's intelligence and his formally acquired knowledge. Such a distinction is important in an argument. A knowledgeable person has at his disposal a great deal of information on one or more topics. That knowledge, however, can serve little or no purpose if intelligence is lacking. An intelligent person is one who is able to recall pertinent data when needed, manipulate ideas readily, and perceive relationships between such data. Theoretically, the more intelligent person, by using inductive and deductive reasoning, should be able to do more with fewer pieces of information—to see more, to generate greater insights, and to come to more meaningful conclusions. There can be little doubt that the advocate who is both knowledgeable and intelligent is a double threat. Soon we shall suggest ways of gauging your opponent's knowledge and intelligence.

Rationality

In many instances, winning or losing an argument is determined by the psychological disposition of your opponent. Without getting into a semantic bog over the meaning of the words *rational* and *irrational,* surely some common-

---

[6] See Gordon W. Allport, *The Nature of Prejudice,* abridged ed. (New York: Anchor Books, Doubleday & Co., Inc., 1958), pp. 6-10.

[7] See Milton Rokeach, *The Open and Closed Mind* (New York: Basic Books, Inc., 1960), p. 135.

sense judgment can be agreed upon. One does not have to be a psychiatrist to know when the person he is arguing with is irrational. Such fairly obvious displays as language degeneration, failure to follow simple logical sequences of thought, and inappropriate emotional outbursts are commonplace symptoms of irrational behavior. If winning your argument depends upon a rational comprehension of the proof you provide, and your opponent lacks the ability to exercise such rationality, victory is virtually impossible. Therefore, at the moment you become aware of your opponent's irrational status, prepare for a speedy withdrawal.

EXTERNAL INDICATORS OF YOUR OPPONENT'S INTERNAL STATE

Unable to get inside another person's mind, we must rely on certain external indicators as cues to his internal state; however, caution should be taken when making inferences based on such indicators. At best they are helpers, not infallible guides, in making judgments. In this section, we present a variety of aids for the advocate. Included are such determinants as age, occupation, group allegiance, education, hobbies and interests, language, paralanguage and kinesics, and body type.

Age

One of the more difficult things to compensate for in an argument is an age difference. All the words in the world seem incapable of erasing the effects of a time differential. Occasionally, however, one encounters a senior citizen or young person who is able to break through the age barrier. How do they do it? Perhaps mentioning some of the characteristics associated with varying stages of life will help you transcend the age barrier. The following are descriptions of men: old, young, and in their prime. Read them carefully, for they come from a master observer, Aristotle.

> To begin with the Youthful type of character. Young men have strong passions, and tend to gratify them indiscriminately. Of the bodily desires, it is the sexual by which they are most swayed and in which they show absence of self-control. They are changeable and fickle in their desires, which are violent while they last, but quickly over: their impulses are keen but not deep-rooted, and are like sick people's attacks of hunger and thirst. They are hot-tempered and quick-tempered, and apt to give way to their anger; bad temper often gets the better of them, for owing to their love of honour they cannot bear being slighted, and are indignant if they imagine themselves unfairly treated. While they love honour, they love

victory still more; for youth is eager for superiority over others, and victory is one form of this. They love both more than they love money, which indeed they love very little, not having yet learnt what it means to be without it—this is the point of Pittacus' remark about Amphiraus. They look at the good side rather than the bad, not having yet witnessed many instances of wickedness. They trust others readily, because they have not yet often been cheated. They are sanguine; nature warms their blood as though with excess of wine; and besides that, they have as yet met with few disappointments. Their lives are mainly spent not in memory but in expectation; for expectation refers to the future, memory to the past, and youth has a long future before it and a short past behind it: on the first day of one's life one has nothing at all to remember, and can look only foward. They are easily cheated, owing to the sanguine disposition just mentioned. Their hot tempers and hopeful dispositions make them more courageous than older men are; the hot temper prevents fear, and the hopeful disposition creates confidence; we cannot feel fear so long as we are feeling angry, and any expectation of good makes us confident. They are shy, accepting the rules of society in which they have been trained, and not yet believing in any other standard of honour. They have exalted notions, because they have not yet been humbled by life or learnt its necessary limitations; moreover, their hopeful disposition makes them think themselves equal to great things—and that means having exalted notions. They would always rather do noble deeds than useful ones: their lives are regulated more by moral feeling than by reasoning; and whereas reasoning leads us to choose what is useful, moral goodness leads us to choose what is noble. They are fonder of their friends, intimates, and companions than older men are, because they like spending their days in the company of others, and have not yet come to value either their friends or anything else by their usefulness to themselves. All their mistakes are in the direction of doing things excessively and vehemently. They disobey Chilon's precept by overdoing everything; they love too much and hate too much, and the same with everything else. They think they know everything, and are always quite sure about it; this, in fact, is why they overdo everything. If they do wrong to others, it is because they mean to insult them, not to do them actual harm. They are ready to pity others, because they think everyone an honest man, or anyhow better than he is: they judge their neighbour by their own harmless natures, and so cannot think he deserves to be treated in that way. They are fond of fun and therefore witty, wit being well-bred insolence.

Such, then, is the character of the Young. The character of Elderly Men— men who are past their prime—may be said to be formed for the most part of elements that are the contrary of all these. They have lived many years; they have often been taken in, and often made mistakes; and life on the whole is a bad business. The result is that they are sure about nothing and underdo everything. They "think," but they never "know"; and because of their hesitation they always add a "possibly" or a "perhaps," putting everything this way and nothing positively. They are cynical; that is, they tend to put the worse construction on everything. Further, their experience makes them distrustful and therefore suspicious of evil. Consequently they neither love warmly nor hate bitterly, but following the hint of Bias they love as though they will some day hate and hate as though they will some day love. They are small-minded, because they have been humbled by life: their desires are set upon nothing more exalted or unusual than what will help them keep alive. They are not generous, because money is one of the things they must have, and at the same time their experience has taught them how hard it is to get and how easy to lose. They are cowardly, and are always anticipating danger; unlike that of the young, who are warm-blooded, their temperament is chilly; old age has paved the way for cowardice; fear is, in fact, a form of chill. They love life; and all the more when their last day has come, because the object of all desire is something we have not got, and also because we desire most strongly that which we need most urgently. They are too fond of themselves; this is one form that small-mindedness takes. Because of this, they guide their lives too much by considerations of what is useful and too little by what is noble—for the useful is what is good for oneself, and the noble what is good absolutely. They are not shy, but shameless rather; caring less for what is noble than for what is useful, they feel contempt for what people may think of them. They lack confidence in the future; partly through experience—for most things go wrong, or anyhow turn out worse than one expects; and partly because of their cowardice. They live by memory rather than by hope; for what is left to them of life is but little as compared with the long past; and hope is of the future, memory of the past. This, again, is the cause of their loquacity; they are continually talking of the past, because they enjoy remembering it. Their fits of anger are sudden but feeble. Their sensual passions have either altogether gone or have lost their vigour: consequently they do not feel their passions much, and their actions are inspired less by what they do feel than by the love of gain. Hence men at this time of life are often supposed to have a self-controlled character; the fact is that their passions have slackened, and they are slaves to the love of gain. They guide their lives by reasoning more than by moral feeling; reasoning being directed to utility and moral feeling to moral goodness. If they wrong others, they mean to injure them, not to insult them. Old men may feel pity, as well as young men, but not for the same reason. Young men feel it out of kindness; old men out of weakness, imagining that anything that befalls anyone else might easily happen to them, which, as we say, is a thought that excites pity. Hence they are querulous, and not disposed to jesting or laughter—the love of laughter being the very opposite of querulousness.

Such are the characters of Young Men and Elderly Men. People always think well of speeches adapted to, and reflecting, their own character: and we can now see how to compose our speeches so as to adapt both them and ourselves to our audiences.

As for Men in their Prime, clearly we shall find that they have a character between that of the young and that of the old, free from the extremes of either. They have neither that excess of confidence that amounts to rashness, nor too much timidity, but the right amount of each. They neither trust everybody nor distrust everybody, but judge people correctly. Their lives will be guided not by the sole consideration either of what is noble or of what is useful, but by both; neither by parsimony nor by prodigality, but by what is fit and proper. So, too, in regard to anger and desire; they will be brave as well as temperate, and temperate as well as brave; these virtues are divided between the young and the old; the young are brave but intemperate, the old temperate but cowardly. To put it generally, all the valuable qualities that youth and age divide between them are united in the prime of life, while all their excesses or defects are replaced by moderation and fitness. The body is in its prime from thirty to five-and-thirty; the mind about forty-nine.[8]

Occupation or Profession

If the adage *similar organisms behave similarly under similar circumstances* could be assigned even partial truth, knowing an opponent's occupation or profession can be useful. Each field of endeavor has its own particular pattern of behavior and thought. Therefore, it tends to draw people of a certain type and mold them in particular ways. Anyone who has had extensive exposure to members of a given occupation or profession will tell you that there are specific characteristics common to a majority of them. Trucking and construction work seldom attract the scholarly type, while theoretical astrophysics generally does. Allow your imagination to run free—conjure the image of a college professor in your mind. What kind of language do you think he would use in everyday speech? What might be his political views? Speculate as to his clothes, literary tastes, and attitude toward art. Now imagine a physician or a lawyer. Could you make similar judgments about her attitudes, values, and beliefs? Of course! The point is simply this: Although we are not dealing with an exact sceince but instead with human nature, we can make reliable inferences about a person on the basis of his occupation or profession.

Group Allegiance

Belonging to an organization suggests some degree of adherence to its principles. A familiar cliché like "the military mind" corroborates such a view. News media continually report the activities of certain organizations. Observing

[8]*Rhetorica*, trans. W. Rhys Roberts, from *The Oxford Translation of Aristotle*, ed. W. D. Ross, Vol. II (1924), 1389a-1390b. Reprinted by permission of The Clarendon Press, Oxford.

a group's behavior allows us to make reasonable judgments about membership. There are organizations dedicated to the overthrow of the government, to the pursuit of religious growth and understanding, to weight loss, to the experience of erotic gratification, and so on. Knowing your opponent's group affiliations adds another dimension to your awareness of his internal state.[9]

Education

Knowing the extent and source of your opponent's education can tell you something about his internal state. The more extensive a person's education, the broader his frame of reference. Likewise, the more critical he is apt to be when evaluating your arguments. Ironically, the more one learns, the less one "knows." Perhaps this explains why educated people at times appear timid and are inclined to possess a more plastic set of attitudes, values, and beliefs.

The institution from which a person graduates also yields information. Some schools, for example, have the reputation of turning out bright students. Moreover, certain political and religious ideologies are both characteristic of and indigenous to particular institutions. The imprint left by such places may last a lifetime.

Hobbies and Interests

Building model ships in bottles, sky diving, chess, mountain climbing, stamp collecting, gourmet cooking, and weight lifting all attract people who seem to share certain personality traits. Does the particular hobby or interest require studied patience, courage, cleverness, a thirst for adventure, curiosity, creativity, or narcissism?

These traits are important considerations in an argument. Would you overlook important details when arguing with a person who thrives on close attention to minutiae? Or assume that you are an extrovert who is loud, gregarious, and prone to touch people when you talk. You are arguing with an opponent who is strongly attracted to a hobby or interest in which there is no physical contact and an extremely low level of sound. In all probability, you will both alienate and offend your opponent because of your loud voice and predisposition toward touching. Bringing polar personalities together in an argument is likely to produce friction. Therefore, we recommend that an advocate *adapt* to his opponent, both in word and deed.

[9] For more information on the impact of group allegiances, see Chapter 10, Argument in a Group.

Language

Researchers in the field of psycholinguistics have established some correlations between personality and language behavior.[10] For instance, people vary in the extent to which they use words that are definitive, emphatic, or colorful, and sentence structures that are complex, repetitive, or grammatically awkward. Think for a moment about the language your friends use. Do word choices denote any idiosyncratic personality traits? Would an excessive use of such words as *I* or *my* or *me* suggest a modicum of egocentricity or insecurity? Would language weighted down with political, religious, sexual, economic, or philosophical buzz words tell anything about its user?

An individual's emotional status can also be detected in his language. A study of suicide notes has established that persons on the verge of self-destruction tend to use short, simple sentences, nondiverse vocabulary, repetitious sentence structures, and few qualifying words.[11] Excited or depressed people are prone to use language appropriate to their mood.

The Listening Side of Language

Your opponent's language may include explicit references to his beliefs, attitudes, and values. Such phrases as "I believe that . . ." and "I am convinced that . . ." signal the announcement of important principles that buttress your opponent's arguments. We advise you to listen very carefully to his statements, for they tell you a great deal about your opponent. Moreover, the outcome of the argument may well depend on how effectively you respond to (and perhaps refute) the points he makes.

Less obvious but equally important are *veiled* references to values and convictions. Your opponent's arguments might rest on unspoken assumptions. His most cherished beliefs might never be stated explicitly. Yet they will lie beneath his chain of reasoning and determinine its outcome.

Here's an example of what we mean by veiled references. During the eighteenth and nineteenth centuries the United States was almost continually involved in dealings with the American Indians. By far the most frequent topic of discussion was land: The white settlers wanted it; the Indians did not want to give it up. Along with warfare and treaty-making, one of the strategies used by the United States was the passage of Removal Bills, bills whose purpose it was to drive Indians off their land by making them subject to the unfriendly laws passed by Indian-hating states within whose territory the Indians resided. When

[10] See Joseph DeVito, *The Psychology of Speech and Language: An Introduction to Psycholinguistics* (New York: Random House, Inc., 1970), pp. 183-93.

[11] *Ibid.*, pp. 191-92.

such bills came before Congress, debates occurred. Defenders of the Indians, motivated by humanitarianism as well as by self-interest, defended the Indians' rights to stay on their land and argued against the Removal Bills. Opponents of the Indians (usually representatives of the states or sections of the country within whose borders the Indians lived) argued for passage of the bills.

An analysis of the arguments advanced in favor of removal (and against the Indians) was conducted by one of the authors of this text.[12] It showed that adversaries of the Indians based their arguments on value assumptions that reflected the white man's frame of reference. A typical argument ran as follows:

> It seems visionary to suppose that . . . claims can be allowed on tracts of country on which [the American Indians] have neither dwelt or made improvements, merely because they have seen them from the mountain or passed them in the chase.[13]

Can you detect the value assumption hidden between the lines of this argument? It is that unless lands are lived on or improved (by farming), they are being ill-used. In other words, occupation or improvement are the only desirable uses to which land can be put.

Many would disagree today. Environmentalists and sophisticated land developers recognize the importance of open space. We now see (after we have polluted the air and filthied the waters that surround us) the worth of so-called "unimproved land." But in the nineteenth century, values were different.

Our point is that at times it is productive to listen for unspoken assumptions beneath your opponents' arguments. By making them explicit and by arguing them explicitly, disagreements can be resolved.

Lest the reader think that our discussion of unspoken assumptions has no relevance to contemporary advocacy, here are a few other examples. The advocate who maintains that adequate welfare payments destroy work incentives *assumes* that welfare recipients who receive adequate payments do not want to work. (Research shows that this isn't true. Most people would rather be off the dole than on it, regardless of the adequacy of the payments.) The person who argues in favor of increasing class size on the grounds that it would make teaching more efficient *assumes* that teaching is a mechanical process, which, like an assembly line, can be speeded up by processing more items per unit of time. The chauvanist who maintains that women who plan to marry shouldn't go to college *assumes* that married women have no need for a college education. As you can

---

[12]Joseph A. Ilardo, "An analysis of the Congressional Debate on the Removal Bill of 1830." (Unpublished Master's thesis, Queens College of the City University of New York, 1966).

[13]Gales and Seaton's *Register of Debates in Congress,* Twenty-First Congress, First Session, "Appendix, Senate and House of Representatives" (Washington, D.C.: Gales and Seaton, 1830), pp. 14-50.

see, many arguments rest on unstated assumptions. By listening for them you can learn a great deal about your opponent and successfully refute his arguments.

The skilled advocate listens for still another set of unstated meanings. His adversary may indirectly reveal *feelings* as he talks. If he is concerned with changing his opponent's opinions, he will listen for the feelings being expressed between the lines and, by responding to them, achieve the desired result.

Suppose you are talking with a friend about discotheques. The name of a local disco comes up, and your friend reveals that under no circumstances would he want to go there. You're surprised and disappointed at his reaction, especially since you had planned to convince him to meet you there with his girlfriend this very night. Your task, of course, is to discover the origin of his reaction. If you were clever, you would get him to talk about his experiences there, then listen carefully for the feelings he is expressing. For example, if he says, "The people who go there are creepy," you might say, "You've had bad experiences there?" Your remark would have the effect of helping him to contact and express his feelings. He might say, "I sure did! Why three weeks ago, I went there with my girlfriend and some guys stole her pocketbook! They took all her money and jammed the pocketbook into a toilet."

You might respond by encouraging him to ventilate his anger. Only then would it be possible to get him to talk rationally about the club. You might then bring to his attention such facts as these: (1) There has been a change of management at the club within the past few weeks. Now the disco is catering to a different crowd. (2) It's unlikely that the same group of thieves would be there tonight, since the police recently arrested a gang that was hitting local discos. (3) Special precautions could be taken by his girl and yours to ensure that no one steals their pocketbooks. In short, reason could be introduced into the discussion, but only *after* your opponent has had the opportunity to ventilate his feelings. By listening for them, you may be able to facilitate such ventilation. However, it is certain that by not listening, you make it impossible.

One of the best ways to detect feelings is by watching your opponent as he speaks. Feelings are often communicated nonverbally, by the way someone looks or sounds. This brings us to the next key to knowing your opponent, paralanguage and kinesics.

Paralanguage and Kinesics

Success in an argument often depends on being able to get behind and between opponent's words. To do this, a knowledge of paralinguistics and kinesics is necessary. The paralinguist concerns himself with *how things are said, the kinesicist* with *how one looks while speaking.* According to one study, although the average person talks for a total of about ten to eleven minutes daily, he continually communicates through movements of eyes and eyebrows, facial expressions, hand gestures, and even by silence.[14] And when we do speak, the meaning of our words is at times contradicted by the intonation or inflection of our voice. Such paralinguistic vocal qualifiers include hesitations, stress placed upon certain words and not others, changes in pitch, rate, and intensity. All these occur constantly when we speak. The alert advocate can use them as cues to his opponent's internal state.

A word of caution: avoid making value judgments about someone's internal state on the basis of *only one* kinesic or paralinguistic cue. Evaluations must be based on both the context in which the cue occurs and other cues occurring with it. For example, crossed arms plus crossed legs plus a frown might equal hostility. Crossed arms plus crossed legs plus a smile might equal complacency. Much like the balancing of chemical equations, the adding or taking away of an element can seriously affect its outcome. A smile by itself has little reliable meaning. On the face of a "con man" it could be very deceiving.

Observe your opponent carefully during your next argument. Watch for signs of anxiety and frustration—nail biting, finger drumming, hand wringing, playing with hair or clothing. This brings to mind a technique used by famous criminal lawyer Clarence Darrow. He knew that the pupils of the eyes normally dilate when a person is under stress. On cross examination, he would fire a loaded question and watch the witness's pupils. If they dilated, he would move in for the kill.

Body Types

Classifying people according to their body types is not new. Men have informally done this for centuries. Hippocrates designated two fundamental types: *phythisic habitus*—having a long thin body—and the *apoplectic habitus*—having a short and thick body.[15] Sheldon, in his book in 1940, divided men into three types: endomorphic, mesomorphic, and ectomorphic; he then assigned to each certain physical characteristics.[16] Since then, studies have begun to appear in which personality and temperament were correlated.[17] The *endomorph* on psychological tests proved to be relaxed, easy-going, and even-tempered. The *mesomorph* was aggressive, assertive, and restless. The *ectomorph* was flexible and adaptable.[18] It should be remembered that none of these are pure types

[14] Gordon Wiseman and Larry Barker, *Speech—Interpersonal Communication* (Scranton, Pa.: Chandler Publishing Company, 1967), p. 216.

[15] H. Harrison Clark, *Application of Measurement to Health and Physical Education* (Englewood Cliffs, N.J.: Prentice-Hall, Inc., 1950), p. 119.

[16] W. H. Sheldon, S. S. Stevens, and W. B. Tucker, *The Varieties of Human Physique* (New York: Harper & Row, Publishers, Inc., 1940).

[17] J. B. Cortes and Florence M. Gatti, "Physique and Motivation," *Journal of Consulting Psychology* XXX (Oct. 1966), pp. 408-14.

[18] C. Wesley Dupertuis and Lelio Franchesini are the researchers. Their findings were reported in the *New York Post,* Sept. 3, 1970, p. 32.

but are mixtures with certain characteristics more dominant than others. While all this may seem rather pseudoscientific to some, serious research is now in progress.

Try looking at your next adversary and see whether or not these generalizations check out. Is the endomorph more passive, calm, and lethargic? Is the ectomorph active, excitable, and tense, with a faster reaction time?[19] Is the mesomorph aggressive, assertive, and restless? We urge you to make personal observations among friends, relatives, and business associates.

STRATEGIES TO BE USED WHEN EXTERNAL CUES FAIL

The techniques presented in this section are considered by the authors to be "heavy artillery." They are recommended for use against the more difficult opponent whose defenses seem resistant to penetration.

What's Your Price?

This technique is designed for the opponent who appears to have a closed mind. It is called for when you have been arguing with someone for a length of time without success. Nothing you have said seems to have made the smallest impression. Here is an example of how to implement it:

Arnold: For God's sake, Pete, we've been arguing this point for three hours and nothing I've said seems to make any difference to you. Exactly what would it take to convince you?

Pete: Well, I would be convinced if you could show me. . . .

You have finally found out what you must do to convince him. Now it is simply a matter of whether or not you can deliver the kind of proof he requires. Of course, instead of naming his price, he might say, "There's nothing you could do or say to change my mind." In such a case you are dealing with a *closed mind,* and there is little you can do about it. As you can see, this strategy is a time-saver: it spares you the expenditure of precious energy on someone whose view is unshakable.

Of Course You're Familiar With . . .

This one is suggested for the opponent whose knowledge of the subject being argued has not been established. You suspect that she might be a phony, pretending to a knowledge she does not possess, but you are not sure. The object is to get her to commit herself on some relevant point. To ask her a direct question might cause her to become hostile or retreat. A better approach is to set a trap like this one:

Tom:	Of course you're familiar with the writing of Camus?
Marianna:	Certainly.
Tom:	Then you know the theme of *Catcher in the Rye?*
Marianna:	(bluffing): Why, er I, er, . . . of course I know it.

Now you have her at swordspoint! Your victim has snapped at the bait. You know that Camus didn't write *Catcher in the Rye,* but she doesn't. Now you must decide her fate. You can either unmask her as a phony—thus achieving the ultimate in oneupsmanship—or string her along like a fish on a hook. It's your move. You can construct your trap in a variety of ways depending upon the person, subject, and situation.

Can I Assume Then . . . ?

The more daring reader might find this technique rather appealing. It invites you to go out on a limb—to take a chance and predict your opponent's reaction to an idea. It exposes suddenly an advocate's attitudes, values, and beliefs. It allows you (if you're clever) to make inferences on the basis of what he has already said.

Nora:	In other words, you think society can never condone immoral acts?
Saul:	That's right!
Nora:	*Can I assume then that* you are opposed to legalizing prostitution?

Voila! You have just baited your opponent, forcing him to either agree or disagree with your prediction about what you think he thinks. If he agrees with your prediction, then you have confirmed your suspicions. If not, then you have learned something and would be wise to find out why your prediction was off target. Possibly you have been arguing till now under a misconception, that is, you have misjudged your opponent. Under such circumstances, it would be advisable to regroup and get back on course.

What Would Your Reaction Be to . . . ?

This, a more subdued version of "Can I assume, then . . . ?," permits eliciting a response from an opponent without going out on a limb. Couched in tentative language, the question allows you to laugh off, if need be, an unexpected answer. It also enables you to deal in hypothetical as well as real cases.

Finally, the question facilitates the introduction of an argument or piece of evidence surreptitiously.

1st Man: *What would your reaction be* to the United States' sharing all its technology with Red China?

or

1st Man: *What would your reaction be* to the prediction that in twenty-five or thirty years, the institution of marriage will be obsolete?

or

1st Man: *What would your reaction be* to a guaranteed minimum annual wage?

This all-purpose strategy is an effective means of exposing your opponent's attitudes, values, and beliefs; the quality of his information; his psychological set; and his degree of open-mindedness. Experiment with this marvelous probe in your next encounter.

WRAP-UP

The first part of this chapter discusses what an advocate needs to know about his opponent: his attitudes, values, beliefs, biases, prejudices, degree of open-mindedness, knowledge, intelligence, and rationality. The second part, in addition to perceptive listening, considers eight indicators of an individual's internal state: age, occupation, group allegiance, education, hobbies and interests, language, paralanguage and kinesics, and body type. We contend that if an advocate makes cautious and conscientious use of these external cues, he can learn most of what he needs to know about an opponent in an argument. Should these cues fail to provide sufficient data, use of the strategies given in the third part is encouraged.

PROBES, PRODS, AND PROJECTS

If an opponent were to analyze you, what conclusions do you imagine he would draw?

How useful and reliable are the author's external cues to an opponent's internal state?

How valid would these external cues be when applied to a foreigner?

Can you justify the authors' quoting of Aristotle so extensively when they claim to be anti-traditional? Are they as avant garde as they want us to believe?

Although this book cautions against stereotyping, the authors have done just that in their discussion of body types, occupations, hobbies, etc. Would you defend or condemn their actions? Why?

How good are you at emulating the roles of others? Arrange for a series of arguments in which the advocates play such roles as doctors, priests, college professors. Make interesting combinations: pair a rabbi with a prostitute, a male college president with a fanatical feminist. What adjustments must be made to play these roles? What can you tell from the external cues about an opponent's internal state?

Pretend that you must argue with some well-known public figure. Based on the advice given in this chapter, prepare your strategy and defend your choice of tactics. With your instructor's permission, ask a classmate to assume the role of your opponent. Now, role-play the argument.

9

AUDIENCE DIAGNOSIS

BEHAVIORAL OBJECTIVES

After reading this chapter, you should have a clearer understanding of

1. how this book's definition of an audience differs from that of other books
2. how the homogeneity or heterogeneity of an audience can be determined by a speaker
3. how to best adapt to a widely varied audience
4. what the term "least common denominator" means in audience analysis
5. how to cope with a hostile or potentially hostile audience
6. what can precipitate hostility in an audience
7. the sources, symptoms, and management of audience apathy

After reading this chapter, you should be able to stand before a completely alien audience and draw certain empirically reliable conclusions about it. Further, based upon these conclusions, you should be able to make appropriate adjustments in your presentation that will strengthen your argument. In short, this section brings to light a variety of audience characteristics that can be diagnosed. Some clues derive from the appearance of the audience; others, from its behavior. It is important to distinguish between an audience and an indivudal listener because when two or more people function together as listeners, they exert an influence on one another. Each becomes part of the context in which communication occurs and a source of stimulation for others.[1] In this chapter we examine some of the dynamics of audience behavior, placing special emphasis on hostility and apathy. Let us begin by defining exactly what an audience is.

DEFINITION OF AUDIENCE

In defining audience, we depart from the traditional formulation and substitute the following:

> *An audience consists of two or more persons who, intentionally or accidentally, initially assume a primarily receptive role in relation to one or more persons who act as senders in a relatively structured verbal or nonverbal interpersonal relationship.*

For a better understanding of the definition, let us examine its elements individually.

Two or more persons who intentionally or accidentally . . . According to our definition, audiences can consist of as few as two people or as many as millions. Moreover, audience members may be such by intention or accident; not every member of an audience assumes such a role intentionally or even willingly. A person can find himself in the midst of a curbside political rally without wanting or meaning to get involved. Or again, he may be a speaker one minute and an audience member the next. (Many a speaker has been displaced by a dissident who has taken over a meeting by commandeering the lectern or microphone.) And then, of course, there's the listener who comes to a meeting to please his wife or placate a professor. As an advocate you should realize that a person's presence in an audience does not necessarily mean that he shares your enthusiasm for the topic to be discussed.

Initially assume a primarily receptive role . . . Listening is a dynamic process. Although audience members may appear passive, they are not necessarily

---

[1] Theodore Clevenger, *Audience Analysis* (Indianapolis: Bobbs-Merrill Co., Inc., 1966), pp. 6-9. According to Rollo May, *Love and Will* (New York: W. W. Norton & Co., Inc., 1969), p. 91, "Our feelings . . . are in a real sense partially *formed by the feelings of the other persons present.* We *feel* in a magnetic field."

so. There is a distinction between receptivity and passivity. A responsible receiver in a communication situation is occupied with a number of activities, including concentrating on what is being said, decoding the message, manipulating ideas sparked by the speaker, and formulating relevant questions. Further, audiences are not *merely* receivers. Through posture, facial expressions, and such, they are constantly sending messages to the speaker.

In relation to one or more persons who act as senders . . . An audience can face one or more senders. When multiple senders are present, their relationship may be cooperative (the actors in a play, work together to convey the playwright's message), competitive (in a heated altercation, participants may speak simultaneously or try to out-shout one another), or a combination of these (a formal debate is both cooperative and competitive).

In a relatively structured verbal or nonverbal interpersonal relationship . . . Although the word audience derives from the Latin *audire,* to hear, it is a gross oversimplification to restrict the function of an audience to hearing alone. A constant exchange of both verbal and nonverbal messages occurs between senders and receivers. Thus, it should be apparent that relationships develop at both verbal and nonverbal levels.

We have emphasized that the speaker-audience relationship is relatively structured in order to point up a basic difference between advocacy directed toward an audience and advocacy carried on in an informal group. More is said in Chapter 10 regarding distinctions between an audience and a group.

CHARACTER OF AN AUDIENCE

Audiences, like people, possess certain characteristics. Just as the advocate needs to discover his opponent's attitudes, values, beliefs, biases, prejudices, open- or closed-mindedness, knowledge, intelligence, and rationality, he must search out these same qualities in his audience. Often the task is more difficult, since a plurality of people usually implies the presence of many shades of opinion. How, we ask, can the extent of an audience's homogeneity or heterogeneity be determined? And once established, how should the audience be dealt with? What's to be done with an audience in which wide variations exist? How should the advocate deal with an apathetic or hostile audience? On the following pages, we delineate principles that can lead to answers to these quesitons.

Internal State and Degree of Homogeneity

The following questions can help you gain insight into an audience's internal state and degree of homogeneity.

1. What is the age distribution of the audience? Already mentioned in Chapter 8, Know Your Opponent, are some of the characteristics common to individuals of various ages. How can this information be useful in an audience analysis? Well, you might ask yourself, "Is my audience primarily composed of young, old, or middle-aged people?" If there are wide variations in age, you will have to decide whether to attempt to reach the entire audience or limit yourself to the group that is most amenable to persuasion.

2. What occupations or professions are represented in the audience? People with similar occupations or professions possess many common traits and probably experience a greater sense of cohesiveness. If you know that members of your audience share some common occupation or profession, you should take advantage of the knowledge. Such areas of mutuality should be used as levers with which to move the mind. If, on the other hand, few or no occupational similarities exist, you will have to turn to another area for information regarding this audience's internal state and degree of homogeneity.

3. What group allegiances do members of your audience hold? Would you approach an audience of predominantly left-wing radicals in the same manner as you would one composed primarily of the Daughters of the American Revolution? Of course not! The advocate should be aware of his audience's group affiliations and should structure his appeals accordingly.

4. What is the educational level of your audience? Nothing offends an audience more than being talked down to. Conversely, misjudging an audience's educational level and talking over its head is equally dangerous. Educated people appreciate having their education acknowledged by the manner in which you address them. The uneducated resent having their deficiency thrown in their faces.

Adapting to an Audience in Which Wide Variance Exists

The advocate who addresses an audience encompassing wide variations in internal state has two alternatives: (1) to address only part of his audience, or (2) to attempt to reach the entire audience by appealing to those things, however few and basic, that his listeners have in common (such as culture or human needs). The first alternative requires deciding which portion of the audience should be addressed and, further, recognizing the risk of partially alienating others in the process. The second alternative requires the determination of a least common denominator.

The choice between these alternatives should be based primarily upon the advocate's goal. What, exactly, is your purpose in addressing this audience? Is it to change as many minds as possible or simply to move those who are undecided? Do you care whether or not certain segments of your audience are not involved? Must you sway every listener? It has been said that smartly expressed goals often dictate the means necessary for achieving them. We cannot overemphasize the importance of an advocate's having his goal clearly in mind. Below are three factors that should be considered when deciding on your goal.

1. Nature of the confrontation. In Chapter 1, Orientation to Argumentation, we distinguished between various types of disagreements according to such criteria as emotionality, open-mindedness, structure, participants' level of education and knowledge, and psychological and physical setting. Each can be of help to you when deciding on your goals. How emotional are members of your audience in relation to you and your topic? How open-minded are they? Are there variations within the audience? If so, you might want to gear your argument to those who are least emotional and most open-minded. How formal will your presentation be? Does the structure impose any limitations on you? For example, if you were allowed only five minutes of speaking time instead of an expected twenty minutes, would you be forced to adjust your goals? Instead of converting your listeners, would you be satisfied with merely creating a reasonable doubt? Th educational level of your audience and their knowledge of your subject may help you to decide on your goals. How technical could a practicing experimental biophysicist be when talking about his field to an audience of high school freshman? Again, what limitations might be imposed on a medical doctor addressing a conference of his colleagues? Finally, your choice of goals might be influenced by the psychological and physical setting in which your argument will be presented. Does an atmosphere of tense excitement surround your speech, or is the climate one of polite indifference? Are you among the first (or last) of many speakers? Is the meeting place large and impersonal or small and intimate?[2]

2. Number of encounters. Will you have more than one opportunity to argue before this audience? If so, will your audience's personality and temperament remain the same or change with each encounter? Will part of your audience be available to you at a later date? Such considerations should influence your choice of goals. We recommend that the arguer be realistic and that he adjust his goals not only to his audience but to the number of times he will confront them. Often the most successful advocacy proceeds slowly, in step-by-step fashion. The advocate leads his audience along gradually, beginning with modest goals and establishing readily accepted conclusions. He builds on these conclusions and gently carries his audience to the end point of his argument.

---

[2] Actors often comment on the effect a theatre has on their perfomances. Many prefer small, intimate theatres to large, impersonal ones. Likewise, audiences differ from day to day. Saturday night audiences are reputed to be less critical than most others.

This is the type of advocacy practiced by Antony in Shakespere's *Julius Caesar,* by Socrates in Plato's dialogues, and by most successful adovocates.[3]

3. Facts of the case. The ethical advocate lets the available facts help determine the goal he chooses. At the same time, he lets the facts help determine those listeners whom he should address. If the facts seem to have appeal for certain members of the audience, the realistic advocate addresses himself primarily to *them* and only secondarily the other auditors.

The Least Common Denominator

Suppose an advocate decides that, in order to appeal to his audience's common interests, he must first find out what they are. While this is not too difficult with a small group, it becomes more of a problem as the group size increases and its members become more unfamiliar.

To use an arithmetic analog, searching for an attribute shared by all members of an audience is like testing for a least common denominator. No matter how different people are, they do have certain fundamental similarities. At a basic level, all people share a common humanity. Hence, they have similar needs, among them the need for love, belonging, security, and a sense of self-worth. If the advocate can adjust his proposal to the fulfillment of these needs, he will increase his probability of success. He might be wise to ask such questions as these: Do members of the audience share the same cultural backgrounds (European vs. Oriental, for example)? Have they had the same religious indoctrination and training? Are they citizens of the "free world" or of communist countries? Do they come from the same part of the country? Questions like these help bring to light areas of audience commonality.

THE HOSTILE AUDIENCE

Hostility (derived from the Latin, *hostilis,* meaning of or like an enemy) may exist or develop in an audience. Understanding its nature helps one to cope with a hostile audience. Let us examine two types of hostility: *actual* and *potential.* By *actual* we mean hostility that, in fact, is present in an audience. It takes two forms—*overt hostility* and *occult hostility.* The former is characterized by linguistic abuse of the speaker and visible signs of disfavor (frowns, sneers, and such). The latter lurks beneath the surface, hidden from view. Newspapers occasionally report a case in which a man, known to be quiet and retiring,

---

[3] For a psychologist's viewpoint on the issue, see William D. Ward, "Opinion Change as Related to Sequence of Degree of Change Suggested," *Psychological Reports,* XIV (1964), 93-94.

suddenly goes berserk and slaughters several innocent people. It is naive to assume that no hostility existed in such a person prior to the attacks. Hostility probably smouldered beneath the surface, ready to erupt, requiring only the right stimulus, applied in the right strength, under the right circumstances. This is what we mean by occult hostility.

An audience is potentially hostile when there is reason to believe that hostility might develop. For example, a liberal Democrat addressing a group of devoutly conservative Republicans might expect hostility to develop. A prison warden addressing a group of convicts might expect the same.

Every audience has the capacity to change. A friendly or an apathetic audience can become *potentially* or *actually* hostile. An actually hostile audience can become friendly. Much depends on what the speaker does to aggravate or alleviate certain feelings harbored by the audience. We have all seen a patient and polite audience turn against a speaker who unexpectedly turns out to be long-winded or offensive. The advocate must be prepared to deal with an audience that changes before his eyes.

Sources of Hostility

Hostility may be prompted by such things as the look on a person's face, the way he walks, the kind of clothes he wears.[4] Other precipitants of hostility are politics, religion, education, ethnology, culture, economics, and unpopular ideas.

1. Politics. A political affiliation provides some people with a sense of security. To argue against such a faction or its principles or even to belong to a rival group is to threaten that security. The personal need for psychological reinforcement will vary from individual to individual. Moreover, it will be reflected by the zeal with which the political persuasion is embraced and by the vehemence with which opponents of such a group are attacked.

2. Religion. For most, religious beliefs are an intensely personal matter and not open to discussion or debate. To contest or deprecate them in any way is to invite hostility. Advocates should exercise extreme care in dealing with an audience's religious preferences. Although many people profess a willingness to talk freely about their religion, their declarations should not always be taken literally. Only experience can teach when and how to discuss religion.

3. Education. Does education—or its lack—produce hostility? Are the educated and the uneducated alienated from one another as are the "haves" and "have-nots"? Does the possession of anything, real or imagined, tend to

---

[4] See Chapter 6, Why People Argue.

breed hostility in susceptible individuals? The authors admit a bias in this direction by answering in the affirmative.

To illustrate how education can be a source of hostility, imagine the following situation. A sales representative, lacking *formal* education but rich in *practical experience,* is invited to address an audience of college professors on the subject of persuasion. At the outset, an invisible wall of intolerance may exist in the minds of the audience. This barrier will remain until the speaker succeeds in establishing his competence to the satisfaction of the professors. In reverse, a university professor addressing an audience of sales representatives might experience similar difficulty.[5]

4. Ethnology. This term refers to those characteristics, customs, languages, and peculiarities that define people of different races and nationalities. Some people use ethnology as a tool with which to incite hostility. Labels like *kikes, wops, niggers,* and *spics* are frequently used by agitators to engender hostility. Inadvertent and unintentional ethnic slurs may also provoke hostility. "Humorous" stories—there were once these two Jews . . . , two Chinamen were sitting in a bar . . . .—expressions in foreign languages, ethnic gestures, and food references—watermelon to blacks, spaghetti-benders to Italians—are a few such excitants. At the risk of sounding stuffy and old-fashioned, we offer a word of advice: Avoid ethnic references unless you're absolutely sure they are in good taste.

5. Culture. Violations of cultural norms often embarrass the outsider. Hall relates the case of an American professor who was invited to teach American history to a group of Japanese university professors.[6] Doubting his effectiveness in communicating with them, he requested an interpreter. To his surprise, by making such a request, he had insulted his audience. In the Japanese culture, all educated men speak English. A number of excellent books on the subject of cross-cultural communication have appeared recently. We recommended them to anyone planning to engage in such a pursuit.

6. Economics. Picture yourself as a member of a ghetto audience shortly to be addressed by a world famous economist on the subject of poverty. He arrives, immaculately dressed, in a long, black, chauffeur-driven limousine. You instantly compare his clothes with yours, his car with yours. How do you react? There you are, a member of an audience of people who are struggling to scrape

---

[5] In World War II, the U.S. Army saw fit to use a man's education as a basis for awarding commissions. A new recruit with a college degree could be sent to Officers' Candidate School and, in ninety days, come out a lieutenant. Those without such education, no matter the reasons, were prejudged as being less capable. The phrase used to describe the college-educated officers was "ninety-day wonders."

[6] Edward T. Hall, *The Silent Language* (Garden City, N.Y. Doubleday & Co., Inc., 1959), pp. 11-12.

together the simple necessities of life. And you see these symbols of affluence. Again, how do you feel? What do you think? Obviously, feelings of hostility are not uncommon in situations such as this. We don't recommend the course of action taken by the ancient Greek politician who donned tattered clothes to fool the poor voters (incidently, he failed), but we advise that the advocate take special notice of both himself and his listeners in order to avoid needlessly antagonizing them by flaunting those external indicators of financial success likely to trigger feelings of hostility.

   7. *Unpopular ideas.* For centuries despots have known that certain ideas are more dangerous than bombs. The precautions taken to prevent their free exchange bear witness to this awareness. Reforms with radically destructive ideas pick away at the very fabric of a political or social order. Hence, in many people's eyes, advocates of unpopular ideas should be silenced because they disturb the *status quo.* It takes a rare kind of courage to argue unpopular ideas before an audience committed to maintenance of the existing state of affairs.

   Two other observations need mentioning. First, ideas, like fashions, go in and out of style. Yesterday's absurd beliefs (the conception of the universe, the evolution of man, the theory of disease) are today's scientific dogma. The advocate of sound ideas who is continually berated by hostile audiences can take solace in the knowledge that men probably much greater than himself (Christ, Galileo, Darwin, Joan of Arc, Freud) have suffered the same fate at the hands of the particular establishments they threatened, yet they ultimately triumphed. The danger is that, after establishing a new order, today's radicals may become tomorrow's despots.

   Second, the popularity of an idea varies with the audience to which it is presented. Certain ideas possess mass appeal, but they may be repulsive to a particular audience. The advocate must consider his audience when gauging whether the idea in question will provoke feelings of hostility.

Symptoms of Hostility

   Occult hostility is not easy to detect because most of its physiological symptoms are not visible to the naked eye (elevated blood pressure, increased flow of adrenalin, an overall in muscle tonus). Here are some symptoms that can signify the presence of occult hostility or of potential hostility that threatens to become actual at any moment: (1) restlessness, (2) intense staring at the speaker, (3) a tense and rigid appearance, (4) a splintering of the audience into small clusters, (5) obvious display of banners, buttons, or insignias that are antithetical to the speaker. Although these symptoms, singly or collectively, are far from being incontrovertible evidence of the presence of hostility, they should put the speaker on notice and prompt him to take whatever precautionary measures he might deem necessary.

Dealing with a Hostile Audience

Hostility should be treated as a doctor treats disease: The advocate should deal not with its symptoms but with its underlying causes. In other words, he should try to understand the reasons for his audience's hostility. Once he does, he can work to overcome the barriers created by politics, religion, education, ethnology, culture, economics, or unpopular ideas.

THE APATHETIC AUDIENCE

Most authors make the point that an apathetic audience is more difficult to cope with than a hostile one. We agree. Total indifference and disinterest pose a special problem for the advocate: He must first create interest, for only then can he begin the persuasive process.

Apathy is a condition of noninvolvement. The apathetic person is detached, indifferent to things around him. He can watch a man collapse on the sidewalk, step over him, and continue on his way. He can meet a strange woman at a party, take her home, and engage in sexual intercourse without ever getting to know anything about her or revealing anything significant about himself.

Sources of Apathy

How do people become apathetic? Certainly they are not born that way. Infants and young children are anything but indifferent to their world. A child who is not keenly tuned in to its environment should give parents cause for alarm. As most children mature, they become progressively less excitable and more detached. What could account for this shift in attitude and life-style? One persuasive explanation is that as an individual grows, he becomes more aware of the complex and anxiety-producing world surrounding him. Concurrently, he realizes that he is powerless to change it. He senses that what he *wants* and *feels* makes no real difference to anyone but himself. Further, what he *does* fails to touch or concern anyone significantly. He is wholly oppressed by the futility of his life. The frustration and anxiety resulting from these insights are painful in the extreme. So, as a defense against them, he stops wanting and feeling. He assumes the attitude of "who cares?" Many such people simply stop asserting themselves—permitting their lives to be mechanically directed by outside forces, exerting absolutely no influence whatsoever on the course and nature of their destiny. The apathetic person is someone who chooses not to care—as a defense against anxiety and frustration.[7]

[7]See Rolo May, *Man's Search for Himself* (New York: Signet Books, 1967), pp. 19-23, and his *Love and Will* (New York: W. W. Norton & Co., Inc., 1969), pp. 27-33.

Other sources of apathy are (1) disinterest in the speaker's topic, and (2) the speaker-speech-audience relationship. More will be said about these in a later section of the chapter.

Symptoms of Apathy

Some of the more characteristic symptoms of an apathetic audience may be: (1) eyes roaming about the room; (2) a posture suggestive of disinterest (slumping or a partial turning away in the seat, arms folded across chest with head hung low); (3) yawning; (4) actual sleeping; (5) reluctance to ask *or* answer questions; and (6) a defiant look in the eyes that seems to say, "Interest me! Go ahead! I dare you!"[8]

Dealing with an Apathetic Audience

Analyzing a problem is often easier than providing a viable solution. One thing seems clear. The speaker must know the source of his audience's apathy. It may derive from a feeling of impotence and frustration, a disinterest in the topic, or the speech-speaker-audience relationship.

1. A feeling of impotence and frustration   Audiences whose apathy results from this condition cannot be argued or talked out of it. Theirs is an emotional condition that cannot be "argued away." Instead of trying to jolt them out of their apathy, use it! Discuss why this emotion is felt. Stir them by demonstrating that they are not powerless—at least insofar as your speech is concerned. Show them that they *can* make a difference by doing what is in their power; demonstrate how their action will produce results.

2. Disinterest in topic   People's interests vary. A topic that stimulates one may bore another. Many topics are overworked by too many harangues so that people no longer listen. This is called the "saturation phenomenon." Speeches about women's liberation or prison reform often evoke such a reaction. The particular subjects are, of course, less important than the fact that this saturation phenomenon exists. Disinterest, then, is a major source of apathy. It is best dealt with by maintaining originality and freshness in your speech and by demonstrating the relevance of your topic.

3. Speech-speaker-audience relationship   An advocate must maintain the interest and attention of his listeners. Yet, few successfully fulfill this responsibility. Some are simply dull: They mumble, speak in monotones, seldom vary

[8] According to May, *Love and Will,* p. 220, the unhealthy person sits dully, staring blankly, doing nothing and asking, "Why doesn't something interest me, reach out to me, grasp me?"

their volume or rate, and generally fail to display the dynamism necessary to hold their audiences.

Many speeches contain basic flaws: (1) the language may be too abstract and dull: "The man fell out of the window" instead of "The big fat man in a dirty, unironed suit came tumbling out of the window, splattering on the sidewalk below." Clearly, the latter paints a more vivid picture in the mind. A speaker must choose his words like an artist chooses colors. (2) The organization may be awkward and confusing. (3) The speech may lack interest value—it may be irrelevant to the audience's needs.[9]

WRAP-UP

This chapter brings to light the complex realities of audience composition and behavior. It begins with a definition that departs from the traditional and that stresses the fortuitous nature of audiences as well as their role in communication. Suggestions are given for determining the character (internal state and degree of homogeneity) of an audiences. We present two alternatives open to the speaker facing an audience in which wide variance exists, and we suggest ways in which the advocate may choose between these alternatives. A discussion of the sources, symptoms, and management of audience hostility and apathy brings the chapter to a close.

PROBES, PRODS, AND PROJECTS

Isn't the definition of audience in this chapter unduly complicated? What do you think?

Does an audience have a mind of its own?

When would a homogeneous audience be easier to handle than a heterogeneous one? When wouldn't it?

Which audience do you think would be easier to persuade, an educated or uneducated one?

What characteristics do political and religious audiences have in common?

How would you prepare yourself before addressing members of a subculture: ex-offinders? homosexuals? handicapped persons? nudists? clones?

[9]For additional advice and information on public speaking, see Bibliography under the heading of Persuasion.

The authors have neglected to talk about friendly audiences. What adjustments might be necessary when arguing before a friendly audience? What does an advocate have to be careful to do before a friendly audience?

Imagine you are going to address the local chapter of the John Birch Society. Go to the library and learn all you can about the organization and its membership. Find out its history, philosophy, the likely characteristics of its members, and other pertinent facts.

Now imagine that you must address a local chapter of one of the following organizations: National Organization for Women, Gay Liberation Front, Ku Klux Klan, Audubon Society, or the Anti-Vivisection League. Research the organization and its membership. Find out all you can about your audience. Prepare an audience diagnosis based upon your findings.

10

ARGUMENT IN A GROUP

BEHAVIORAL OBJECTIVES

After reading this chapter, you should have a better understanding of

1. why it is so important to learn how to get along and, if need be, argue effectively in groups
2. the different relationships that can develop between an individual and a group
3. some of the group roles typically encountered (for example, information-provider, ringmaster, idea refiner, peacemaker)
4. what is meant by "group purpose"
5. group norms—unspoken and unwritten codes of proper thought and behavior that are consciously or unconsciously established by groups to facilitate social interaction and are enforced by group pressures
6. some aspects of verbal and nonverbal interaction as they occur in group argumentation

There are people who behave one way when alone, another way in a group. Why? Why does the mere mention of a group situation elicit fear and anxiety in some and exhilaration in others? In this section we take a deep and diversified look into the group profile and to it add the element of *argument*. We hope it will yield an insight that will help the reader in his next group encounter.

We are living in an age of groups. Whether the cause is political, curricular, economic, or religious, the rally cry is the same: "Organize!" Because so much of our arguing takes place in a group context, it is essential to understand the factors that operate when people argue in groups.[1]

You may wonder how groups differ from audiences. The basic difference is in level of formality. The speaker-audience situation is relatively formal and structured. Barring the unusual, there is comparatively little exchange or verbal interaction between speaker and audience. The speaker is the primary sender; those exchanges that take place are often cumbersome and crude (heckling, shouts, and so on). But group discussion implies relatively informal dialogue; there are many opportunities for immediate and easily arranged exchanges among participants. The channels are open. The whole idea of argument in a group is to achieve some good by permitting the free, open, and cooperative exchange of ideas. From experience, we find that this ideal is not always attained. Some groups fail miserably at making the slightest progress while others succeed admirably. Why? Some individuals seem to thrive in a group setting while others pale. You may feel comfortable in one group and awkward in another. Why? In this chapter, we consider the major factors accounting for these often observed phenomena. By understanding the dynamics of group argument, your ability to handle conflicts in a group setting will be enhanced.

Definition of Group

Although there are many possible definitions of the word *group,* for our purposes we define it as follows:

> *A group is a body composed of individuals*
> *who occupy or assume various roles and*
> *status positions and who share a common*
> *purpose, in the accomplishment of which*
> *they establish and enforce group norms and*
> *interact both verbally and nonverbally.*

---

[1] Our concern in this chapter is with interpersonal argument in a group setting. We leave for treatment elsewhere the interesting phenomenon whereby group is pitted against group: a teacher's union against a school board; a militant political group against a law enforcement agency; and so on. People with strong opinions no longer need to stand alone; they can become members of a group. They can thus preserve their anonymity while they have their views expressed for them without great personal risk. One can simply pay dues and vicariously have a spokesman do his arguing for him.

This definition suggests the divisions of the chapter. Below, we discuss each of the elements in our definition. Our treatments are basic, and the reader is encouraged to further his knowledge by consulting the excellent sources listed in the Bibliography under the heading of Group Dynamics and Argumentation.

INDIVIDUALS, STATUS POSITIONS, AND ROLES

As already explained, an individual carries with him into an argument the sum of his life experience. In a group setting, certain traits that an individual brings may assume greater-than-usual importance. These include:

1.   personality attributes
2.   attitude toward the group
3.   feelings about other group members

Certain personality variables are extremely important in group argument. Some people are *other-directed*, meaning that they tend to look outside themselves for advice about what to believe and how to behave. By contrast, others are *inner-directed* and self-reliant. Still others are *tradition-directed*.[2] These tendencies can exert much influence on group argument: The other-directed person might seem cooperative and pleasant to one individual but spineless and dependent to another. The same two persons might see the inner-directed individual as obstinate and closed-minded on the one hand but strong and assertive on the other. These attitudes can exert considerable influence on group climate and the course of an argument.

Some individuals may come into a group willingly; others may have been appointed reluctantly. This will often affect their attitude toward the group. You have doubtless encountered the reluctant group member who acts as though the world were against him. Whether or not it is, he is almost certain to succeed in turning it against him.

How important is the group to individual members? Does it matter a great deal to them? Or are they members because they have nothing better to do? If they don't take the group seriously, it cannot succeed in exerting much influence on them: They will remain disruptive and uncooperative even in the face of group efforts to reshape their behavior. So we see that the group's importance to individual members can seriously affect the course and outcome of group deliberations.

Groups may be composed of strangers or acquaintances. Each of these

[2] The classifications come from a landmark work, David Reisman, Nathan Glazer, and Reuel Denny, *The Lonely Crowd* (New Haven, Conn.: Yale University Press, 1950).

alternatives poses different problems. A worker appointed to serve on a committee with four people he has never met must be concerned with such things as (1) establishing his competence and determining theirs, (2) assuming his proper position in relation to the others and seeing that they do the same in relation to him, and (3) analyzing and drawing conclusions about the other members' personalities, values, biases, and so on. Although many of these tasks are carried out unconsciously, they nonetheless require an expenditure of energy. Moreover, they must be accomplished on a *continuing* basis: Precisely because of the informality of group argment, roles and status positions in the group must evolve; they are not usually prearranged.

A group composed of acquaintances poses different problems. Usually we know the characteristic behavior pattern of friends in our circle: Joe may be the crowd's worrywart; Cathy, the joker; Emily, the high-status leader; and Milton, the peacemaker. These roles and positions may be carried over into a group. This is not necessarily bad, but sometimes conflicts arise when two members vie for the same position. This can happen when a boss appoints a committee, designating someone else as leader. During deliberations, he may unconsciously assume his regular leadership position, thereby offending the appointed leader. More often than not this sort of thing is very subtle and subsurface. It takes experience to detect what is going on, provide a remedy, and thereby ensure the group's well-being.

Status positions can also impede discussion by discouraging healthy difference of opinion. Members may be reluctant to disagree with a high-status member. In general, the better a group functions, the less the tendency to "pull rank." The ideal group attitude can be phrased like this: "The group is working together to accomplish some common objective. Rank and status mean far less than the quality of contributions made. Group members are equally responsible for the outcome of the group's deliberations."

Much fascinating research has been done on the topic of role behavior.[3] We present some of the typically encountered group roles so that you may be aware of them and learn to deal with those disturbing the functioning of the group. The *information provider* ("According to my research . . . .") is the fellow who does his homework and provides accurate and pertinent data for the group's deliberations. He is a valuable asset. The *ringmaster* ("Hold it! Let the guy finish.") is the member who facilitates the exchange of ideas by giving everyone a fair chance to speak. He is often a master of tact and timing.

The *idea refiner* ("What this means is . . . .") clarifies and coordinates information provided by other members. He has a sharp mind and is able to see fine distinctions and subtle interrelationships between ideas. He may point out contradictory or conflicting evidence and bring important disagreements to the attention of the group. He is indispensable to a really excellent discussion.

[3]We recommend especially the work of Erving Goffman. (See Bibliography under Group Dynamics and Argumentation.)

The *peacemaker* ("Please! Don't let's argue.") serves the group by working to keep disagreement focused on ideas rather than people. He tries to resolve interpersonal conflict, comes to the defense of those under personal attack, soothes hurt feelings, and prevents the group from deteriorating to the point of arguing personalities. A frequent ally of his is the *encourager* ("C'mon fellas, we can do it.") He looks on the bright side and tries to keep the group's spirits up. He is quick to compliment someone for a valuable contribution, and he enjoys reminding the group that members are working as a team.

Earlier in the book, the *aggressor* ("Boy! What a dumb remark that was!") was described as an individual who enjoys initiating arguments. He thrives in a group setting, carrying his behavior beyond its usual bounds. He is the loud, vicious critic. He enjoys deflating others, is quick to ridicule or jeer, and delights in arguing personalities rather than ideas. He tends to deprecate the entire group, and he flaunts an air of superiority. Needless to say, he is both offensive and disruptive. When someone assumes this role, the peacemaker and the encourager must work overtime. At times it is best for the group to ignore the aggressor (if possible); at other times, it is best to stop the discussion and let the group try to determine the source of the aggression. This may be opening a Pandora's Box, however, since the aggression may have deep psychological origins. If all else fails, the group can exert social pressures to silence or even exclude the aggressor.

The *stopper* ("Why don't we just give up . . . .") blocks all progress. Whenever the group seems to be gaining momentum, he raises an objection or points to a "fly in the ointment." He enjoys stymieing the group. A master of the game "Why Don't You, Yes But,"[4] he tries to thwart the group by being contrary at every turn. Often the *stopper* goes unnoticed for some time; he may pass as a sincere and well-meaning perfectionist. Sooner or later, however, he is unmasked and his true colors revealed. He is usually best dealt with by being told that perfection is a goal seldom achieved and that the group must do the best it can under existing circumstances. If he accepts this admonition, the group can proceed normally. If not, it may be necessary to exert the same social pressures that can bring the aggressor into line.

The *joker* ("Did you hear the one about . . .") is the group comedian. He takes nothing seriously, thrives on horseplay, and enjoys being the center of attention. To a point, he provides a valuable service to the group, relieving tension and helping group members maintain a sense of humor and perspective. But carried too far, his joking becomes annoying and disruptive.

The *martyr* ("No! No! Ignore me! It's all right!") makes himself conspicuous by displaying chargrin when others disagree with him or when his comments are not met with a blare of trumpets and a display of fireworks. He suffers in silence but communicates his suffering nonverbally. He may stifle the

---

[4] See Eric Berne, *Games People Play* (New York: Grove Press, Inc., 1964), pp. 115-22.

group by sulking visibly, until someone asks, "What's the matter, Henry? Did one of us hurt your feelings?" This question, which thrusts him into the center of the group's attention (secretly, what the martyr wanted all along), is an invitation to a long and tedious exchange about Henry's feelings. It often goes like this:

Ben:	What's the matter, Henry? Did one of us hurt your feelings?
Henry:	No, not really.
Ben:	What do you mean, "not really"?
Henry:	I mean it doesn't matter.
Ben:	It matters . . . of course it matters!
Henry:	Please. I don't want to make a fuss. . . .

Such a dialogue can go on for hours with the group sinking deeper and deeper into a bog. Members should try to prevent the martyr from disrupting the group. State firmly that everyone has the right to argue in defense of his ideas, but make it clear that sulking won't be tolerated. The *know-it-all* ("It's simple! All you do is . . .") dominates the discussion. He believes that, like Moses, he alone can lead the group to Truth, so why should anyone else be given a chance to speak? His tactics are transparent and can best be dealt with by insisting that everyone be given an opportunity to present his ideas.

GROUP PURPOSE

Groups usually have one primary purpose. Generally, they fall into two basic categories: (1) those in which interaction is an end in itself; and (2) those in which interaction is a means to an end. Under the first category fall social groups, therapy groups (including sensitivity and encounter groups), and learning groups. Their members profit individually by the interaction that occurs. Although the groups may produce changes in individuals that are reflected outside the group, these changes are reflected *individually*. The group as a unit accomplishes nothing beyond its own interaction.

The second category includes problem-solving and action groups. They exist to serve some purpose outside the group itself. Individual self-improvement is *not* the primary goal of this kind of group. Rather, it exists to either recommend or take action with regard to some specific extra-group dilemma. For example, a problem-solving group might meet to recommend ways of improving the educational system or to investigate solutions for the problem of air pollution. When they are done with their deliberations, some outside body expects an accounting: They are to have produced some tangible product (perhaps a policy, or a report).

We must add that one group may serve many purposes during its life cycle: It may be a social group one minute, a problem-solving one the next, and a therapeutic one the next. But a single overriding purpose stands out. It is important for all members to know and share the common group goal or else basic misunderstandings and conflicts are sure to arise. Consider how awkward and inappropriate it would be for an individual in a social group to demand that others support their casual statements with up-to-the-minute evidence. By comparison consider how foolish a member of a problem-solving group would appear if he concentrated on nothing but the here-and-now feelings of group members. Both examples show that sharing a common purpose is essential to efficient and profitable group argument.

Occasionally one or more members may know and accept the group purpose but harbor a *private* goal that competes with the group's goal. This can be referred to as a *hidden agendum.* A young lady may join a theatre group to meet men (hidden agendum) as well as to act. A worker may join a committee with the hope of impressing his boss. A husband may join the PTA to please his wife and convince his child's principal of the family's concern. So long as these hidden agenda remain secondary to the group's overriding purpose, they do no harm. But when they emerge as equally important to or more important than the group goal, they can be disruptive. It is a good idea, then, not only to know and share the group's common purpose but to become aware of your personal reasons for joining. This may help you maintain a sense of perspective.

The group's purpose may seriously influence interpersonal relations and the group flow. You may know and like an individual as a friend, but you may not respect him as an intellectual equal. Should you discover him sitting next to you on a crucial committee, you might fail to extend to him the proper respect. For this reason, a judicious selection of members in the light of the group purpose can be critical. As one politician put it, he would prefer to have on his staff a group of distant and stoic intellectuals rather than genial incompetents. This is why teachers often avoid a familiarity with their students: A friendly social relationship may impede their effectiveness as teachers.

GROUND RULES: GROUP NORMS AND SOCIAL PRESSURES

Whenever people interact socially, they establish norms. Norms provide structure for social interaction. As explained earlier, they may be explicit, written down and condified (the formal laws of a society), or implied and unwritten (cultural mores). For our purposes, group norms may be defined as follows: Group norms are unspoken and unwritten codes of proper thought and behavior that are consciously or unconsciously established by groups to facilitate social interaction and are enforced by group pressure. To build on an earlier analogy, norms are like laws, and social pressures are like the legal institutions that enforce them.

It is important to recognize that there are two kinds of norms: (1) those that govern behavior, and (2) those that govern thought. The first kind controls such interactional patterns as forms of correct behavior, minor rituals, and proper signals of status and rank. For example, most groups develop norms regarding rudeness and vulgarity. These are often taboo and are discouraged by negative reinforcement: The guilty party's behavior is conditioned away by group indications of displeasure. Of course, in certain groups vulgarity, rudeness, and insult are allowed. Norms are amoral, meaning that they are generally established by the group without moral considerations.[5] Practical (and often unconscious) considerations are the only ones made: "Do members function comfortably with this norm?" and "Does the norm allow us to accomplish our task efficiently?" are two examples. This means that you may despise working with a particular group because you do not accept its behavioral norms. Surely you can recall the club meeting you attended with enthusiasm only to come away thoroughly disappointed. Perhaps its members were artificially polite or incredibly rude to one another. Your discomfort may have arisen because you could not tolerate this behavioral group norm. *People tend to join and support those groups with whose norms they are most comfortable.*

The second kind of norm may be more pernicious; it exerts an influence on members' thinking. Most members may believe, for example, that teachers should be obliged to take loyalty oaths. Consequently, people disagreeing with that view are given the choice of either being forced into thinking the majority's way or being punished for their "offense." This, in a nutshell, is the whole issue of freedom of thought and speech.[6] Groups may coerce *all* members into accepting and supporting a particular view. Hence, the constant warnings, emanating from such provocative authors as George Orwell and William Whyte, against "group-think" and the "big brother" mentality. As libertarians have explained, a group or society that silences minority thinkers ultimately hurts itself by limiting its own range of input. We cannot enter into a lengthy discussion of the advantages and disadvantages of freedom of speech. Suffice it to say that such freedom is essential to democratic group process and is an ideal toward which all small groups should strive. We later discuss in more detail the

[5] Social anthropologists have written much about the relationships between cultural norms and morality. The issue is quite complicated, and the reader is advised to consult the writings of Clyde Kluckhohn and others. We can say with some certainty, however, that within a given society, the norms of smaller groups generally conform (with minor variations) to those of the society at large.

[6] Perhaps the most eloquent appeal for civil liberties was written in John Stuart Mill's *On Liberty, Representative Government, and the Subjection of Women,* especially Chapter 2, On the Liberty of Thought and Discussion. See Bibliography under Group Dynamics and Argumentation.

advantages and disadvantages of conformity and the options open to members who cannot accept a group's norms.

Social Pressures and Conformity

Conformity is a subject that has concerned thinkers for centuries. When must we conform? When must we not? Do we ever have an obligation to rebel? The answers are complex. We can set down no simple rules of thumb, but we can describe some of the more reliable findings about conformity and list the four options open to the nonconformist.

In the context of this chapter, we define *conformity* as *the act or process of adhering to the behavioral or cognitive norms of a group.* It has been experimentally established that people vary greatly in the extent to which they conform to group wishes.[7] In a classic experiment, Samuel Asch found that certain individuals under certain conditions would allow a large majority of group members to actually change their perceptions of physical phenomena.[8] Other researchers have demonstrated that groups to which an individual is most attracted exert the most influence on him,[9] that an individual threatened with demotion in a group is more likely to conform to group pressure,[10] and that greater influence is exerted by groups to which a member has belonged for some time and with which he plans to remain closely associated.[11] In the light of these findings it is important to consider the advantages and disadvantages of conformity so that we may better understand the consequences of our own behavior and the behavior we induce in others.

As far as the group as a whole is concerned, conformity ensures a smoothness of operation. Behavioral conformity allows the group to concentrate on ideas rather than on operational mechanics and social interaction. To the individual, conformity provides a sense of security and belonging, of fitting in unobtrusively. In a 1964 interview, Che Guevara (trained in psychoanalysis) remarked that "revolutionaries are not normal people." By this he implied that they possess not only dedication but a capacity to function outside the established order of things.[12] They do, of course, conform to the norms of their

[7] Harriet Linton and Elaine Graham, "Personality Correlates of Persuasibility," in Carl Hovland and Irving Janis, *Personality and Persuasibility* (New Haven: Yale University Press, 1959), pp. 69-101.

[8] See Samuel Asch, *Social Psychology* (Englewood Cliffs, N.J.: Prentice-Hall, Inc., 1952), Chapter 16.

[9] See A. Hare, *Handbook of Small Group Research* (New York: The Free Press, 1962).

[10] L. Zeff and M. Iverson, "Opinion Conformity in Groups under Status Threat," *Journal of Personality and Social Psychology* III (1966), 383-89.

[11] H. Gerard and G. Rotter, "Time Perspective, Consistency of Attitude and Social Influence," *Journal of Abnormal and Social Psychology* LXII (1961), 565-72.

[12] Transcript of broadcast aired over radio station WBAI, April, 1964.

particular "out-group." Perhaps it is a question of which groups best serve our needs, including our needs for belonging and security.

Form or structure always carries with it both advantages and disadvantages. So it is with conformity, since it invariably occurs in relation to some structure. Too rigid an insistence on it may drive out certain, often valuable individuals or perhaps inhibit their participation. If too many members conform too strictly, the group might be robbed of good ideas, healthy disagreement, and welcome variety. It is unfortunate, but groups in which there is excessive conformity are dull. They tend toward entropy, which Norbert Weiner considers the likely end of the universe.

> It is highly probable that the whole universe around us will die the heat death, in which the world shall be reduced to one vast temperature equilibrium in which nothing really new ever happens. There will be nothing left but a drab uniformity out of which we can expect only minor and insignificant local fluctuations.[13]

For certain individuals, conformity with group norms and expectations can be achieved only at the expense of personal frustration, aggravation, or a decline in respect for other members or the group as a whole. The resultant decline in participation is often followed by complete withdrawal from the group.

It is difficult to identify "proper" norms or the "proper" amount of pressure to conform. Much depends on the people in the group, its size, its task, internal and external pressures (such as time limits), and the style of leadership followed.

Suppose you are in a group whose norms are unsatisfactory. Perhaps they foster inefficiency, encourage irresponsibility, or stifle participation. What can you do about it? Four options are open to you: (1) conform unwillingly, (2) change the norm, (3) leave the group, or (4) be a deviant and pay the consequences. The first and third alternatives need no further elaboration. The second and fourth do. How can you change norms? There are no simple guidelines, but sometimes it is possible to begin the process by verbalizing the norm and pointing out its undesirable effects. This may be enough to motivate the group to change. Other times (if sensitive feelings might be hurt by too bold an approach) you might align yourself with members who share your view and together make a joint effort to change the norm. For example, if the norm allows unsupported assertions and invalid evidence to go unchallenged, you and your supporters might agree to respectfully cross-examine one another when one of you presents such data. Perhaps by setting a good example you can indirectly affect a change. Again, norms can sometimes be altered by asking a

[13]Norbert Wiener, *The Human Use of Human Beings,* 2nd ed., rev. (Garden City, N.Y.: Anchor Books, Doubleday & Co., Inc., 1954), p. 31.

qualified and objective observer to recommend changes she deems appropriate. This is the kind of service performed by industrial efficiency experts, marriage counselors, and psychological consultants. This technique is especially efficacious when group members sense that something is wrong with the way the group is functioning, but they cannot quite puzzle it out.

The fourth option (be a deviant and pay the consequences) can also facilitate the changing of undesirable norms. Sometimes one bold person can affect highly desirable changes. The price may be great, as it was for Socrates and Christ. At the very least the group will exert social pressures (such as admonitions or frowns of displeasure). More extreme measures include physical violence and expulsion from the group. At any rate, the advocate should be aware of the options open to him and should choose one or more after considering the consequences of each.

ASPECTS OF VERBAL AND NONVERBAL INTERACTION IN GROUPS

Many of the same interactional patterns described in our chapters on Why People Argue and Audience Diagnosis occur in groups. However, there are a few that, if not unique to groups, at least tend to manifest themselves more openly in that context. One of those is clique (subgroup) formation. Within a group there may be two or more factions whose members provide mutual support. Nothing can be more disconcerting to an advocate than to get immediate and contradictory feedback. As he argues, his remarks are met by nods of support, frowns of disapproval, and blank stares. How is he to interpret this contradictory data? Perhaps if he knows that the nodders are members of one clique, the frowners of another, and the starers of a third, he can better interpret his perceptions. Advocates in groups should guard against the establishment of too many widely divergent cliques. This fragmentation can seriously impede group effectiveness. Try to understand the reasons for clique formation; usually members of cliques seek out one another for support that is not provided by the group as a whole. If you can eliminate the source of the problem, you have solved it.

Another aspect of group interaction is leadership style. This component often exerts a profound influence on group deliberations. Is the responsibility for leadership vested in one person? Or is it shared by all members of the group? How directive is the leadership? Does dictatorship prevail? Total freedom? Decisions on these matters depend on the group's purpose, the time at its disposal, and the people present. Each style of leadership has its assets and liabilities. It should be selected and perhaps tailored to suit the needs of the group. And, finally, the advocate should try to be sufficiently flexible to function comfortably under any leadership style.

WRAP-UP

In this chapter we have presented several major factors capable of affecting interpersonal argument in groups. Expressed were the ways in which an individual's personality traits, attitudes toward the group, and attitudes toward other discussants can significantly influence interpersonal relations and group progress. A brief examination of status and role behavior included reference to typical roles assumed by group members (information provider, idea refiner, encourager, aggressor, martyr) and methods of coping with group members who assume destructive roles.

Groups were classified according to their overall purpose, and the phenomenon of *hidden agendum* was explored. Further discussion stressed conformity of behavior and thought in groups, and it touched on some of the issues related to conformity. Also noted were a few aspects of verbal and nonverbal interaction in groups (clique formation, leadership).

PROBES, PRODS, AND PROJECTS

Is your behavior in groups consistent with your behavior outside of them?

In what way does group affiliation destroy individuality and self-confidence?

Are the people who join groups more suggestable than those who don't?

Are most of the groups you belong to run democratically or autocratically?

Wouldn't you agree that most "leader types" share a great many physical and psychological characteristics?

Aren't there times when the democratic process shouldn't be used?

Could a group of ten good men do positively terrible things collectively? Would you believe that ten bad men could do wonderful things together?

We all play roles daily. But is an individual the sum of the roles he plays? Or is he something more?

Opponents seldom respond to what you have said but rather to what they think you said. To dramatize this human tendency, select two people and a middleman. Seat them facing one another with the middleman between them. The object is to argue through the middleman. Absolutely no direct communication is permitted between the advocates. Anything they wish to say to each other must be whispered to the middleman who will, in turn, relate it. Our attention here is on the middleman. We are anxious to see how accurately he transmits the messages given him. Does he add to or subtract from the messages in any way, shape, or form? This exercise may illustrate how people innocently distort what they hear and pass it on as gospel. It can also show how difficult and frustrating it is to argue through a third party (when represented by a lawyer, for example).

On a designated day, all students should bring a blindfold to class. With blindfolds in place and seated in a circle, members of the class should initiate a group argument on a prearranged topic. After fifteen minutes of visual deprivation—that is, not being able to see, have the students remove their blindfolds and discuss their reactions to this probject. Consider such things as increased or decreased gesturing activity, changes in voice volume, alteration in distance between advocates, levels of courtesy, speech speed, and touching.

EPILOGUE

A knowledge of argumentation does not automatically convey the ability to argue effectively, just as familiarity with the alphabet does not imply the capacity to read, spell, or write. In both instances, a good deal more than knowing the fundamentals is required.

In this book we have set down the essentials of argument. Mastery of these essentials should result in a significant improvement in the ability to argue. The extent of improvement depends, of course, on inherent flare for argument, motivation, ability to see relationships and manipulate ideas, emotional disposition, and competitive spirit. All contribute to an individual's potential as an advocate.

The authors now take this opportunity to reiterate some of the highlights of the work.

1. You Cannot Argue Conclusions— Only How They Were Arrived at

To do this, the advocate must become thoroughly familiar with the nature of proof, and he must learn to analyze arguments with the care and precision of a surgeon.

2. Most Arguments Are Not Won on the Basis of What Is Said

This may not apply to arguments in such pure sciences as mathematics and physics, but it *is* true of most everyday arguments. You will recall our mention of paralanguage and kinesics in Chapter 8, Know Your Opponent. Paralanguage, we said, involves the study of *how* people say things; it's not the words they speak but how they speak them that is critical—volume, pitch, hesitations, rhythms, stress placed on certain words, pauses, and the use of such insertions as "er," "ah," and "um." Kinesics, on the other hand, focuses on a speaker's body movements and gestures—that is, facial expressions, posture, finger and toe tapping, direct and indirect eye contact, and so on. The influence of all these paralinguistic and kinesic cues should not be overlooked by the advocate.

3. Most People Are Guilty of Being "Fuzzy Thinkers"

The majority of advocates expect their opinions to be accepted without question. Therefore, carefully constructed questions, designed to determine the support for claims, can be effective strategic devices. Most untrained advocates substitute verbiage for substance. A simple question such as "What's your point?" often pierces their smoke screen.

4. You Can't Win until You Determine Proof Requirements

This is perhaps one of the most important principles of argumentation. Too frequently, arguments begin before the advocates determine the proof required to support their views. A necessary preliminary to argument, therefore, is to analyze the proposition you are advancing and to clarify what is required to establish it logically. Second, we recommend that you analyze your opponent and determine what it would take to change his mind. Even better, if true conflict resolution is to be achieved, both of you should clarify early in the disagreement exactly what proof would be required for each of you to accept the other's point of view. Only after such preliminaries are disposed of can you begin to engage in productive argumentation.

5. Listening Wins Arguments

Contrary to popular opinion, successful argumentation often depends more on critical listening than glib oratory.

To be effective, all arguments must be responsive to the case being advanced by the opposition. Faulty listening habits can lead an advocate to such things as drawing erroneous conclusions, making unwarranted assumptions, and advancing misguided and irrelevant arguments. Consequently, developing the ability to listen, rather than merely hear, is essential. It should be borne in mind that hearing is nothing more than transmitting sound from your environment to your brain; *listening,* however, is the phenomenon of transforming what you hear into meaningful units of thought. Thus, the superior advocate must be a good listener.

BIBLIOGRAPHY

AUDIENCES

Anderson, Martin P., Lewis Wesley, and James Murray. *The Speaker and His Audience,* New York: Harper & Row, Publishers, Inc., 1964.

Bauer, Raymond A. "The Communicator and the Audience." In *People, Society and Mass Communication*, edited by Lewis A. Dexter and David M. White. New York: Macmillan Publishing Co., Inc., 1964.

_____. "The Obstinate Audience." *American Psychologist* XIX (1964): 319-28.

Clevenger, Theodore. *Audience Analysis.* Indianapolis: Bobbs-Merrill Co., Inc., 1966.

Festinger, Leon. *Conflict, Decision and Dissonance.* Stanford, Calif.: Stanford University Press, 1964.

Hollingworth, H. L. *The Psychology of the Audience.* New York: American Book Company, 1935.

Pease, Raymond B. "The Audience as the Jury." *Journal of Public Speaking* III (1917): 218-33.

Smelser, Neil J. *Theory of Collective Behavior.* New York: The Free Press, 1963.

Woolbert, Charles H. "The Audience." *Psychological Monographs* XXII (1916): 37-54.

BELIEFS, ATTITUDES, AND VALUES

Albert, Ethel M. "The Classification of Values: A Method and an Illustration." *The American Anthropologist* LVIII (1956): 221-48.

Allport, Gordon W. *The Nature of Prejudice.* Abridged ed. New York: Anchor Books, Doubleday & Co., Inc., 1958.

Berry, Thomas E., ed. *Values in American Culture: Statements from Colonial Times to the Present.* New York: Odyssey Press, 1966.

Boulding, Kenneth. *The Image.* Ann Arbor, Mich.: University of Michigan Press, 1956.

Brown, Roger. *Social Psychology.* New York: The Free Press, 1965.

Dobkin, Milton. "Social Values and Public Address: Some Implications for Pedagogy." *Western Speech* XXVI (1962): 140-46.

Dodd, Stuart C. "On Classifying Human Values: a Step in the Prediction of Human Valuing." *American Sociological Review* XVI (1951): 645-53.

Ehninger, Douglas. *Influence, Belief, and Argument: An Introduction to Responsible Persuasion.* Glenview, Ill.: Scott, Foresman & Co., 1974.

Heider, Fritz. "Attidues and Cognitive Organization." *Journal of Psychology* XXI (1946): 107-12.

_____. *The Psychology of Interpersonal Relations.* New York: John Wiley & Sons, 1958.

Insko, Chester A. *Theories of Attitude Change.* Englewood Cliffs, N.J.: Prentice-Hall, Inc., 1967.

Kluckholn, Clyde. *Anthropology and the Classics.* Providence: Brown University Press, 1961.

_____. "Common Humanity and Diverse Cultures." In *The Human Meaning of the Social Sciences,* edited by Daniel Lerner. New York: Meridian Books, 1959.

Kluckholn, Richard, ed. *Culture and Behavior.* New York: The Free Press, 1962.

_____. "Toward a Comparison of Value-Emphases in Different Cultures." In *The State of the Social Sciences,* edited by Leonard D. White. Chicago: University of Chicago Press, 1956.

Maslow, Abraham H. "Fusion of Facts and Values." *American Journal of Psychoanalysis* XXIII (1963): 117-31.

Newcomb, Theodore. "An Approach to the Study of Communicative Acts." *Psychological Review* LX (1953): 393-404.

_____. "Individual Systems of Orientation." In *Psychology: A Study of a Science,* edited by S. Koch. Vol. III. New York: McGraw-Hill Book Co., Inc., 1959.

Paulson, Stanley F. "Social Values and Experimental Research in Speech." *Western Speech* XXVI (1962): 133-40.

Rokeach, Milton. *Beliefs, Attitudes, and Values: A Theory of Organization and Change.* San Francisco: Jossey-Bass, Inc., Publishers, 1968.

Sherif, Carolyn, Mazafer Sherif, and Roger E. Nebergall. *Attitude and Attitude Change*. Philadelphia: W. B. Saunders Co., 1965.

Steele, Edward D. "Social Values, the Enthymeme and Speech Criticism." *Western Speech* XXVI (1962): 70-75.

Steele, Edward D., and Charles W. Redding. "The American Value System: Premises for Persuasion," *Western Speech* XXVI (1962): 83-91.

BODY TYPES

Cortes, Juan B., and Florence M. Gatti. "Physique and Motivation." *Journal of Consulting Psychology* XXX No. 5 (Oct. 1966): 408-14.

_____. "Physique and Propensity." *Psychology Today* IV (1970): 42ff.

Fisher, Seymour. *Body Image and Personality*. Princeton, N.J.: D. Van Nostrand Co., 1958.

Lowen, A. *Physical Dynamics of Character Structure*. New York: Grune & Stratton, 1958.

Rolf, Ida. "Structural Integration." *Systematics* 1 (1963): 66-83.

Sheldon, W. H., S. S. Stevens, and W. B. Tucker. *The Varieties of Human Physique*. New York: Harper & Row, Publishers, Inc., 1940.

FALLACIES

Bentham, Jeremy. *Bentham's Handbook of Political Fallacies*. Revised, edited and with an introduction by Harold A. Larrabee. Baltimore: Johns Hopkins Press, 1952.

_____. *The Book of Fallacies*. In *The Works of Jeremy Bentham,* edited by John Bowring. Vol. II. Edinburgh: William Tait, 1838-1843.

Fearnside, Ward W., and William B. Holther. *Fallacy: the Counterfeit of Argument*. Englewood Cliffs, N.J.: Prentice-Hall, Inc., 1959.

Schopenhauer, Arthur. "The Art of Controversy." In *The Essays of Arthur Schopenhauer*. Trans. by T. Bailey Saunders. New York: John Wiley & Sons, n.d.

Thouless, Robert H. *Straight and Crooked Thinking*. New York: Simon & Schuster, Inc., 1932.

GENERAL ARGUMENTATION

Baker, George P., and Henry B. Huntington. *The Principles of Argumentation*. Revised ed. Boston: Ginn and Co., 1905.

Brock, Bernard L. "The Comparative Advantage Case." *Speech Teacher* XVI (March 1967): 118-23.

Brock, Bernard L., James W. Chesebro, John F. Cragan, and James F. Klumpp, *Public Policy Decision-making: Systems Analysis and Comparative Advantages Debate*. New York: Harper & Row, Publishers, Inc., 1973.

Brockriede, Wayne, and Douglas Ehninger. "Toulmin on Argument: An Interpretation and Application." *Quarterly Journal of Speech* XLVI (1960): 44-53.

Castell, Alburey. *A College Logic: an Introduction to the Study of Argument and Proof.* New York: Macmillan Publishing Co., Inc., 1935.

Cragan, John F., and Donald C. Shields. "The Comparative Advantage Negative." *Journal of the American Forensic Association* VII (Spring 1970): 85-91.

Ehninger, Douglas, and Wayne Brockriede. *Decision by Debate.* New York: Dodd, Mead & Co., 1963.

Flesch, Rudolph. *The Art of Clear Thinking.* New York: Harper & Row, Publishers, Inc., 1951.

Freeley, Austin J. *Argumentation and Debate: Rational Decision Making.* 4th ed. Belmont, Calif.: Wadsworth Publishing Company, Inc., 1976.

Huber, Robert B. *Influencing Through Argument.* New York: David McKay Co., Inc., 1963.

Lichtman, Allan J., and Daniel M. Rohrer. "A General Theory of the Counterplan." *Journal of the American Forensic Association* XII (Fall 1975): 70-79.

Miller, Gerald, and Thomas Nilsen, eds. *Perspectives on Argument.* Chicago: Scott, Foresman & Co., 1968.

Mills, Glen E., *Reason in Controversy*, 2nd ed. Boston: Allyn & Bacon, 1968.

Murphy, Richard, "The Ethics of Debating Both Sides." *The Speech Teacher* VI (January 1957), 1-9.

O'Neill, James M., Craven Laycock, and Robert L. Scales. *Argumentation and Debate.* New York: Macmillan Publishing Co., Inc., 1917.

Rieke, Richard D., and Malcolm O. Sillars. *Argumentation and the Decision Making Process.* New York: John Wiley & Sons, Inc., 1975.

Smith, Craig R., and David M. Hunsaker. *The Bases of Argument: Ideas in Conflict.* Indianapolis: Bobbs-Merrill Co., Inc., 1972.

Terry, Donald R., et al. *Modern Debate Case Techniques.* Skokie, Ill.: National Textbook Co., 1970.

Thomas, David A., ed. *Advanced Debate Readings in Theory. Practice and Teaching.* Skokie, Ill.: National Textbook Co., 1975.

Thompson, Wayne. *Modern Argumentation and Debate: Principles and Practices.* (New York: Harper & Row, Publishers, Inc., 1971).

Toulmin, Stephen. *The Uses of Argument.* New York: Cambridge University Press, 1958.

Windes, Russel, and Arthur Hastings. *Argumentation and Advocacy.* New York: Random House, Inc., 1965.

Wood, Roy V. *Strategic Debate.* Skokie, Ill.: National Textbook Co., 1968.

Zarefsky, David. "The 'Traditional Case'-'Comparative Advantage Case' Dichotomy: Another Look." *Journal of the American Forensic Association* VI (Winter 1969): 12-20.

Ziegelmueller, George W., and Charles A. Dause. *Argumentation: Inquiry and Advocacy.* Englewood Cliffs, N.J.: Prentice-Hall, Inc., 1975.

GROUP DYNAMICS AND ARGUMENTATION

Allen, Vernon L. "Situational Factors in Conformity." In *Advances in Experimental Psychology*, Vol. 2, edited by Leonard Berkowitz. New York: Academic Press, Inc., 1965.

Asch, Solomon E. "Effects of Group Pressure upon the Modification and Distortion of Judgments." In *Groups, Leadership, and Men*, edited by H. Guetzkow. Pittsburgh: Carnegie Press, 1951.

Bales, Robert F. *Personality and Interpersonal Behavior.* New York: Holt, Rinehart & Winston, Inc., 1970.

Barnlund, Dean, and Franklyn Haiman. *The Dynamics of Discussion.* Boston: Houghton Mifflin Co., 1960.

Bennis, Warren G., Edgar H. Schein, David E. Berlew, and Fred I. Steele, eds. *Interpersonal Dynamics: Essays and Readings on Human Interaction.* Homewood, Ill.: Dorsey Press, Inc., 1964.

Berne, Eric. *Games People Play.* New York: Grove Press, Inc., 1964.

_____. *The Structure and Dynamics of Organizations and Groups.* Philadelphia: J. B. Lippincott Co., 1963.

Bormann, Ernest G. *Discussion and Group Methods: Theory and Practice.* 2nd ed. New York: Harper & Row, Publishers, Inc., 1975.

Brilhart, John K. *Effective Group Discussion.* Dubuque, Iowa: William C. Brown Co., Publishers, 1967.

Burgoon, Michael, Judee K. Heston, and James McCroskey. *Small Group Communication: A Functional Approach.* New York: Holt, Rinehart & Winston, 1974.

Cartwright, Dorwin, and Alvin Zander, eds. *Group Dynamics: Research and Theory.* 2nd ed. Evanston, Ill.: Row, Peterson, 1960.

Cathcart, Robert S., and Larry A. Samovar, eds. *Small Group Communication.* Dubuque, Iowa: William C. Brown Co., Publishers, 1970.

Collins, Barry E., and Harold Guetzkow. *A Social Psychology of Group Processes for Decision-Making.* New York: John Wiley & Sons, 1964.

Fisher, B. Aubrey. *Small Group Decision Making: Communication and the Group Process.* New York: McGraw-Hill Book Co., 1974.

Goffman, Erving. *The Presentation of Self in Everyday Life.* New York: Doubleday & Co., Inc., 1959.

Goldberg, Alvin A., and Carl E. Larson. *Group Communication: Discussion Processes and Applications.* Englewood Cliffs, N.J.: Prentice-Hall, Inc., 1975.

Gouran, Dennis S. *Discussion: The Process of Group Decision-Making.* New York: Harper & Row Publishers, Inc., 1974.

Grove, Theodore G. "Attitude Convergence in Small Groups." *Journal of Communication* 15 (1965): 226-38.

Gulley, Halbert E., and Dale G. Leathers. *Communication and Group Process: Techniques for Improving the Quality of Small Group Communication.* 3rd ed. New York: Holt, Rinehart & Winston, Inc., 1977.

Hare, A. Paul, Edgar F. Borgatta, and Robert F. Bales, eds. *Small Groups: Studies in Social Interaction.* New York: Alfred A. Knopf, Inc., 1955.

Homans, George C. *The Human Group.* New York: Harcourt Brace Jovanovich, Inc., 1950.

Ilardo, Joseph A. "An Analysis of the Congressional Debate on the Removal Bill of 1830." Unpublished Master's thesis, Queens College of the City University of New York, 1966.

Janis, Irving L. "Groupthink." *Psychology Today* 5 (1971): 43-46.

Kahn, Robert L., and Elise Boulding, eds. *Power and Conflict Organizations.* New York: Basic Books, Inc., 1964.

Lott, Albert J., and Bernice E. Lott. "Group Cohesiveness as Interpersonal Attraction: A Review of Relationships with Antecedent and Consequent Variables." *Psychological Bulletin* LXIV (1965): 259-309.

Mill, John Stuart. *On Liberty, Represenative Government, and the Subjection of Women.* Introduction by Millicent G. Fawcett. London: Oxford University Press, 1873.

Phillips, Gerald M. *Communication and the Small Group.* Indianapolis: Bobbs-Merrill Co., Inc., 1966.

Raven, Bertram R., and Jeffrey Z. Rubin. *Social Psychology: People in Groups.* New York: John Wiley & Sons., Inc., 1976.

Riesman, David, Nathan Glazer, and Reuel Denny. *The Lonely Crowd.* New Haven: Yale University Press, 1950.

Rogers, Carl. *Encounter Groups.* New York: Harper & Row, Publishers, Inc., 1970.

Rosenfeld, Lawrence B. *Human Interaction in the Small Group Setting.* Columbus, Ohio: Charles E. Merrill Publishing Co., Inc., 1973.

Shaw, Marvin E. *Group Dynamics: The Psychology of Small Group Behavior.* 2nd ed. New York: McGraw-Hill Book Co., 1976.

Simmel, George. *Conflict and the Web of Group Affiliations.* Trans. by Kurt H. Wolf and Reinhard Bendix. New York: The Free Press, 1955.

Steiner, Claude. *Scripts People Live.* New York: Grove Press, Inc., 1974.

Thibaut, John, and Harold Kelly. *The Social Psychology of Groups.* New York: John Wiley & Sons, Inc., 1959.

Whyte, William, Jr. "Groupthink." *Fortune* XLV (1952): 114ff.

LANGUAGE AND SEMANTICS

Alexander, Hubert G. *Meaning in Language.* Glenview, Ill.: Scott, Foresman & Co., 1969.

Alston, William P. *Philosophy of Language.* Foundations of Philosophy Series. Englewood Cliffs, N.J.: Prentice-Hall, Inc., 1964.

Black, Max, ed. *The Importance of Language.* Englewood Cliffs, N.J.: Prentice-Hall, Inc., 1962.

Bloomfield, Leonard. *Language.* London: George Allen and Unwin Ltd., 1935.

Bronstein, Arthur J., Claude L. Shaver, and Cj Stevens. *Essays in Honor of Claude M. Wise.* Hannibal, Mo.: Standard Printing Co., 1970.

Condon, John C. *Semantics and Communication.* New York: Macmillan Publishing Co., Inc., 1966.

Hayakawa, S. I. *The Use and Misuse of Language.* New York: Fawcett World Library, 1962.

_____. *Language in Thought and Action.* New York: Harcourt Brace Jovanovich, Inc., 1952.

Korzybski, Alfred. *Science and Sanity.* Lakeville, Conn.: Institute of General Semantics, 1948.

Whorf, Benjamin. *Language, Thought and Reality.* Cambridge, Mass.: Technology Press, Massachusetts Institute of Technology, 1956.

LIBRARY RESEARCH AND REPORT WRITING

Hook, Lucyle, and Mary V. Gaver. *The Research Paper.* 3rd ed. Englewood Cliffs, N.J.: Prentice-Hall, Inc., 1962.

Pugh, Griffith T. *Guide to Research Writing.* 2nd ed. Boston: Houghton Mifflin Co., 1963.

Turabian, Kate. *A Manual for Writers.* Chicago: University of Chicago Press, 1967.

Winchell, Constance M. *Guide to Reference Books.* 8th ed. Chicago: American Library Association, 1967.

MOTIVATION AND PERSONALITY

Adorno, T. W., E. Frenkel-Brunswick, D. J. Levison, and R. N. Sanford. *The Authoritarian Personality.* New York: Harper & Row, Publishers, Inc., 1950.

Barron, Frank. "Some Personality Correlates of Independence of Judgment." *Journal of Personality* XXII (1952): 287-97.

Berkowitz, L., and R. M. Lundy. "Personality Characteristics Related to Susceptibility to Influence by Peers or Authority Figures." *Journal of Personality* XXV (1956): 306-16.

Bonner, Hubert. *Psychology of Personality.* New York: Ronald Press, Co., 1961.

Borgatta, E. F., and W. W. Lambert, eds. *Handbook of Personality Theory and Research.* Chicago: Rand McNally & Co., 1968.

DeVito, Joseph. *The Psychology of Speech and Language: An Introduction to Psycholinguistics.* New York: Random House, Inc., 1970.

Ferullo, Robert J. "The Self-Concept in Communication." *Journal of Communication* XIII (1963): 77-86.

Goffman, Erving. *The Presentation of Self in Everyday Life.* New York: Doubleday & Co., Inc., 1959.

Hovland, Carl, and Irving Janis. *Personality and Persuasibility.* New Haven, Conn.: Yale University Press, 1969.

Ilardo, Joseph A. "Ambiguity Tolerance and Disordered Communication: Therapeutic Aspects." *The Journal of Communication,* 23 (December, 1973), 371-91.

Leventhal, Howard, and Stanley Perloe. "Relationship Between Self-Esteem and Persuasibility." *Journal of Abnormal and Social Psychology* LXIV (1962): 385-88.

Lewin, K. *A Dynamic Theory of Personality.* New York: McGraw-Hill Book Co., 1935.

Lindzey, Gardner, ed. *Handbook of Social Psychology.* 2 vols. Reading, Mass.: Addison-Wesley Publishing Co., Inc., 1954.

Linton, Harriet B. "Dependence on External Inference: Correlates in Perception, Attitudes and Judgment." *Journal of Abnormal and Social Psychology* LI (1955): 502-7.

Maslow, Abraham H. *Toward a Psychology of Being.* Princeton, N.J.: D. Van Nostrand Co., 1962.

Murray, Edward J. *Motivation and Emotion.* Englewood Cliffs, N.J.: Prentice-Hall, Inc., 1964.

Perls, Fritz. *Gestalt Therapy Verbatim.* New York: Bantam Books, Inc., 1971.

Powell, Frederick. "Open- and Closed-Mindedness and the Ability to Differentiate Source and Message." *Journal of Abnormal and Social Psychology* LXV (1962): 61-64.

Rokeach, Milton. *The Open and Closed Mind.* New York: Basic Books, Inc., 1960.

Teitzman, Peter, and Thomas Fenaughty. "Personal Impulse and the Adolescent Actor." Unpublished paper, 1977.

NONVERBAL COMMUNICATION

Birdwhistell, Ray. *Kinesis and Context.* Philadelphia: University of Pennsylvania Press, 1970.

Eisenberg, Abne M. *Living Communication.* Englewood Cliffs, N.J.: Prentice-Hall, Inc., 1975.

Eisenberg, Abne M., and Ralph R. Smith, Jr. *Nonverbal Communication.* Indianapolis: Bobbs-Merrill Co., Inc., 1971.

Hall, Edward T. *The Silent Language.* Garden City, N.Y.: Doubleday & Co., Inc., 1959.

_____. *The Hidden Dimension.* New York: Anchor Books, Doubleday & Co., Inc., 1969.

Hayes, Alfred S. "Paralinguistics and Kinesics: Pedagogical Perspectives." In *Approaches to Semiotics,* edited by Thomas Sebeok, et al. The Hague: Mouton, 1964.

Mahl, George, and Gene Schulze. "Psychological Research in the Extralinguistic Area." In *Approaches to Semiotics,* edited by Thomas Sebeok, et al. The Hague: Mouton, 1964.

Mehrabian, Albert. "Orientation Behaviors and Nonverbal Attitude Causation." *Journal of Communication* 17 (1967): 331.

———. "Communication Without Words." *Psychology Today* 11(1968): 53.

Ogilvie, Mardel, and Norma Rees. *Communication Skill: Voice and Speech.* New York: McGraw-Hill Book Co., 1970.

Trager, George L., and Henry L. Smith, Jr. *An Outline of English Structure.* Washington: American Council of Learned Societies, 1957.

PARLIAMENTARY PROCEDURE

Hellman, Hugo E. *Parliamentary Procedure.* New York: Macmillan Publishing Co., Inc., 1966.

Robert, Henry, and Sarah C. Robert. *Robert's Rules of Order, Newly Revised.* Glenview, Ill.: Scott, Foresman & Co., 1970.

Sturgis, Alice F. *Standard Code of Parliamentary Procedure.* New York: McGraw-Hill Book Co., 1950.

PERSUASION

Abelson, Herbert I. *Persuasion: How Opinions and Attitudes Are Changed.* New York: Springer Publishing Co., Inc., 1959.

Abernathy, Elton. *The Advocate: A Manual of Persuasion.* New York: David McKay Co., Inc., 1964.

Anderson, Kenneth, and Theodore Clevenger. "A Summary of Experimental Research in Ethos." *Speech Monographs* XXX (1963): 59-78.

Aronson, Elliott, and Burton Golden. "The Effect of Relevant and Irrelevant Aspects of Communicator Credibility on Opinion Change." *Journal of Personality* XXX (1962): 135-46.

Bettinghaus, Erwin P. *Persuasive Communication.* New York: Holt, Rinehart & Winston, Inc., 1968.

Bostrom, Robert N., and Raymond K. Tucker. "Evidence, Personality and Attitude Change." *Speech Monographs* XXXVI (1969): 22-27.

Brembeck, Winston, and William S. Howell. *Persuasion: A Means of Social Influence.* 2nd ed. Englewood Cliffs, N.J.: Prentice-Hall, Inc., 1976.

Brown, J. A. C. *Techniques of Persuasion.* Baltimore: Penguin Books, Inc., 1963.

Cronkhite, Gary. *Persuasion: Speech and Behavioral Change.* Indianapolis: Bobbs-Merrill Co., Inc., 1969.

Dobbs, James M. "Self-Esteem, Communicator Characteristics and Attitude Change." *Journal of Abnormal and Social Psychology* LXIX (1964): 173-81.

Erickson, Erik. *Ghandi's Truth.* New York: W. W. Norton & Co., Inc., 1970.

Hubert, Robert B. *Influencing through Argument.* New York: David McKay Co., Inc., 1963.

Insko, Chester. *Theories of Attitude Change.* Englewood Cliffs, N.J.: Prentice-Hall, Inc., 1967.

Meyerhoff, Arthur E. *The Strategy of Persuasion: The Use of Advertising Skills in Fighting the Cold War.* New York: Coward, McCann & Geohegan, Inc., 1965.

Minnick, Wayne C. *The Art of Persuasion.* 2nd ed. Boston: Houghton Mifflin Co., 1968.

Oliver, Robert. *The Psychology of Persuasive Speech.* 2nd ed. New York: Longman, Inc., 1957.

Ostermeier, Terry. "Effects of Type and Frequency of Reference upon Perceived Source Credibility and Attitude Change." *Speech Monographs* XXXIV (1967): 137-44.

Pear, Tom H. *The Moulding of Modern Man.* London: George Allen and Unwin Ltd., 1961.

Scheidel, Thomas M. *Persuasive Speaking.* Glenview, Ill.: Scott, Foresman & Co., 1967.

Schweitzer, Don. "The Effect of Presentation on Source Evaluation." *Quarterly Journal of Speech* LVI (1970): 33-39.

Sharp, Henry, and Thomas McClung. "Effect of Organization on the Speaker's Ethos." *Speech Monographs* XXXIII (1966): 182-83.

Sherif, Carolyn, Muzafer Sherif, and Roger Nebergall. *Attitude and Attitude Change.* Philadelphia: W. B. Saunders Co., 1965.

Wilson, John F., and Carroll C. Arnold. *Public Speaking as a Liberal Art.* 4th ed. Boston: Allyn & Bacon, Inc., 1978.

PROOF: EVIDENCE AND REASONING

Becker, Samuel L. "Research on Emotional and Logical Proofs." *Southern Speech Journal* XXVIII (1963): 198-207.

Bettinghaus, Erwin P. *The Nature of Proof.* 2nd ed. New York: Bobbs-Merrill Co., Inc., 1972.

Bostrom, Robert N., and Raymond K. Tucker. "Evidence, Personality and Attitude Change." *Speech Monographs* XXXVI (1969): 22-27.

Clarke, Edwin L. *The Art of Straight Thinking.* Englewood Cliffs, N.J.: Prentice-Hall, Inc., 1934.

Dewey, John. *How We Think.* Boston: D. C. Heath & Co., 1933.

McCroskey, James C. "The Effects of Evidence in Persuasive Communication." *Western Speech* XXXI (1967): 180-99.

Newman, Robert P., and Dale R. Newman. *Evidence.* Boston: Houghton Mifflin Co., 1969.

Tracey, John E. *Handbook of the Law of Evidence.* Englewood Cliffs, N.J.: Prentice-Hall, Inc., 1952.

STATISTICS

Bormann, Ernest G. *Theory and Research in the Communicative Arts.* New York: Holt, Rinehart & Winston, Inc., 1965.

Huff, Darrell C. *How To Lie with Statistics.* New York: W. W. Norton & Co., Inc., 1954.

Moroney, M. J. *Facts from Figures.* Baltimore: Penguin Books, Inc., 1956.

Zeisel, Hans. *Say It with Figures.* New York: Harper & Row, Publishers, Inc., 1947.

VIOLENCE AND CONFLICT

Arendt, Hannah. *On Violence.* New York: Harcourt Brace Jovanovich, Inc., 1970.

Brown, Richard M. *American Violence.* Englewood Cliffs, N.J.: Prentice-Hall, Inc., 1970.

Doolittle, Robert J. *Orientations to Communication and Conflict.* Palo Alto, Calif.: Science Research Associates, 1976.

Filley, Alan C. *Interpersonal Conflict Resolution.* Glenview, Ill.: Scott, Foresman & Co., 1975.

Hamilton, Charles V., et al. *Dialogue on Violence*, edited by George Vickers, Indianapolis: Bobbs-Merrill Co., Inc., 1968.

Jandt, Fred E. (ed.) *Conflict Resolution Through Communication.* New York: Harper & Row, Publishers, Inc., 1973.

Jones, Howard Mumford. *Violence and Reason: A Book of Essays.* New York: Atheneum Press, 1969.

INDEX